Scalatra in Action

DAVE HRYCYSZYN
STEFAN OLLINGER
ROSS A. BAKER

MANNING
Shelter Island

For online information and ordering of this and other Manning books, please visit
www.manning.com. The publisher offers discounts on this book when ordered in quantity.
For more information, please contact

Special Sales Department
Manning Publications Co.
20 Baldwin Road
PO Box 761
Shelter Island, NY 11964
Email: orders@manning.com

Manning Publications Co.
20 Baldwin Road
PO Box 761
Shelter Island, NY 11964

Development editor:	Karen Miller
Technical development editor:	Barry Polley
Copyeditor:	Andy Carroll
Proofreader:	Katie Tennant
Technical proofreader:	Andy Hicks
Typesetter:	Gordan Salinovic
Cover designer:	Marija Tudor

ISBN 9781617291296
Printed in the United States of America
1 2 3 4 5 6 7 8 9 10 – EBM – 21 20 19 18 17 16

brief contents

contents

preface

Most web frameworks have a lot of assumptions built into them. When you're building whatever the framework designers envisaged, they work very well. But if you need to depart from their happy paths, all that prescriptiveness starts to work against you.

Full-stack web frameworks with server-side rendering, using a relational database are common, and in the past I used them all the time. But over time, I progressively departed from using their standard components.

I began to build web APIs and microservices, often using nonrelational data stores, asynchronous requests, and server-push technologies. I was installing more dependencies to layer extra functionality on top of already large and complex frameworks. Simple tasks were difficult, because I was fighting against the basic assumptions of the frameworks I was using.

Then I discovered Scalatra. The language was unfamiliar at first, but the friendly community and incredibly simple HTTP DSL made it easy to get started.

Suddenly I was working in the environment I always wanted. The Scala language gave me all the speed and correctness benefits of static typing without the Java or C# boilerplate, a simple and productive language syntax akin to Ruby or Python, and access to a wealth of high-quality libraries.

Scalatra, with its minimalistic style, does one thing well: it makes HTTP actions trivially easy to express. Beyond that, it gets out of your way. This makes it easy to pick and choose from tens of thousands of Java and Scala libraries to build exactly the application you need.

We wrote this book to bring this minimal style of application development to a wider audience. The web's not new technology any more, and if the history of computing tells us anything, it's that common tasks get simpler over time.

The modern internet wouldn't be much fun if people sent input using punched cards and had to wait several hours to get their output back, as though it were the 1960s. We think that the acrobatics coders go through to quickly set up high-performance HTTP interfaces to their programs are similarly outdated. It's not 1996 anymore. HTTP can be easy.

Scalatra is one of the easiest ways to build a web application. This book will show you pretty much the entirety of the framework in the first four chapters. The other nine chapters explain how to integrate with other interesting components, customize the framework, and deploy your applications. Because really, it's not about us: it's about you, your ambitions, and the next thing you want to make.

DAVE HYRCYSZYN

acknowledgments

We'd like to collectively thank everyone at Manning, especially Karen Miller, Michael Stephens, Ozren Harlovic, Rebecca Rinehart, Candace Gillhooley, and Ana Romac. And thanks to Christina Rudloff, who helped us get started.

We'd also like to thank our technical editor, Barry Polley, and our technical proof-reader, Andy Hicks. Their help was invaluable. The MEAP reviewers provided great feedback: Brian Hanafee, Jeff Condal, Chuck Daniels, Christian Horsdal, Ronald Tischliar, M. Marc-Philippe Huget, Ramsés Morales, Craig Aspinall, Helmuth Breiten-fellner, Adam Slysz, Alain Couniot, Carlos Aya, Emre Kucukayvaz, Charles Feduke, Alberto Quario, Scott Dierbeck, Dimitrios Liapis, and Dr. Dan Klose.

Dave: I want to thank Tanya Gouthro, Bettina Wittneben, and Katrin Hellermann, who encouraged me to go for it. Thanks also to employers and friends past and present, including Dave Else, Pete Boyle, Rebecca Simmonds, and Ramsey Khoury, who set me up to experiment with weird technologies as part of my job. And I thank my parents, Bill and Carol, who stimulated my career in tech by encouraging me to mess with computers, guns, exploration, and music (happily not all at the same time).

Ross: I'd like to thank Jim Plush, who reached out from California all the way to Indiana and gave me the opportunity to turn my hobby into a part of my daily job. Also thanks to my wife, Brooke, and children, Will and Cara, who let me continue to write about and work on my hobby after hours on said job.

Stefan: I thank my friends and family for their support—especially my parents, Edwin and Irmgard, as well as my sister, Patricia. Also thanks to the University of Trier for a good learning environment. Big thanks to the Scala community for the continuous evolution of the language and the ecosystem.

The whole Scalatra core crew has been incredibly supportive and helpful, especially Ivan Porto Carrero. Early contributions and enthusiasm from Ivan, Jared Armstrong, and Mikko Nylen were part of the mix that got the book off the ground. Thanks, guys!

Lastly, thanks from all of us to everyone who contributes code to framework, and to everyone who uses Scalatra. We hope you enjoy it as much as we do.

about this book

Scalatra is an incredibly easy way to start building HTTP applications. A small but dedicated base of coders uses it, but the interesting thing is that it has a huge total user base: from BBC, Tesco, and McLaren data systems to Box.com, IGN, and Netflix APIs, this little framework has a reach that's out of proportion to its developer numbers. Written by three long-time Scalatra contributors, *Scalatra in Action* takes Scalatra development out of the realm of relatively elite coders and shows a wider audience the simplicity, scalability, and ease of use that have made Scalatra the framework of choice for big organizations doing weird and wonderful things with HTTP.

Roadmap

The book is divided into three parts:

- Part 1 starts with core Scalatra functionality. Chapter 1 gives you a brief taste of what it's like to build an application with Scalatra, and you'll write a small sample application. Chapter 2 provides a broader overview of Scalatra development, and chapters 3 and 4 cover the two core Scalatra concepts—defining HTTP routes and executing actions on HTTP input—in more detail.
- Part 2 deals with common development tasks that aren't necessarily part of the Scalatra core framework. You'll learn how to integrate with external libraries to extend Scalatra's core capabilities. Chapter 5 deals with JSON handling. Chapter 6 demonstrates how to handle file uploads and serve files to clients, and chapter 7 goes into the details of HTML templating. Chapters 8 and 9

cover testing and application deployment, and then chapter 10 explores data
storage and querying.

▪ Part 3 takes on advanced topics. Chapter 11 deals with securing your application using HTTP sessions and authentication strategies. Chapter 12 discusses
asynchronous programming, demonstrating how to use Scala's advanced support for concurrent programming. Finally, chapter 13 shows you how to build,
secure, and document your APIs using the Swagger framework, which has
become the world's most popular way to represent REST APIs.

There's also an appendix, which walks you through a full development setup including installation, code generation, building and running code, and setting up your
favorite IDE.

Who should read this book?

Readers of this book should be familiar with an object-oriented programming language such as Java, Ruby, Python, C#, or Scala. We don't expect that you have a lot
of previous Scala (or Java) experience. We try to provide a gentle introduction to the
Scala language at the same time we're explaining how to do HTTP development
using Scalatra.

We assume that you have a basic familiarity with standard web programming concepts (HTTP requests and responses, basic database knowledge) and that you want to
learn how to do web coding in Scala. This isn't a general introduction to programming. It's also not a book on the Scala language. See *Scala in Action* by Nilanjan Ray-
chaudhuri (Manning, 2013) for a good introductory text on Scala.

Code conventions

This book provides full example listings, which include everything you should need to
learn Scalatra. Source code in listings or in text is in a `fixed-width font like this` to
separate it from ordinary text. Scala method names, component parameters, object
properties, and XML elements and attributes in text are also presented using `fixed-
width font`.

When it's written down, code can be verbose. In many cases, the original source
code (available online) has been reformatted; we've added line breaks and reworked
indentation to accommodate the available page space in the book. In rare cases, even
this wasn't enough, and listings include line-continuation markers. Additionally, comments in the source code have often been removed from the listings when the code is
described in the text. Code annotations accompany some of the source code listings,
highlighting important concepts.

Source code downloads

All source code for this book is freely available via Manning at www.manning.com/
books/scalatra-in-action, and also on GitHub at https://github.com/scalatra/scalatra-
in-action. If you get stuck with any of the example code in the book, check out the source
code using Git and run it—a running application can often be worth many lines of code
in a book! But try to type in as much of the code as you can, instead of copying and past-
ing it from the GitHub repository. It'll help embed the concepts in your mind.

About the authors

Dave Hrycyszyn helps large organizations use emerging technologies for innovation.
He has spent the past two decades designing and building software systems that are
used by several hundred million people worldwide. He's director of strategy and technology at the digital consulting firm Head: https://headlondon.com.

Stefan Ollinger likes to computationally hoist and crunch information. He is an active
Scalatra contributor.

Ross A. Baker is a senior cloud engineer, a Scalate committer, and an organizer of the
Indy Scala meetup.

about the cover illustration

The figure on the cover of *Scalatra in Action* is captioned "Girl from Novi Vinodolski, Croatia." The illustration is taken from a reproduction of an album of Croatian traditional costumes from the mid-nineteenth century by Nikola Arsenovic, published by the Ethnographic Museum in Split, Croatia, in 2003. The illustrations were obtained from a helpful librarian at the Ethnographic Museum in Split, itself situated in the Roman core of the medieval center of the town: the ruins of Emperor Diocletian's retirement palace from around AD 304. The book includes finely colored illustrations of figures from different regions of Croatia, accompanied by descriptions of the costumes and of everyday life.

Dress codes and lifestyles have changed over the last 200 years, and the diversity by region, so rich at the time, has faded away. It's now hard to tell apart the inhabitants of different continents, let alone of different hamlets or towns separated by only a few miles. Perhaps we have traded cultural diversity for a more varied personal life—certainly for a more varied and fast-paced technological life.

Manning celebrates the inventiveness and initiative of the computer business with book covers based on the rich diversity of regional life of two centuries ago, brought back to life by illustrations from old books and collections like this one.

Part 1

Introduction to Scalatra

This book begins by examining Scalatra's core functionality. Chapter 1 gives you a taste of what it's like to build a small application with Scalatra. Chapter 2 provides a broader overview of Scalatra development, and chapters 3 and 4 discuss defining HTTP routes and executing actions on HTTP input.

Introduction

This chapter covers

- Recognizing what Scalatra is good at
- Writing a simple Hello World web application
- Using microframeworks versus full-stack frameworks

Scalatra is a lightweight web framework written in the up-and-coming new language, Scala. It offers extremely fast development and execution speeds for HTTP applications.

If you're a Java coder who's curious about Scala or looking for a productivity gain, Scalatra offers a perfect opportunity: it's easy to get started with, and if you're already running your web apps in servlet containers, you can drop in a Scalatra application without any fuss. You can be up and running in a few minutes, building simple and intuitive HTTP interfaces to new or existing software.

On the other hand, maybe you're a Perl, PHP, Python, or Ruby coder looking for a massive performance boost. Perhaps you've built a large system and want the refactoring benefits of type safety without Java boilerplate. Scalatra is the simplest way to jump into Scala web development. You get easy access to tens of thousands of battle-tested Java libraries with a simple and familiar HTTP routing DSL wrapped around them.

1.1   What's Scalatra good at?

Scalatra can replace other web development frameworks for most tasks. This book will guide you through all the major aspects of building a web application, starting with an overview in chapter 2 and breaking down the details in chapters 3 through 11.

Mobile app development on Android and iOS has exploded over the past half decade. At the same time, single-page in-browser development frameworks such as Backbone.js, Ember.js, and AngularJS are rapidly gaining in popularity.

All of this means a lot of clients still make heavy use of web technologies but aren't the traditional browser clients we've seen for the past 20 years. Scalatra is a perfect fit for these clients. It's easy to install, lightweight, and fast. It lets you design and build out high-performance web APIs quickly, and it's integrated with special tools to produce beautiful, functional, and correct API documentation.

Another major area of internet innovation recently is in the realm of server-push technologies. Scalatra incorporates advanced constructs for event-driven programming, so you can easily push information into your users' browsers—they see constantly updated information without having to refresh the page. This technology has the potential to turn the web upside-down.

Finally, in some cases people are using full-sized frameworks for the bulk of their web development functionality, and they bust out Scalatra for specific, high-performance actions. This means it's relatively easy to try it out in an isolated part of your system. You can use Scalatra to solve performance hotspots or wrap a legacy set of class libraries in a shiny new HTTP layer.

1.2   Hello World

Scalatra is simple. All you need to do is add a small configuration file and download and run one command, and you have a running web application. The following listing illustrates just how simple a Scalatra program can be.

Listing 1.1   Scalatra in action

```
package com.example.yourapp
import org.scalatra._

class HelloWorld extends ScalatraServlet {
  get("/") {
    "Hello world"
  }
}
```

When you run this code on your local machine, you can type `http://localhost:8080/` into your browser and see the text "Hello world" in return, as shown in figure 1.1.

There's a lot more to learn, but that simple code expresses the essence of Scalatra. You define a *route*, which is a combination of an HTTP verb (`get`) and a URL route

Figure 1.1 "Hello world" **output**

matcher (/), which executes a block of code on the server and returns the result (in this case, the string "Hello world"). The next listing explains things line by line.

Listing 1.2 Anatomy of "Hello world"

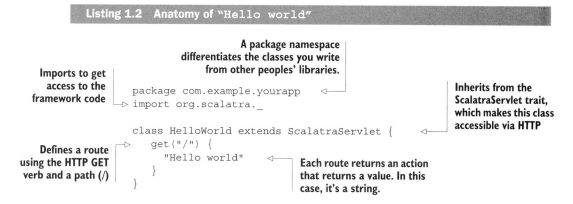

As you can see, Scalatra applications can be very small. What do all of these big organizations see in it? The interesting thing is that there isn't a single answer to that question, because Scalatra is a microframework.

1.3 *Microframeworks vs. full-stack frameworks*

Most web programmers are used to full-stack frameworks. In general, these try to solve all the problems you'll commonly encounter, and to do so within the confines of a fairly unified codebase. Despite their obvious differences, Spring, Symfony, Ruby on Rails, Django, and the Play Framework all share something: they make the assumption that you won't often need (or even want) to step out of the environments they provide.

Microframeworks are different.

Instead of trying to provide for your every need, microframeworks try to do a few things well. In Scalatra's case, you get a great way of expressing HTTP actions, a lot of optional modules for common tasks, and an easy way to bolt on additional libraries to accomplish whatever you want.

The microframework approach is a candid admission by the Scalatra authors that they don't have a clue what you're going to build. It'll probably be related to HTTP, but your choices beyond that—of data stores, template libraries, testing frameworks, strategies for asynchronous requests and responses, server push, message queuing systems, and API documentation—are up to you. Maybe you don't need half the things on that list. Maybe you need all of them, but you want to choose each library yourself.

This lean way of doing things allows you to build up exactly the right capabilities for the job at hand and keeps the amount of extra code in your project to a minimum. If you're building a full-sized web application, like a social network app or an e-commerce application, you can use Scalatra as a full model-view-controller stack, with an HTML templating system and an object-relational mapper for database access. Conversely, if you're building a small, high-performance system, such as an API that routes incoming request data to other systems, or an authorization server, you can import only what's needed to do so.

The lean nature of the resulting codebases means fewer lines of code to maintain. If you structure things well, this can mean speedier development, better performance, and lower maintenance costs than a full-stack framework.

1.4   How does Scalatra compare with other Scala web frameworks?

Scalatra isn't your only choice when it comes to HTTP development in Scala. Other popular frameworks include Lift and Play. Of these three, why would you choose Scalatra? It comes down to trade-offs in several main areas: application development style, the aforementioned microframework versus full-stack approach, and deployment.

1.4.1   Scalatra is a lean MVC framework

Let's consider Scalatra versus Lift first. Unlike the other frameworks, Lift doesn't use the popular *model-view-controller* (MVC) pattern for organizing code. Instead, it offers a *view-first* approach, which many programmers aren't familiar with. Whatever the merits of view-first versus MVC, sometimes familiarity is a big win, especially if you're coming from another MVC framework.

Both Play and Scalatra, in contrast, use the more popular MVC pattern. With Play, you get a larger and more featureful framework than Scalatra. Play favors convention over configuration, so it seeks to decrease the number of decisions you'll typically need to make. Stay on the happy path, and it arguably provides more initial development speed than Scalatra.

But if you stray from Play's application structure or library choices, you may find yourself wanting more flexibility. Scalatra gives you the freedom to curate every library choice and be in complete control of your application's structure.

The other main thing to consider is how you'll host your application when it's built.

1.4.2 *Scalatra runs on servlets*

Once you build your application, you'll need to deploy it to a server in order to make it available to the world. Lift and Scalatra are both designed to be deployed in standard Java servlet containers: Tomcat, JBoss, and Jetty are popular examples. Play, on the other hand, deploys on newer technology: the Netty network application framework. Again, there are various pros and cons to consider.

Netty, which uses the new Java NIO APIs, is a relatively fresh technology and is theoretically more performant. But the subject is complicated, with Netty winning against servlets for some workloads and losing for others.

In contrast to Netty, servlet containers aren't sexy, but they're battle-hardened and have great tooling. Additionally, many people know how to configure them, tune them, and keep them running in production.

One last consideration: many workplaces still mandate servlets for web deployments. In these cases, the ability to deploy on servlets may be make-or-break for Scala adoption.

We hope this is enough to provide a fair overview of possible choices. Now let's write some Scalatra code.

How much Scala do you need to know to read this book?

We write this book under the assumption that Scala is a new language and that there aren't many Scala programmers yet. We suspect that we'll need to teach you a bit about Scala at the same time we teach you Scalatra. We know how daunting it can be to be suddenly thrust not just into the land of Scala, but also into the world of the JVM, if you're coming from another environment. We'll provide a well-lit path for you.

At the same time, Scala is a large language with many concepts that may be unfamiliar to you. Unfortunately, we don't have enough room in this book to provide a full language reference. You should get a copy of *Scala in Action* (Manning, 2013) to read alongside this book if you haven't yet read an introductory book on the Scala language.

1.5 *Installing Scalatra*

Before we can move on to the rest of the book, you'll need to have a running installation of Scalatra. You can find installation instructions in the appendix. It includes full instructions for getting Scalatra installed and for setting up your development environment. If you haven't yet installed Scalatra, take some time now to get set up.

Once you're ready, let's generate, build, and run a traditional Hello World example. The first thing you'll need to do is generate an application skeleton. How does project generation work?

Although you can set up your project almost any way you want, the normal thing to do when starting a new project is to use a tool called giter8 (or g8 for short). giter8 retrieves project templates from Git repositories. The standard Scalatra project template lives in a repository on the popular coding website GitHub, at https://github.com/scalatra/scalatra-sbt.g8.

When you run the g8 command, giter8 will ask you a series of questions about the project you'd like to create. It will then retrieve the standard project skeleton from GitHub, inject the information you provided into the retrieved files, and save them on your machine.

1.5.1   *Generating a new project*

Run the following code in your terminal:

```
g8 scalatra/scalatra-sbt
```

This checks out a prebuilt application skeleton for you (from GitHub) and asks you some questions about your application. giter8 will ask you the following questions when generating a project. Press Enter to accept the default value for each question:

```
$ g8 scalatra/scalatra-sbt
        organization [com.example]:
        name [My Scalatra Web App]:
        version [0.1.0-SNAPSHOT]:
        servlet_name [MyScalatraServlet]:
        package [com.example.app]:
        scala_version [2.11.6]:
        sbt_version [0.13.8]:
        scalatra_version [2.4.0]:
```

giter8 will take your answers to these questions and write them into the build.sbt file for your application, so you can change them in that file later. Table 1.1 gives a basic rundown of what the questions mean.

Table 1.1   Generating a project

g8 question	What it means
organization	Used for publishing. Should be the reverse of a domain name you control. If you don't own a domain, com.github.username is a popular choice.
package	All Scala code belongs in a package. The Scala Style Guide recommends that your packages start with your organization. This convention is used across multiple JVM languages and gives your project a globally unique namespace.
name	The name of your project. g8 generates a project into a folder of this name, and the artifacts you publish will be based on this name.
servlet_name	The name of your servlet. This might be something like BlogServlet, BlogController, or just Blog.
scala_version	The version of Scala your project is built with. When in doubt, use the default.
version	The version number of your project. This is entirely up to you, but we like semantic versioning.

Once you've answered the questions, your answers are applied to the giter8 templates, and the project skeleton is saved on your local system.

> **Check for giter8 templates to speed things up**
> Quite a few Scalatra giter8 templates are available for various purposes. If you're looking to find out how to integrate Scalatra with some other library, do a bit of searching on GitHub, and you may be pleasantly surprised.

1.5.2 Downloading dependencies and building the app

Enter the top-level directory of your new application, and type ./sbt. sbt will take a while to respond, especially the first time. sbt looks at the dependencies defined in the file project/build.scala and downloads Scala, a Scala compiler, Scalatra, and a small set of dependencies of the Scalatra application. That single three-letter command gives you a full web development environment! Once sbt has finished downloading everything, you'll get an sbt prompt, which looks like this: >.

1.5.3 Starting the Hello World application

Let's start the Hello World application:

```
jetty:start
```

That will compile the application and start a web server running on http://localhost:8080. When you see some output like this, you'll know it's running:

```
Started
ServerConnector@5f164c1{HTTP/1.1}{0.0.0.0:8080}
```

Visit it in your browser—you'll see output similar to that in figure 1.2. The first request will be slow, because the application sets itself up for the first time; subsequent requests will get faster and faster as the JVM optimizes code paths for your machine.

We can now take a quick look at the application code. Open the file src/main/scala/com/example/app/MyScalatraServlet.scala. You'll see the code in the following listing; this is a simple Scalatra app containing a single HTTP route.

Figure 1.2 Hello World in your browser

Listing 1.3   Your first Scalatra application

```
package com.example.app

import org.scalatra._
import scalate.ScalateSupport

class MyScalatraServlet extends MyScalatraWebAppStack {

  get("/") {
    <html>
      <body>
        <h1>Hello, world!</h1>
        Say <a href="hello-scalate">hello to Scalate</a>.
      </body>
    </html>
  }

}
```

1.5.4   *Making changes and seeing them in your browser*

Let's change the code so that the response is the same as the original Hello World example that started this chapter. Change the output from an XML literal to a string:

```
get("/") {
  "Hello world"
}
```

Save the file and refresh your browser. The example hasn't changed.

Scala needs to recompile the program in order to make your changes appear. Doing this manually every time you make a change to your source code would be pretty awful, so there's a handy way to make your changes appear automatically.

Back at the sbt console, type this:

```
~jetty:start
```

From this point on, every time you change your code, sbt will automatically recompile the application code to make your changes visible. It will then reload the server. When that's done, you'll see this information in your console:

```
[success] Total time: 1 s, completed 01-Feb-2014 23:38:44
3. Waiting for source changes... (press enter to interrupt)
```

Click Refresh in your browser, and you should see your changes. When you're only modifying web assets, you can run the ~webappPrepare task, which leads to faster turn-around times.

How do I stop?

When you want to stop the reloader, press the Enter key. If you want to stop serving your application, type `jetty:stop`. To get out of the sbt console, type `exit`.

Finally, let's change the URL matcher. Change this

```
get("/") {
  "Hello world!"
}
```

to this:

```
get("/hello") {
  "Hello world!"
}
```

Visit it in your browser, at http://localhost:8080/hello. You're done!

1.6   *Summary*

- Microframeworks let you structure things exactly to your liking.
- Scalatra applications are generated using the command g8.
- The Scala build command sbt will download a functioning Scala environment.
- Scalatra comes prebundled with a web server so you can get started coding without a lot of setup.
- You can define HTTP actions with very little code.

A taste of Scalatra

This chapter covers

- Understanding the framework's major features
- A brief introduction to the concept of routing
- Sending parameters to a Scalatra application

As an introduction to building applications with Scalatra, let's start with a basic page-retrieval system and then move on to more-advanced functionality. Because it's your first app, we'll keep the initial requirements fairly simple. You want to be able to visit URLs in the browser, retrieve data from a data store, format the data into styled HTML, and display the page. These are the sorts of common tasks that can be accomplished by pretty much any web framework. In this case, you'll build a site that displays food-related text.

2.1 Your first Scalatra application

Let's try generating a Scalatra application. Scalatra code generation is handled by a utility called g8, which grabs application templates from the internet, customizes them, and saves them on disk for you. To use g8, type the following on the command line:

```
$ g8 scalatra/scalatra-sbt.g8
    organization [com.example]:
    name [My Scalatra Web App]: Scalatra CMS
    version [0.1.0-SNAPSHOT]:
    servlet_name [MyScalatraServlet]: PagesController
    package [com.example.app]: com.example.cms
    scala_version [2.11.6]:
    sbt_version [0.13.8]:
    scalatra_version [2.4.0]:
```

When you run the g8 command, you're asked some questions about your application, in the order shown. Once you answer the last question, giter8 creates your project for you, and you can run the project using the ./sbt command:

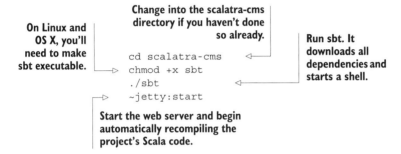

Your application is now running, although it doesn't do anything yet. Let's turn to the user interface, so you can see something happen.

> **Installation**
> If you haven't yet installed g8, conscript, and sbt, make sure you read the installation instructions in the appendix before proceeding any further in the book.

2.2 Designing the UI

Next you'll build an HTML user interface for your application. It's often best to start by visualizing the interface you want, so figure 2.1 shows a quick sketch of the user interface you'll achieve.[1]

The page is pretty simple. You can see a title at the top, a summary below that, and body text at the bottom. The application will run at the web address http://localhost:8080/pages, and you'll retrieve the page via its slug, bacon-ipsum, which you can see in the address bar.

---

[1] We copied the text from the fabulous http://baconipsum.com. If your tastes run in a different direction, you can always head over to http://veggieipsum.com, or the canonical http://lipsum.com.

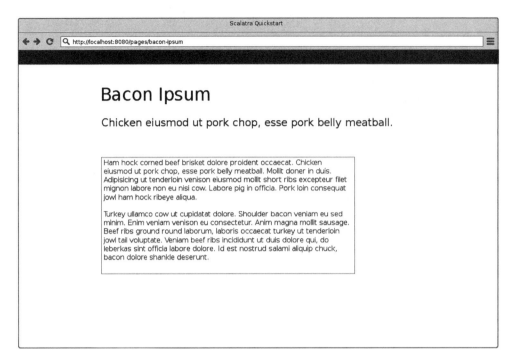

Figure 2.1   Bacon Ipsum

2.3   *What's in a Scalatra project?*

At its core, Scalatra is nothing more than a way of routing HTTP requests in order to execute blocks of code on the server. Almost everything else comes from external libraries, which are regular JAR files containing packaged JVM bytecode. Scalatra handles HTTP requests and responses; for all other functionality, you choose from the vast array of Scala (and Java) libraries and use them as building blocks for your application.

Figure 2.2 shows the relationship between the various components, with some commonly used external libraries grouped by function. The default g8 template gives you the Scalatra core DSL, Scalate templating, the Specs2 testing library, a logger, and a Jetty web server to run your project. You're free to customize the application stack, using the libraries that suit your needs. Your application can use zero or more of the libraries from any given group. To add a library to your application, add a new dependency line in the `libraryDependencies` section of the file project/build.scala (see the appendix for more on this).

When you generate a project using g8, Scalatra sets up a project as shown in figure 2.3. The `PagesController` class, which is the class file you'll do most of your work in (shown in listing 2.1), is found in src/main/com/example/cms/PagesController.scala. It looks much like the Hello World application you generated in chapter 1.

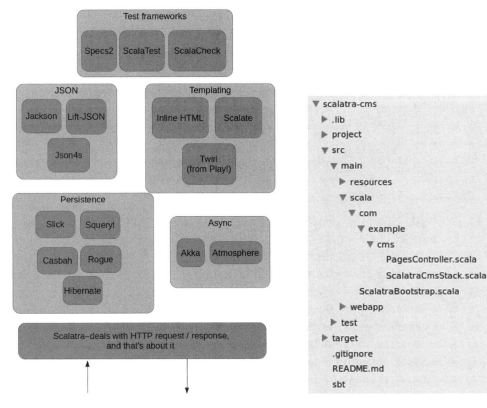

Figure 2.2 Scalatra and a few related technologies

Figure 2.3 A new Scalatra project

Listing 2.1 Generated PagesController

```
package com.example.cms

import org.scalatra._
  import scalate.ScalateSupport

class PagesController extends ScalatraCmsStack {

  get("/") {
    <html>
      <body>
        <h1>Hello, world!</h1>
        Say <a href="hello-scalate">hello to Scalate</a>.
      </body>
    </html>
  }

}
```

Defines a package name to group code

Imports everything in another package. The _ here is equivalent to * in Java or C#.

Imports a single class from another package

You should be able to visit your application at http://localhost:8080. It doesn't look like much yet, but that will change. Before working on the user interface, though, you should think about the data you want to show.

2.4   Building the data model

Data is fundamental to most applications, so let's begin building Scalatra CMS by defining the data model. All you need to start with is a simple Scala case class. If you believed the application was going to grow significantly, you could create some new package namespaces and files for your models to live in, but in this case you'll keep things simple. Drop the following code into the end of PagesController.scala:

```
case class Page(slug:String, title:String, summary:String, body: String)
```

A Scala case class automatically creates accessors for all the properties listed in the constructor. So in the case of the Page class, you can get all the properties with which you initialize an instance.

The Page class has a title, a summary, and main body text. It also has a slug, which allows you to retrieve the page.

You could store the page data in a database such as PostgreSQL or MySQL. Like other web frameworks, Scalatra can do this, and you'll find out how in chapter 9. For the moment, you'll set up the simplest possible data store for your pages: an immutable List containing Page data. Let's make some pages now.

You'll make two pages: one for Bacon Ipsum lovers, and another for veggies. Drop the code from the next listing into the end of the PagesController class file, after the case class Page definition.

Listing 2.2   A simple data storage mechanism

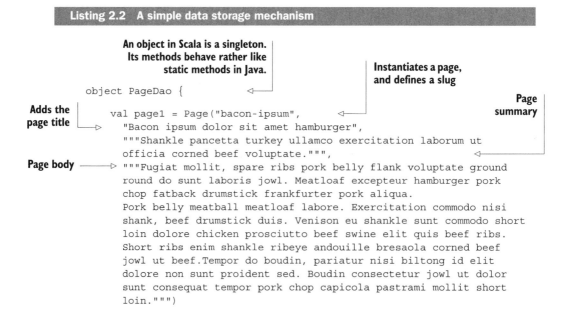

**Another
page, again
starting
with a slug,
and repeat** ┌──▷

```
val page2 = Page("veggie-ipsum",
    "Arugula prairie turnip desert raisin sierra leone",
    """Veggies sunt bona vobis, proinde vos postulo esse magis napa
    cabbage beetroot dandelion radicchio.""",
    """Brussels sprout mustard salad jícama grape nori chickpea
    dulse tatsoi. Maize broccoli rabe collard greens jícama wattle
    seed nori garbanzo epazote coriander mustard.""")

  val pages = List(page1, page2)   ◁──── Defines a list of pages
}
```

Classes in Scala aren't allowed to define static methods—but you can get roughly the same effect by defining an `object`. Listing 2.2 sets up a Scala `object` called `PageDao`. You can call `PageDao.pages` directly, without explicitly instantiating anything, just like a static method in Java or C# or a class method in Ruby.

2.5 Retrieving pages

Now that you have some pages stored, you need a way to retrieve them. Scalatra is an implementation of Ruby's Sinatra DSL in Scala, and when it comes to dealing with HTTP, it looks almost identical to Sinatra. You make methods available over HTTP by setting up routes, and you execute code, called *actions*, inside the routes.

2.5.1 A page-retrieval route

There are several different types of routes, and most of them correspond to an HTTP verb—your choices are GET, POST, PUT, and DELETE, along with a few others for specific situations. You'll see more about routes in chapter 3. For now, let's define a route that you can use to retrieve your pages.

The route needs to GET a page, identified by the page's slug. Delete the entire `get("/")` action, which currently looks like this:

```
get("/") {
  <html>
    <body>
      <h1>Hello, world!</h1>
      Say <a href="hello-scalate">hello to Scalate</a>.
    </body>
  </html> }
```

Replace that code with a page-retrieval route, which looks like this:

```
get("/pages/:slug") {

}
```

Let's break that down. The route starts with `get` and defines a route matcher (pages/:slug). The `:slug` portion of the route matcher tells Scalatra that you're defining a parameter in the URL, so anything submitted at the `:slug` part of the URL is treated as input to the route.

You're running this web app on http://localhost:8080. Any HTTP GET request to the path http://localhost:8080/pages/anything-at-all will match the route and cause the route's body, or action code, to execute.

2.5.2 A page-retrieval action

Let's fill in the action so your web application starts to do something useful. Enter the body of the action as shown next.

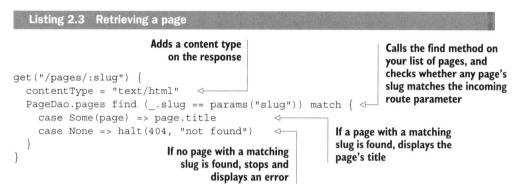

Listing 2.3 Retrieving a page

```
get("/pages/:slug") {
  contentType = "text/html"
  PageDao.pages find (_.slug == params("slug")) match {
    case Some(page) => page.title
    case None => halt(404, "not found")
  }
}
```

Adds a content type on the response

Calls the find method on your list of pages, and checks whether any page's slug matches the incoming route parameter

If a page with a matching slug is found, displays the page's title

If no page with a matching slug is found, stops and displays an error

There's quite a bit going on here. The route's action uses the find method from Scala's List class. The _ may look strange if you haven't seen it before; although the _ symbol has many different uses in Scala, in this case it's used as a wildcard pattern. Every Page object instance in the PageDao.pages list is iteratively sent to the match function, and if a Page's slug matches the params("slug"), the match block yields that Page's title. If no matching page is found, the match block calls halt and returns an HTTP 404 status code.

Time to try it out. Save your work, and ensure that you've enabled automatic compilation. You know your data store contains pages with the slugs bacon-ipsum and veggie-ipsum, so choose the one that matches your preference and retrieve it in a browser. For our part, we chose http://localhost:8080/pages/bacon-ipsum. Type your chosen address into a browser address bar, and you'll get back something like figure 2.4, displaying the page title.

Figure 2.4 Following a route in the browser

Figure 2.5   Generating a 404 message

Next, let's try using a slug that you know doesn't exist: http://localhost:8080/pages/ pizza-ipsum. This time, you'll see the "not found" message you defined in the case None => halt(404, "not found") matcher in your controller, as shown in figure 2.5.

Finally, let's try a route that doesn't exist: http://localhost:8080/foo/bar. The behavior is slightly different. You'll see something like figure 2.6.

In this case, you're shown the default Scalatra error-handling page, because no matching routes were found. This one is subtly different from the /pages/pizza-ipsum route in figure 2.5. Although you didn't define a Page with the slug pizza-ipsum, the URL path /pages/pizza-ipsum did match the route get("/pages/:slug") defined in your application. You defined your own 404 message to be shown when the page wasn't found. The URL path /foo/bar doesn't match any of the routes you defined in the controller class, and it falls through to the default Scalatra 404 page, which lets you know that no routes were matched.

Where are the tests?

You may have noticed that we're not using any automated tests here. You can find a short introduction in section 2.7. In chapter 8 you'll see how to write tests in Scalatra in detail.

Now that you've got a handle on hitting route matchers and sending simple text back in response, let's look at how to render more-complex content for display in a browser.

Figure 2.6   The default Scalatra 404 page

2.6   *Rendering the page*

The get("/pages/:slug") action does its job and shows you the page title, but it's not likely to win any design awards. Let's fix that by rendering an HTML page to the browser.

2.6.1   *A quick introduction to Scalate*

Scalatra has a number of different ways of rendering HTML, and you'll get full coverage of the options in chapter 7. For the moment, let's use the Scalate template engine, which is probably the most common way of doing templating in Scalatra.

Scalate supports multiple templating styles. We'll use the Scala Server Pages (SSP) style, which is similar to Java's Velocity or Ruby's ERB template engines.

First, let's change the output of the page-retrieval action so that it renders a page instead of merely displaying the page's title. You can do this by changing the body of the page-retrieval action so it contains the code from the following listing.

Listing 2.4   Using Scalate from an action

```
get("/pages/:slug") {
  contentType = "text/html"
  PageDao.pages find (_.slug == params("slug")) match {
    case Some(page) => ssp("/pages/show", "page" -> page)    ⟵── Renders a page instead of just printing a page title
    case None => halt(404, "not found")
  }
}
```

The ssp method attempts to render a template, and it passes the page from your PageDao to the template. In order for this to work, you need to make a template for displaying pages.

The default Scalatra project structure includes a webapp folder, which holds your application's static assets (images, CSS, and JavaScript) and also provides a place for you to keep your HTML templates, in the WEB-INF/templates folder. Figure 2.7 gives you an idea of where this sits in the project's structure.

By default, g8 generated two template files, default.jade and hello-scalate.jade, both of which use the Jade templating style. You'll use the SSP style instead, so delete both of the .jade files. Create a pages directory to hold page-related templates and a show.ssp template file, as shown in figure 2.8. The contents of show.ssp should look like the next listing.

Figure 2.7   Views in your project structure

Listing 2.5 Initial page template

```
<%@ import val page: com.example.cms.Page %>

<div class="row">
  <div class="span6">
      <h2><%= page.title %> </h2>
      <p class="lead"><%= page.summary %></p>
      <p><%= page.body %></p>
  </div>
</div>
```

If you're coming from a dynamic language such as Python, Ruby, or PHP, you may be surprised by the first line. Like most other things in Scala, variables in Scalate templates are statically typed, and you need to explicitly define all template variables and their types before you can use them. The `import` statement ensures that this template has access to your `com.example.chat.Page` class. `val page` declares a page variable so Scalate knows how to access the `page` being passed to it from the page-retrieval action.

Figure 2.8 Create a show.ssp template.

With the page template in place, you can view http://localhost:8080/pages/bacon-ipsum in your browser. You see the page's title, summary, and body displayed, as shown in figure 2.9

2.6.2 Adding a layout

You can quickly make things look nicer by wrapping the page template in a layout that includes some boilerplate CSS. Open the layouts folder, and create a new file called default.ssp containing the contents of listing 2.6. By convention, Scalate will use this file as the layout for your pages/show.ssp template. It will wrap the contents of listing 2.6 around the HTML output of each of your controller's actions, inserting the action's output into the layout at the point where the layout says `<%= unescape(body) %>`.

Figure 2.9
Template output
using SSP

Listing 2.6   A Scalate layout

```
<%@ val body:String %>
<html>
  <head>
    <title>Scalatra CMS</title>
    <!-- Bootstrap -->
    <link href="/css/bootstrap.min.css" rel="stylesheet" media="screen">
    <style type="text/css">
      body {
        padding-top: 60px;
      }
    </style>
  </head>
  <body>
    <div class="navbar navbar-inverse navbar-fixed-top">
      <div class="navbar-inner">
        <div class="container">
          <a class="btn btn-navbar" data-toggle="collapse"
            data-target=".nav-collapse">
            <span class="icon-bar"></span>
            <span class="icon-bar"></span>
            <span class="icon-bar"></span>
          </a>
          <ul class="nav">
            <li>
              <a class="brand" href="#" id="server">
                Scalatra CMS
              </a>
            </li>
          </ul>
        </div>
      </div>
    </div>

    <div class="container">

      <%= unescape(body) %>

    </div> <!-- /container -->
  </body>
</html>
```

This is a fairly unexceptional layout based on the popular Twitter Bootstrap framework. Download the referenced CSS and JavaScript from http://getbootstrap.com/2.3.2/, and put them into your application's webapp/css, webapp/js, and webapp/img folders. Refresh the page in your browser, and you should get a result like figure 2.10.

You now have a much better-looking result. The output of the action get("/pages/:slug") is inserted into the default SSP layout you just defined.

When a page is found, the get("/pages/:slug") action calls ssp("/pages/show", "page" -> page). The HTML generated out of views/pages/show.ssp is then inserted into the default.ssp layout at the point where it says <%= unescape(body) %>.

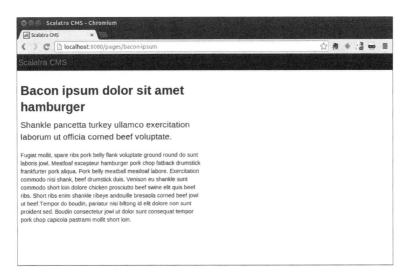

Figure 2.10   Adding a layout

Now that you've been introduced to templating, it's time to turn your attention to another important tool: automated testing.

2.7   Writing tests

Scalatra has integrations for the major Scala test frameworks: ScalaTest, Specs2, and ScalaCheck. Which one to use is mostly a matter of personal taste. You'll get a full tour of Scala testing libraries in chapter 8, but for the moment let's test the /pages/bacon-ipsum route using the Specs2 library, which is used by default in Scalatra's g8 template.

2.7.1   Writing your first test

When you generated your project, you may have noticed that the src folder containing your application's source code has two subdirectories: main and test. So far, you've done everything in the application's main directory, which contains the application itself. Now let's explore the test directory, which you can see expanded in a file browser in figure 2.11.

If you open the test directory tree, you'll see that when you generated your PagesController, g8 automatically generated a matching test file called PagesControllerSpec. Open that now.

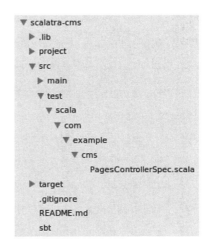

Figure 2.11   You've got tests!

The default generated test looks like this:

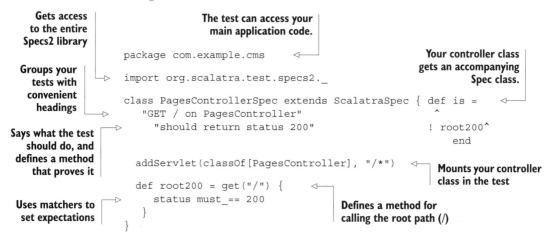

Gets access to the entire Specs2 library

The test can access your main application code.

Groups your tests with convenient headings

Your controller class gets an accompanying Spec class.

Says what the test should do, and defines a method that proves it

Mounts your controller class in the test

Uses matchers to set expectations

Defines a method for calling the root path (/)

```
package com.example.cms

import org.scalatra.test.specs2._

class PagesControllerSpec extends ScalatraSpec { def is =
    "GET / on PagesController"
        "should return status 200"                    ! root200^
                                                       end

    addServlet(classOf[PagesController], "/*")

    def root200 = get("/") {
        status must_== 200
    }
}
```

This is a Specs2 acceptance test designed to exercise the `PagesController`. In its present form, it's not much use, though, because it's not testing a route that you've defined. There's a test for the root path of the servlet (/), but there's no test for the route `get("/pages/:slug")` you're interested in testing.

First, change the route being tested to GET /pages/:slug, as shown in the following listing, so you're testing the correct route.

Listing 2.7   Testing the /pages/:slug route

Tests the /pages/:slug route

Calls the pagesWork method to test whether pages work

Follows the correct route, with a slug you know exists

```
package com.example.cms

import org.scalatra.test.specs2._

class PagesControllerSpec extends ScalatraSpec { def is =
    "GET /pages/:slug on PagesController"
        "should return status 200"                    ! pagesWork^
                                                       end

    addServlet(classOf[PagesController], "/*")

    def pagesWork = get("/pages/bacon-ipsum") {
        status must_== 200
    }

}
```

Let's take a closer look at the structure of the test. The def `pagesWork` function is fairly self-explanatory: it's a regular Scala method that follows the `get("/pages/bacon-ipsum")` route in the `PagesController` and gets access to the resulting response `status` and the response `body`. The `! pagesWork^` part probably deserves a bit more explanation, though.

Specs2 uses the `^` operator to separate your test headings into a series of tests that it can then output into your test runner. The `!` operator tells Specs2 that you'd like to

run the `pagesWork` method to prove the assertion that hitting the pages route `should
return status 200`. The 200 HTTP status, of course, is the web server status, which
denotes a successful request. As you add more tests, you'll slowly build out the list of
assertions, adding more spec lines that call methods using `!` and separated by `^`.

2.7.2 Running your tests

Let's try running the new test. In a new terminal window, run `./sbt` again so you have
a fresh `sbt` prompt running. Then type `~ test` to execute all test code in your application. Additionally, because the command is prefaced with `~`, it watches your filesystem
for changes, recompiles, and reruns the `test` command whenever you make a change
in your application. You'll see output like figure 2.12: there's a green success indicator
after every passing test, and an overview message about the entire test run (in this
case, a green success message).

```
[info] PagesControllerSpecGET /pages/:slug on PagesController+ should return status 200
[info] Total for specification PagesControllerSpec
[info] Finished in 730 ms
[info] 1 example, 0 failure, 0 error
[info] Passed: Total 1, Failed 0, Errors 0, Passed 1
[success] Total time: 2 s, completed 26-Jan-2014 17:32:41
1. Waiting for source changes... (press enter to interrupt)
```

Figure 2.12   Test output

2.7.3 Adding another test

To round things out, let's add one more test. When hitting the `get("/pages/:slug")`
route, you can expect to see the word *Bacon* in the response body. Check that it's there
by adding the following test code.

Listing 2.8   Setting an expectation on the response body

```
package com.example.chat

import org.scalatra.test.specs2._

class PagesControllerSpec extends ScalatraSpec { def is =
  "GET /pages/:slug on PagesController"
    "should return status 200"                     ! pagesWork^       Adds a new
    "shows the word 'Bacon' in the body"           ! containsBacon^   expectation
                                                     end

  addServlet(classOf[PagesController], "/*")

  def pagesWork = get("/pages/bacon-ipsum") {
    status must_== 200
  }                                                    Sets up a new
                                                       assertion function,
  def containsBacon = get("/pages/bacon-ipsum") {      and tries the route
    body must contain("Bacon")
  }                              Specifies that the body must
}                               contain a known string
```

If you're still running your ~ `test` terminal, then sbt should automatically recompile your test code and run it.

Before moving on to deployment, it's a good idea to see a failing test (because that's what you're supposed to write first). Generally speaking, there are two cases you'll encounter over and over when testing: code errors and test failures.

CODE ERRORS

You may see syntax errors in either the code being tested or the test code itself. Try generating error output by opening your `PagesController` and dropping some garbage into the body of the class. We typed the word *foo* right before the end of the class and saved the file; our tests ran, and the compiler displayed the error shown in figure 2.13. (Remember to take the *foo* out of your `PagesController` class body before you continue!)

Figure 2.13   A compile error in the test terminal

TEST FAILURES

The application may compile and run but not meet the expectations you've set up. To see what happens, change the `containsBacon` function in your `PagesControllerSpec` so that it looks like this (substitute the word *flowers* instead of *Bacon* in the assertion testing the response body):

```
def containsBacon = get("/pages/bacon-ipsum") {
  body must contain("flowers")
}
```

You'll see output like that in figure 2.14.

You're told that although the code compiled and everything ran without problems, the expectation that the response body contains the word *flowers* wasn't met. Your application is "working" insofar as it's not throwing a 500 error. But it's not doing what the test is asserting about the way the application should behave. Set that test assertion back to *Bacon*, and bask in the warm glow of a test suite running green.

2.8   *Getting ready for deployment*

Now that your app has some basic tests, you may want to deploy it so you can show off what you've done. You'll see a full breakdown of deployment options in chapter 9. For the moment, we'll show you only the basics of exporting a deployable copy of your application.

First, stop automatic compilation in your sbt console by pressing the Enter key. Then type `package` and press Enter again. sbt packages your application into a *WAR file*—a *web application archive.* This is a self-contained export of your entire application, including

```
[error]       </div>
[error]       </div>
[error]       </div> <!-- /container -->
[error]       </body>
[error]       </html>' doesn't contain 'flowers' (PagesControllerSpec.scala:18)
[info]
[info] Total for specification PagesControllerSpec
[info] Finished in 801 ms
[info] 2 examples, 1 failure, 0 error
[error] Failed: Total 2, Failed 1, Errors 0, Passed 1
[error] Failed tests:
[error]         com.example.cms.PagesControllerSpec
[error] (test:test) sbt.TestsFailedException: Tests unsuccessful
[error] Total time: 3 s, completed 26-Jan-2014 17:38:41
4. Waiting for source changes... (press enter to interrupt)
```

Figure 2.14   A failure of expectations

the Java bytecode, templates, and other resources needed to run it, all zipped up into a single file. When packaging is complete, sbt will tell you where it put the file, with console output as shown in figure 2.15. In our case, the file ended up at target/scala-2.10/scalatra-cms_2.10-0.1.0-SNAPSHOT.war.

```
> package
[info] Compiling Templates in Template Directory: /home/dave/Desktop/chapter02/src/main/webapp/WEB-INF/templates
SLF4J: Failed to load class "org.slf4j.impl.StaticLoggerBinder".
SLF4J: Defaulting to no-operation (NOP) logger implementation
SLF4J: See http://www.slf4j.org/codes.html#StaticLoggerBinder for further details.
[info] Packaging /home/dave/Desktop/chapter02/target/scala-2.11/chapter-2-scalatra-cms_2.11-0.1.0-SNAPSHOT.war ...
[info] Done packaging.
```

Figure 2.15   Packaging a WAR file

Once the WAR file has exported, you can drop it into a servlet container (Tomcat, JBoss AS, and Glassfish are popular open source containers), or you can upload to a platform such as Jelastic, which takes care of the infrastructure for you. You'll see detailed deployment instructions in chapter 9.

2.9   Summary

- Routes, route parameters, actions, and template rendering work together in a Scalatra application. We'll go into these in greater detail in future chapters.
- Adding a layout can give your application a consistent look and style.
- Scalatra serves static CSS, JavaScript, and image files from inside the webapp directory.
- Automated tests ensure the correctness of your code. You can easily distinguish between test failures and broken application code by watching for compilation errors.
- Scalatra applications can be exported as self-contained WAR files for production deployments.

Routing 3

This chapter covers
- Defining a route
- Choosing the right HTTP method
- Matching path expressions
- Exploring advanced routes

Scalatra is often referred to as a web framework. This is fair. Scalatra ably handles requests from a web browser and responds with dynamically generated HTML. But *web framework* fails to tell the whole story. We prefer to call Scalatra an *HTTP framework*. This distinction is subtle but important.

Scalatra often serves applications unrelated to web clients. It's used for RESTful services that may serve a mobile application or integrate internal systems. One user even uses Scalatra to provide an interface to his home heater. This is all made possible by Scalatra's firm embrace of HTTP.

Routes are the glue that binds HTTP requests to the blocks of Scala code that implement your application logic. New Scala developers with HTTP experience should find immediate comfort in Scalatra's HTTP DSL. If you're new to HTTP, don't despair. Although full coverage of HTTP is out of scope for\this book, we'll cover enough to empower you to make the right decisions when designing your HTTP API.

In this chapter, we'll demonstrate routing with a simple music service.[1]

3.1 Anatomy of a route

Routes are declared directly in the body of your Scalatra application. Let's look at an example in figure 3.1.

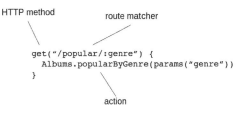

Figure 3.1   Anatomy of a route

A Scalatra route is composed of three main components:

- *The HTTP method*—This is required. HTTP supports only eight methods, and we'll cover them all in section 3.2.
- *The route matcher*—The route is matched by a single *path expression*. Route matchers are flexible in number and type. Matchers are discussed in section 3.3.
- *The action*—This is also required, and it's the block of code responsible for handling the request and generating a response. Actions will be discussed in chapter 4.

Now that you understand the syntax of a route, let's go into detail about how to define it. We'll start with a discussion of methods.

3.2 Choosing the right method

HTTP supports just eight methods. Making it simpler still, a couple of these methods derive their semantics from other methods. This controlled vocabulary allows clients and servers to have certain expectations of each other, regardless of the application.

Unfortunately, these expectations can't be enforced by the Scala compiler. Choosing the right method and implementing it according to convention is a crucial part of writing an HTTP API.

> **TIP** Consumers of your API will tend to consume a lot of APIs and will have certain expectations. Your API may be combined with other APIs in a mashup. The *principle of least astonishment* applies to HTTP as much as it does to your lower-level code. Learn the conventions and follow them, and your API will stand a greater chance of success.

3.2.1 The CRUD methods

With few exceptions, application developers eventually need to deal with persistence. Whether that storage is a trusty old SQL engine or cutting-edge cloud storage, a CRUD pattern inevitably emerges in most applications. The mapping between CRUD and HTTP methods is not quite one-to-one (as shown in table 3.1), but it's simple to implement a CRUD service over HTTP.

---

[1] We might not topple iTunes or Amazon Music, but we'll have a good time name-checking our favorite artists.

Table 3.1 CRUD-to-HTTP method mapping

CRUD operation	HTTP method
Create	▪ POST ▪ PUT
Read	▪ GET
Update	▪ PUT ▪ PATCH
Delete	▪ DELETE

> **NOTE** Method names are uppercase in the HTTP protocol but, following the Scala Style Guide (http://docs.scala-lang.org/style/), always use lowercase in Scalatra code.

HTTP doesn't know about rows in relational databases, documents in MongoDB, or any other data store's implementation. When we speak of CRUD in a Scalatra service, we're referring to *resources*. We'll discuss how URIs are matched in section 3.3 and map them to the persistence layer in chapter 10. But first, we'll discuss how the HTTP methods would be mapped to the CRUD operations of a resource that represents an artist in our music service.

GET

GET is the most familiar of the HTTP methods. When a user enters an address in the browser's location bar, a GET request is submitted. Simple hyperlinks generate a GET request. The class in the following listing creates a route that fetches information about an artist by name.

Listing 3.1 Fetching an artist with get

```
class RecordStore extends ScalatraServlet {
  get("/artists/:name/info") {
    Artist.find(params("name")) match {
      case Some(artist) => artist.toXml
      case None => status = 404
    }
  }
}
```

Don't worry about the :name path expression or the action body for now. These will be discussed in detail in section 3.3.1 and chapter 4, respectively. The focus here is to get a feel for choosing the correct method.

Use GET in the following situations:

▪ *When you're implementing a read-only operation, such as the R in CRUD*—A GET action must not have any observable side effects. It's fine to populate a cache from a GET action, but it would be inappropriate to modify the document being retrieved.

- *When the request can be submitted repeatedly*—Building on the read-only nature, the application should be prepared to handle identical GET requests. It need not respond identically if an intervening event changes the application's state. For web interfaces, ask yourself if your application is prepared for a user who leans on the F5 key.

- *When the response should be bookmarkable or indexed in search engines*—Whenever you see a link in a search engine, it's a GET request. Your bookmarks all represent GET requests. The QR code on the back of your company's T-shirt generates a GET request. If the URL is meant to be shared, think GET.

POST

The default method of a web form is POST, but POST isn't limited to web forms. The request body may contain any arbitrary data, described by the Content-Type header of the request. Other common POST bodies include JSON, XML, and images. Special handling for JSON bodies is discussed in chapter 5.

The following listing declares a route to add a new artist to the database via a POST.

Listing 3.2   Adding a new artist with `post`

```
class RecordStore extends ScalatraServlet {
  post("/artists/new") {
    val artist = parseArtist(request)
    Artist.save(artist)
    val location = s"/artists/${artists.name}"
    Created(artist, headers = "Location" -> location)      ⊲⎯⎯ Generates a 201
  }                                                                Created response with
                                                                   Location header

  def parseArtist(implicit request: HttpServletRequest): Artist =
    Artist(
      name = Artist.fromParam(params("name")),
      nationality = params("nationality"),
      isActive = params("isActive").toBoolean      ⊲⎯⎯ Reads the artist from the request
    )                                                    parameters. Input parsing is
  }                                                      covered in chapter 4.
}
```

A typical POST action parses the request body, creates a new resource on the server, and responds with a pointer to the new resource. All HTTP responses include a status code to inform the client of the result of the request.

The default is 200 OK, which is appropriate for successful GET requests. This POST resulted in the creation of a resource, so you respond with a Created action result. This sets the response status to 201 Created, along with a Location header. The header points to a URL at which your new artist can be fetched via a subsequent GET request. Action results are discussed in depth in section 4.6.3.

Use POST in the following cases:

- *When implementing create operations, such as the C in CRUD*—In this usage, a POST action reads the request body according to its Content-Type header and adds a new resource to the application.
- *When the server is responsible for generating a URI for the created entity*—It's bad form to allow POSTs on resources that don't already exist. A POST request often hits a parent URI and responds with a Location header giving the URI of the newly created resource. This is similar to autogenerating a key in a database when a record is inserted.
- *When you're implementing a write operation, and nothing else seems to fit*—POST is a good default choice, because it's the only CRUD method that's not *idempotent*. A client should be able to resubmit a GET, DELETE, or PUT request and expect the same result. A POST offers no such guarantee and is thus more flexible in its implementation. This is the reason why web browsers issue a warning when a POST request is resubmitted.

WARNING   HTML forms only support GET and POST, requiring scripting for a browser client to submit methods such as PUT or DELETE. Some corporate proxies rigidly reject anything but a GET or POST. In these circumstances, it's tempting to treat all non-GET operations as POSTs. A better alternative is introduced in section 3.2.3.

PUT

PUT requests are most similar to POST. The PUT body should overwrite the resource at the specified URI. The following listing updates an existing artist with PUT.

Listing 3.3   Updating an artist with put

```
class RecordStore extends ScalatraServlet {
  put("/artists/:name"/) {
    val artist = parseArtist(request)
    Artist.update(params("name"), artist)
    NoContent()                                          Sets the status to 204
  }                                                      No Content

  def parseArtist(implicit request: HttpServletRequest): Artist = {
    Artist(
      name = Artist.fromParam(params("name")),
      nationality = params("nationality"),
      isActive = params("isActive").toBoolean          Reads the artist from the request, using
    )                                                  the same method as in listing 3.2
  }
}
```

PUT requests tend to look a lot like POSTs: you parse the input, modify the data store, and return. In fact, parsing the input is usually identical between PUT and PUT routes for a given type.

In contrast to the POST handler in listing 3.2, here you return a NoContent status. Instead of regurgitating a representation of the resource identical to the request body, NoContent signals to the client that the update was successful, and there's nothing left to be said in the response body.

Use PUT in the following cases:

- *When implementing update operations, such as the U in CRUD*—All the same techniques used to read a POST request body are available to PUT. It's not uncommon for a POST and a PUT action to share code.
- *When implementing create operations, such as the C in CRUD when the URI is known*—Note in the CRUD mapping table that a create operation can be implemented as either a POST or a PUT. The correct choice depends on whether the resource's URI is fully known to the client. Unlike a POST, a PUT can be executed on a new URI. Use PUT if the client assigns the identifier, or POST if the server does.

> **PATCH**
>
> There is an RFC for PATCH requests. A PATCH is like PUT, but instead of overwriting the resource, it partially modifies the existing resource. PATCH should only be used for updates, not for creates.
>
> PATCH is not part of the HTTP 1.1 specification, but it's fully supported by Scalatra.

DELETE

A DELETE request is structurally closest to a GET. It comes with no request body, but like a GET may use query strings and headers to refine itself. The following listing declares a route to delete an artist.

Listing 3.4   Removing an artist with `delete`

```
class RecordStore extends ScalatraServlet {
  delete("/artists/:name") {
    if (Artist.delete(params("name")).isDefined)
      NoContent()
    else
      NotFound()
  }
}
```

If an artist was deleted, responds with 204 No Content

Returns an option: Some if the artist was found to delete, None if not

If no artist was found, responds with 404 Not Found

In most services, confirmation would be handled on the client side. It's assumed that anybody who hits this URL is authorized (covered in chapter 11) and really means it.

Like the POST action in listing 3.2, here you return a NoContent on success. It's useful to let the client know whether the operation was successful, so you introduce a conditional and respond with NotFound if no artist was found to delete.

Use DELETE in the following case:

- *When implementing delete operations, such as the D in CRUD*—This is the most obvious of the CRUD methods. Indeed, it's the only one whose CRUD name matches its HTTP name.

The perils of not following the rules

Many web developers ignore anything beyond the familiar GET and POST. This can be a security risk if the rules aren't followed.

In one infamous case, an application implemented delete with simple hyperlinks (GET requests). Much to the horror of the development team, they found their content was gone. The culprit? Google's web spider, which dutifully followed every delete link on the page to index the site.

HTTP services are often consumed by clients that aren't considered at the time of development. This is why it's important to follow conventions and use the methods as they're intended.

3.2.2 *The lesser-known methods*

The vast majority of APIs need to worry themselves only with the CRUD methods discussed in the previous section. Still, Scalatra aims to be a complete HTTP framework, and it's good to know about the other methods.

HEAD

A HEAD request should be handled like an otherwise identical GET request, except that it shouldn't return a body. The following listing declares special handling for a HEAD request to an artist.

Listing 3.5   Optimizing HEAD requests with an explicit HEAD

```
class RecordStore extends ScalatraServlet {
  head("/artists/:name/info") {
    contentType = "text/json"
    if (Artist.exists(params("name"))) Ok()
    else NotFound()
  }
}
```

Where the GET request in listing 3.1 needs to load the artist to render the info, a HEAD request only needs to verify its existence. You're able to override the default behavior with a more efficient implementation.

Use HEAD in this case:

- *When the default implementation is suboptimal*—Because a HEAD response can be derived from a GET, Scalatra gives it to you for free by calling GET with a null response writer.[2]

Premature optimization

We should forget about small efficiencies, say about 97% of the time: premature optimization is the root of all evil.

—Donald Knuth

Most applications shouldn't implement HEAD directly. Doing so is error-prone, and unless the GET action is known to be slow, it's a form of premature optimization.

On the other hand, a client may execute a HEAD request to determine whether a previously fetched resource has been modified. This is especially common when the client is a caching proxy. If headers such as Last-Modified or Content-MD5 have changed, the client may execute a GET request for the full body. Recalculating a timestamp or especially a digest can be expensive, so if the resource is known to be unchanged on the server side, it may make sense to return these headers as cached values in a custom HEAD route.

OPTIONS

An OPTIONS request, like HEAD, is implemented in terms of other methods. It's expected to return an Allows header so clients understand which other methods are supported for a particular path.

The following listing shows that a call to delete Frank Zappa will not be supported by the delete call.[3]

Listing 3.6 Returning the supported methods with options

```
class RecordStore extends ScalatraServlet {
  get("/artists/:name") {
    Artist.find(params("name")) match {
      case Some(artist) => artist.toXml
      case None => status = 404
    }
  }

  delete("/artists/:name") {
    val name = params("name")
    if (name == "Frank Zappa")
      MethodNotAllowed()                    ⟵  405 is the standard HTTP
    else if (Artist.delete(name).isDefined)     status code for invoking a
                                                method that isn't allowed.
```

---

[2] Actually, this functionality is provided by the underlying servlet container. Scalatra's philosophy is to build on existing standards where possible.

[3] If a music service doesn't carry Frank Zappa, it's not worth running.

```
      NoContent()
    else
      NotFound()
  }

  options("/artists/Frank_Zappa") {
    response.setHeader("Allow", "GET, HEAD")   ←───┐  Note the absence
  }                                                 │  of DELETE.
}
```

OPTIONS requests on lesser artists will fall through to the default and return an Allow header of GET, HEAD, DELETE.

Use OPTIONS in these cases:

- *When the default implementation is incorrect*—By default, Scalatra searches its routing table, seeking a matching route for each HTTP method. Instead of executing the action, as with other methods, it constructs an Allow header with all the matching methods.

    In some cases, the user might want to customize the methods. A delete method may be supported for some resources matched by a given route, but others may be protected from deletion. A customized view can be generated by explicitly overriding the OPTIONS route.

- *For security*—Every bit of unnecessary information a service exposes potentially gives an attacker another clue to break into your application. Options are considered rather harmless by most, but some users would prefer to not give this information away at all.

The following listing declares a route that forbids all requests with method option.

Listing 3.7   Forbidding all OPTIONS requests

```
options() {                ←───  A method with no path matches
  Forbidden()              ←───  everything. Learn more in section 3.3.3.
}

                                 Returns HTTP status 403, indicating
                                 the request is forbidden
```

Methods unsupported by Scalatra

There are two standard HTTP methods we haven't discussed:

- A TRACE request echoes the request back as the body of the response. The implementation of this method is rigidly defined by spec. Scalatra inherits a default implementation through the servlet container and thus doesn't provide a method to customize the behavior.
- CONNECT requests are used in SSL tunneling, which is not relevant to Scalatra. Scalatra handles these requests by issuing a 404 response. Like TRACE, this behavior is not overridable.

3.2.3   *Overriding the methods*

The preceding sections describe the perfect world where the client speaks the entire HTTP standard. It won't surprise veteran web programmers that implementations often fall short of the published standard.

Many web browsers support a subset of the HTTP methods GET and POST. This is adequate for web browsers that simply need to get pages and post form data. But as the line blurs between web APIs and websites, this is inadequate. You'd like to support browsers as first-class clients of our APIs.

This isn't a new problem, and various ad hoc solutions have been developed. A popular one is to look for a special _method parameter in a POST request. If present, the request is interpreted with the parameter. This is a fair solution on the client side, but it quickly becomes tedious for a Scalatra application.

> **Listing 3.8   Method override example**

```
class RecordStore extends ScalatraServlet {
  delete("/artists/:name") {
    if (Artist.delete(params("name")).isDefined)      ◁──┐
      NoContent()
    else
      NotFound()
  }                                                        Duplicate
                                                           calls
  post("/item") {
    params.get("method") match {
      case Some("delete") =>
        if (Artist.delete(params("name")).isDefined)  ◁──┘
          NoContent()
    else
      NotFound()
      case None =>
        val artist = parseArtist(request)
        Artist.save(artist)
        val location = s"/artists/${artists.name}"
        Created(artist, headers = "Location" -> location)
    }
  }
}
```

Note how the deleteArtist call is repeated in listing 3.8. Even if the delete logic is extracted, you'd still need to repeat the call in both the DELETE route and the POST's "delete" condition.

What you want is a way to transparently rewrite the request before routing occurs. Scalatra provides this functionality out of the box with MethodOverrideSupport. In addition to the _method body parameter, MethodOverrideSupport observes the X-HTTP-Method-Override header, a convention adopted by many JavaScript frameworks.

Listing 3.9   Using method-override conventions

```
class RecordStore extends ScalatraServlet with MethodOverrideSupport {
  delete("/artists/:name") {
    val name = params("name")
    if (Artist.delete(name).isDefined)
      NoContent()
    else
      NotFound()
  }
  post("/item") {
    val artist = parseArtist(request)
    Artist.save(artist)
    val location = s"/artists/${artist.name}"
    Created(artist, headers = Map("Location" -> location))
  }
}
```

Declares that this servlet supports the method-override conventions

This is now the only call to deleteArtist.

This now has one responsibility: handling POST.

Listing 3.9 shows an example of Scalatra's *stackable modifications*, where additional behaviors can be composed onto the core with mixin traits.

3.3   Route matchers

If HTTP methods declare the type of action to be performed, then route matchers declare the resources on which the action is to be performed. They describe which requests an action runs on and extract parameters to further describe the request to the action.

Unlike the tightly constrained HTTP methods, route matchers can take many forms and match an unlimited number of resources. Three types of route matchers are supported out of the box:

- Path expressions (string)
- Regular expressions
- Boolean expressions

We'll examine each of these in detail, and later show you how to create your own.

3.3.1   Path expressions

The most common type of route matcher is the *path expression*. A path expression always starts with a / character and refers to the mount point of your application.

In this chapter, assume that your application is mounted at http://localhost:8080, and that your servlet is mounted to /* within your application. More complex deployments are covered in chapter 5.

> **NOTE** Scalatra is a portmanteau of *Scala* and *Sinatra*, the Ruby framework that inspired it. Rubyists may find the path expression syntax familiar. This is not coincidental.

STATIC PATH EXPRESSIONS

In the following listing, you'll see a *static path expression*. This path expression declares
a literal path to match.

Listing 3.10   Static path expression

```
class RecordStore extends ScalatraServlet {
  get("/artists") {                              <————————— /artists is the route matcher.
    <artists>
      Artist.getAll.map { artist =>              <———————
        <artist href=""/artists/${artist.name}$quot;>        Action code that lists
          ${artist.name}                                      each artist ID. Actions
        </artist>                                             will be discussed in
      }                                                       detail in chapter 5.
    </artists>
  }
}
```

With this route, a GET request to http://localhost:8080/artists fetches a list of all the
artists in the system. A resource can be an individual item or a collection of items.
Static routes are ideal for referring to a collection of a items—though the collection of
artists may be dynamic, the collection maintains a static resource identifier. Static path
expressions are an ideal fit for static URIs.

The /artists resource only links to the individual artists. Each artist is a resource
with its own URI. The following listing adds a static route per artist.

Listing 3.11   Routes with static path expressions

```
class RecordStore extends ScalatraServlet {
  get("/artists/Bruce_Springsteen/info") {
    showArtist("Bruce Springsteen")
  }

  get("/artists/Charles_Mingus/info") {
    showArtist("Charles Mingus")
  }

  get("/artists/A_Tribe_Called_Quest/info") {
    showArtist("A Tribe Called Quest")
  }

  def showArtist(name: String) = {
    Artist.find(name) match {
      case Some(artist) => artist.toXml
      case None => NotFound()
    }
  }
}
```

In listing 3.11, a GET request to http://localhost:8080/artists/Bruce_Springsteen/info would fetch information about Bruce Springsteen. It's a nice start, but notice how repetitive the routes are. The action repeats a part of the request path, and each artist's action is almost identical to the others. It would be difficult to maintain a fully stocked music shop this way. Further, you wouldn't want to modify and redeploy your application every time an artist was added to your inventory. It would be nice if you could *parameterize* the paths.

PATH PARAMETERS

Listing 3.12 introduces *path parameters*. A path parameter called name is declared by preceding it with a colon character. Instead of literally looking for "/:name", the colon signals Scalatra to capture that portion of the request path as a parameter, which is made available to the route.

Listing 3.12   Path parameter example

```
class RecordStore extends ScalatraServlet {
  get("/artists/:name/info") {                  ⟵————————— :name declares a path parameter.
    showArtist(params("name"))           ⟵
  }                                                        params("name") evaluates
                                                           to the name from the
  def showArtist(name: String) = {                         request path.
    Artist.find(name) match {
      case Some(artist) => artist.toXml
      case None => status = 404
    }
  }
}
```

The example in listing 3.12 is much cleaner. With dynamic names, you can add to the Artist data store without touching the Scalatra application. Working with path parameters is discussed in depth in chapter 4.

Path parameters are matched according to the following rules:

- A path parameter is never an empty string. At least one character must be matched.
- A path parameter matches everything up to the next special character: /, ?, or #.

Table 3.2 shows some hypothetical URIs for the path expression /artists/:name/info, whether they'd match, and the value of the extracted parameter.

Table 3.2   Some examples of matching /artists/:name/info

URI	Matches?	Name param
http://localhost:8080/artists/Radiohead/info	Yes	Radiohead
http://localhost:8080/artists/AC/DC/info	No	
http://localhost:8080/artists/AC%2FDC/info	Yes	AC/DC

> ### URL encoding
>
> It's possible to use special characters like / in a path parameter, but they must be percent-encoded (http://en.wikipedia.org/wiki/Percent-encoding). AC/DC doesn't match in table 3.2 because the name parameter stops matching at /, leaving the literal /DC where /info is expected. By percent-encoding the / as %2F, the slash is absorbed as part of the path parameter, and it's then decoded as / when exposed to the application as a param.

OPTIONAL PARAMETERS

A ? in a path expression makes the previous *character* or *path parameter* optional. The following listing demonstrates an optional trailing slash.

Listing 3.13 Trailing slash

```
class RecordStore extends ScalatraServlet {
  get("/artists/?") {
    <artists>${Artist.fetchAll().map(_.toXml)}</artists>
  }
}
```

The "/artists/?" expression would match a request to both of these:

- http://localhost:8080/artists
- http://localhost:8080/artists/

A trailing slash can be significant in a URI, but humans are apt to overlook it. If your application's URI is likely to be typed by a person rather than provided by a machine, supporting trailing slashes is good practice.

> **WARNING** In the literal URI, ? marks the beginning of the *query string*, which is not part of the path matched by Scalatra. In a path expression, ? marks the previous token as optional. It's unrelated to matching the query string.

This technique is taken one step further in the next listing and is also applied to a path parameter.

Listing 3.14 Optional format suffix

```
class RecordStore extends ScalatraServlet {
  get("/artists/:name/info.?:format?") {          ◁─────   First ? applies to the literal
    Artist.find(params("name")) match {                    period (.) character. Second ?
      case Some(artist) =>                                 applies to the format param.
        params.get("format") match {
          case Some("json") => artist.toJson
          case _ => artist.toXml
        }
  }
```

```
        case None => NotFound()
      }
    }
  }
}
```

Table 3.3 gives some examples of how the route in listing 3.14 would match various requests. In all the examples, the route matches, but only in some is a `"json"` format parameter defined.

Table 3.3   Format examples

URI	Format param
http://localhost:8080/artists/Otis_Redding/info	undefined
http://localhost:8080/artists/Otis_Redding/info.json	`"json"`
http://localhost:8080/artists/Otis_Redding/info.xml	`"xml"`
http://localhost:8080/artists/Otis_Redding/info.	undefined
http://localhost:8080/artists/Otis_Redding/infojson	`"json"`

The last two examples in table 3.3 may come as a surprise. Both the literal . and the parameter that follows are optional, and the matching of one doesn't depend on the presence of the other. This is acceptable for many applications, but too permissive for some. Finer-grained control can be obtained with regular expression matching or Rails path pattern parsing.

SPLAT SUPPORT

Path expressions also support *splat* parameters. Splat parameters are nicknamed for the * character that declares them.

Listing 3.15   Splat example

```
class RecordStore extends ScalatraServlet {
  val downloadPath = "/srv/media"

  get("/downloads/*") {              ◁──────────── * declares the splat param.
    val path = params("splat")       ◁──────┐
    new File(downloadPath, path))    ◁──┐    │  params("splat")
  }                                     │    │  references the portion of
}                   Returning a File sends the │  the path captured by *.
                    file as the response. │
```

Listing 3.15 implements a download section of the site. In this route, you use a single `/downloads/*` route to serve files under a virtual filesystem. You could have used `/downloads/:name`, but recall that named parameters match up until the next / character in a URL. A splat parameter frees you from this restriction, so that you can match a path in an arbitrary directory structure.

3.3.2 Regular expressions

> *Some people, when confronted with a problem, think "I know, I'll use regular expressions." Now they have two problems.*
>
> —Jamie Zawinski

Path expressions are a simple, satisfactory solution to the majority of routing needs, but they're limited in what they can express. *Regular expressions* provide the needed expressivity at the expense of a steeper learning curve. A full tutorial on regular expressions is beyond the scope of this book, but we'll show you how a not-too-scary regular expression can solve a rather complicated problem.

In our music shop, we'd like to create a route to show the best albums of either a year or an entire decade:

- For a year, we expect a four-digit number.
- For a decade, we expect a four-digit number ending in 0, followed by an s.

We could attempt to route these requests with a simple path expression like "/best-of/:when". The problem is that the same route would need to handle both the year and the decade list. Furthermore, if the parameter were neither a year nor a decade, the route would still match. We want to both capture and *validate*. Regular expressions excel at validating special syntax as part of the match.

Conceptually, we have two routes: one for years and one for decades. The following listing shows how to use regular expressions to express these as two separate routes.

Listing 3.16 Regular expression route

```
class RecordStore extends ScalatraServlet {
    get("""/best-of/(\d{4})""".r ) {          Defines a regular expression
        val Seq(year) = params("captures" )
        // Load albums by year                 captures is a special parameter name for accessing the groups of a regular expression.
    }

    get("""/best-of/(\d{3}0)s""".r ) {
        val Seq(decade) = params("captures"
        // Load albums by decade
    }
}
```

In both expressions, /best-of/ does a simple literal match. (\d{4}) and (\d{3}0)s declare the syntax for a year and a decade, respectively. Let's tear apart the latter:

- \d matches a digit, 0–9.
- {3} repeats the previous expression (\d) exactly three times.
- 0 is a literal 0.
- () declares a *capture group*. The characters matched by the expression inside the capture group are made available to the route under the param name "captures". In this case, you capture exactly three digits followed by a zero.

> **What makes a regular expression in Scala?**
>
> We could just as well have written the regular expression `"""/best-of/(\d{4})"""`.r as `new Regex("/best-of/(\\d{4})")`, but the former is more idiomatic in Scala. How does it work?
>
> Certain special characters in a string literal, such as \ and ", can be disabled by enclosing the string in triple quotes. This syntax comes in handy with regular expressions, which tend to contain several backslashes. But merely triple quoting still yields a string, not a regex.
>
> Scala also provides an implicit method `r` on `StringLike`, which compiles the string into a regex. Without the `.r` call, the string would be interpreted by Scalatra as a path expression.

Table 3.4 shows how various URIs might be matched by the routes declared in listing 3.16.

Table 3.4　Year and decade URI examples

URI	Route matched	`param("captures")`
http://localhost:8080/best-of/1967	Year	1967
http://localhost:8080/best-of/1960s	Decade	1960
http://localhost:8080/best-of/1967s	None	

Internally, Scalatra compiles path expressions down to regular expressions. For those who grok regex, table 3.5 explains how Scalatra's path expressions map to regular expressions.

Table 3.5　Path expression–to–regular expression translation

Path expression	Regex equivalent
`:param`	`([/*#?]+)`
`?`	`?`
`*`	`(.*?)`
`()`	`\(\)` [a]

a. `()` are not special characters in a path expression. Only the characters already listed are special in a path expression.

3.3.3　*Boolean expressions*

The third and final type of route matcher in Scalatra's core is the *Boolean expression*. A Boolean expression is any arbitrary Scala expression that returns a Boolean value. The expression is evaluated at request time, with the current request in scope.

Unlike path expressions and regular expressions, a Boolean expression can't extract any parameters. Its role is to act as a guard. So far, all of our routes have taken a single route matcher, but Scalatra supports any number of route matchers in a given route. Most commonly, a Boolean expression will act as a guard condition, adding an extra constraint to a path or regular expression. A route matches if, and only if, all of its route matchers match.

Formal definition of "match"

A route matcher returns an `Option[Map[String, Seq[String]]]`. An `Option` can be `Some` map of extracted parameters, or `None`. A route matches if and only if all of its route matchers return `Some`. The extracted parameters are merged into a single map, and these are the route parameters passed to the action.

But how do our types translate into this `Option`?

- A path expression or regular expression returns `Some` extracted route parameters if the expression matches the request URI.
- A Boolean expression returns `Some` empty map of route parameters if the expression evaluates to `true`. As already stated, Booleans don't extract parameters. If the expression evaluates to `false`, the route matcher returns `None`, and the route doesn't match.

Consistent with `forall` on an empty collection, a route with no matchers always matches. To match all `POST` requests, you might write a route with an empty list of route matchers (such as `post()`).

The following listing defines two routes: one for mobile users and one for everybody else.

Listing 3.17 Matching mobile requests

```
class RecordStore extends ScalatraServlet {
  get("/listen/*".r, isMobile(request))) {            Responds with a mobile-
    StreamService.mobile(params("splat"))             friendly stream
  }

  get("/listen/*".r, !isMobile(request))) {           Responds with a richer
    StreamService.desktop(params("splat"))            stream for desktops
  }

  def isMobile(request: HttpServletRequest): Boolean = {
    val lower = request.getHeader("User-Agent")       A naive browser
    lower.contains("android") || lower.contains("iphone")  sniffer. There are
  }                                                    free databases and
}                                                      subscription APIs to
                                                       do this properly.
```

The route code in listing 3.17 could just as well have been written as a single route:

```
get("/listen/*".r) {
  if (isMobile(request.getHeader("User-Agent"))) {
    StreamService.mobile(params("splat"))
  } else {
```

```
        StreamService.desktop(params("splat"))
    }
}
```

The Boolean guard neatly keeps all the request-related logic together in the route matchers, and lets the route action focus on a single thing. But it's fine to keep the branching logic in the action if you prefer. In Scalatra, as with Scala, there's usually more than one way to do it.

> **WARNING** Boolean expressions support arbitrary snippets of code, as long as the return type is correct. These snippets may be evaluated on each request as Scalatra attempts to find a matching route. It's important that these expressions be free of side effects, or failed matches could change the state of your application. Your Boolean guards should always be read-only operations.

We've now taken a tour of the three primitive route matchers in Scalatra. In the next section, we'll look at some more-advanced use cases.

3.4 Advanced route matching

By now, you should have a good grasp of the basic building blocks of a route. As your applications grow larger, you might run into routes that overlap, or find a corner case that just isn't handled well by the basic routing structures. In this section, we'll cover these more complicated scenarios.

3.4.1 Conflict resolution

In the spirit of guessable URIs, you'd like your users to be able to type an address to look up their favorite bands. But is it "Smashing Pumpkins" or "The Smashing Pumpkins"?[4] This is a common problem, but one you can solve easily with overlapping routes.

The following listing defines a splat route that overlaps the info and album routes.

Listing 3.18 Article normalizer

```
class RecordStore extends ScalatraServlet {
    get("/artists/:name/info") {                  ⟵——————— This route is matched third.
        Artists.findByName(params("name"))
    }

    get("/artists/:name/albums/:album") {         ⟵—— This route is matched second.
        Albums.findByName(artist = params("name"), name = params("album"))
    }

    get("/artists/The_:name/*") {                 ⟵—— This route is tried first.
        redirect("/artists/%s/%s".format(params("name"), params("splat")))
    }
}
```

---

[4] Check out the covers of *Siamese Dream* and *Mellon Collie and the Infinite Sadness*. Even the band doesn't know.

What happens when a request matches two routes? Scalatra looks for matching routes from the bottom of your application, and works its way to the top.

WARNING   Scalatra routes applications from the bottom up. Sinatra, and most other frameworks inspired by Sinatra, route from the top down. This is to allow routes declared in a child class to override routes declared in a parent.

Figure 3.2 demonstrates how the client interacts with Scalatra given the music store in listing 3.18.

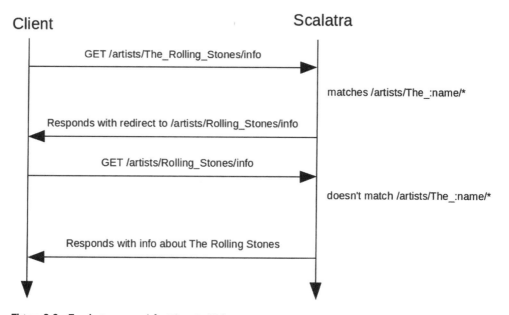

Figure 3.2   **Tracing a request for** `The_Rolling_Stones`

When a request comes in for `/artists/The_Rolling_Stones/info`, the top and bottom routes match. Because Scalatra routes from the bottom up, `/artists/The_:name/*` is matched. This triggers the redirect response. The client immediately requests `/artists/Rolling_Stones/info`. Scalatra, as always, matches the request from the bottom up.[5] The redirected request finally matches `/artists/:name/info`, which generates the desired response.

3.4.2   *Rails-style path expressions*

As already mentioned, Scalatra is heavily influenced by the Sinatra framework, but Sinatra-style path expressions aren't the only game in town. Ruby on Rails[6] uses an alternate syntax—one that lends itself a little better to the format example introduced in listing 3.14.

---

[5]   Redirects are stateless. Scalatra neither knows nor cares that the original request was rewritten.

[6]   Technically, it's the Ruby Rack::Mount::Strexp module.

Listing 3.19 Rails matcher

```
class RecordStore extends ScalatraServlet {
  implicit override def string2RouteMatcher(path: String) =     Overrides the
    RailsPathPatternParser(path)                                 existing string

  get("/artists/:name/info(.:format)") {                        Supports an info route
    // Load artist info according to the format                 with an optional format
  }
}
```

Listing 3.19 demonstrates the use of Rails-style path expressions. The implicit `string2RouteMatcher` method overrides the inherited `ScalatraServlet`.

What type are route matchers, anyway?

Route matchers extend the `org.scalatra.RouteMatcher` trait. `ScalatraServlet` inherits protected methods that perform *implicit conversions* of strings, regular expressions, and Boolean expressions to `RouteMatcher`. You can extend the DSL to support arbitrary types by creating your own implicit conversions to `RouteMatcher`.

The expression is very similar to the standard path expressions. Instead of using ? to make the previous token optional, the Rails style uses () to make its entire contents optional. This allows you to express that, if there is a period, the format must also be provided.

Table 3.6 takes the URIs from table 3.3 and shows how the Rails routes can lock down two typically undesirable matches.

Table 3.6 Rails-style format examples

URI	Sinatra /artists/:name/ info.?:format?	Rails /artists/:name/ info(.:format)
/artists/Otis_Redding/info	Yes	Yes
/artists/Otis_Redding/info.json	Yes	Yes
/artists/Otis_Redding/info.xml	Yes	Yes
/artists/Otis_Redding/info.	Yes	No
/artists/Otis_Redding/infojson	Yes	No

3.5 Summary

- Choosing the correct HTTP methods results in APIs that act in accordance with prevailing standards.
- It's important to choose intuitive URIs for application resources. You can use Scalatra's route resolution to create concise code.

Working with user input

In the previous chapter, we focused on route matchers. You saw how Scalatra takes an incoming URL, decomposes it into its constituent parts, and matches it to a block of code in your application. But route matching is only part of the overall request-response cycle. We'll give you the whole life story of a request in this chapter so you can start responding to incoming HTTP requests and do some useful work. Let's start with an overview.

4.1 The life of a request

In Scalatra, each incoming HTTP request that hits your server is answered with an HTTP response. What happens when an HTTP request hits your application?

First, Scalatra checks the URL's path (including path parameters) to see whether it has a matching route. Assuming a matching route is found, the following things happen:

1 Params are extracted and placed in a `params` map, so that you can use them inside the route's action.
2 `before` filters are executed, so you can do preprocessing.
3 The body of the route's action code is executed.
4 `after` filters are executed.
5 The response is written and returned to the requesting agent.

If no matching route is found, Scalatra will run a special method called `notFound`, so you can customize the response. Usually this involves setting a 404 response status, but you're free to do whatever you like.

You saw how routing works in chapter 3, so let's move on to look at the route body, which is called an *action* in Scalatra.

4.2   Routes and actions

The URL http://localhost:8080/hackers/ada-lovelace might map to the following route.

Listing 4.1   Retrieving info about specific hackers

```
package com.constructiveproof.hackertracker

import org.scalatra._
import scalate.ScalateSupport

class HackersController extends HackerTrackerStack {
    get("/hackers/:slug") {
        // Code to retrieve info about this hacker
        // Code to display information about this hacker
    }
}
```

Defines a route matcher → (points to `get("/hackers/:slug")`)

The code inside the route is called an action. → (points to the `// Code to retrieve info about this hacker` line)

The block of code inside a route matcher is called *action code* or an *action*. In a forms-based CRUD application, you might retrieve some data and then render a view inside the action. In an API, you might accept incoming data, use it to create a new object, and then return the newly created object as JSON. In either case, the action is where your application goes to work for you.

One of the things that your actions need is a way to read incoming HTTP input, so that your program can react appropriately. There are multiple ways that an HTTP application typically receives input. Let's take a look at how Scalatra handles HTTP parameters.

4.3   HTTP parameter handling in Scalatra

HTTP parameters are key-value pairs, with the key and value separated by an equals sign: `key1=first-value&key2=second-value`. Parameters can be received by your application in several different ways, which we'll go over in a moment. Once your application receives HTTP parameters as input, they get turned into a Scala `Map`, and they become available for you to use in your action code using the `params` method.

> **NOTE** If you're new to Scala, a `Map` is like Ruby's `Hash`, Python's `dict`, JavaScript's `object`, or Java's `Map`. It's a data structure that stores and retrieves values by key.

If your application receives the parameters `key1=hello&key2=world`, you'll be able to access the values `hello` and `world` by calling `params("key1")` and `params("key2")` inside your route actions. When accessed using the `params` method, all parameters are of type `String` unless you explicitly force them to be something different.

Now let's turn our attention to the various ways you can read HTTP parameters. Excluding file uploads for the moment (we'll cover those in chapter 6), there are three kinds of HTTP parameters that you'll typically want to read inside your actions:

- Query string parameters
- Path parameters (sometimes known as *route* parameters)
- Form parameters (sometimes inaccurately called *POST* parameters)

Let's take a look at how some familiar real-world applications use parameters, and then look at how to model them in a Hacker Tracker application.

4.3.1 Query string parameters

Query string parameters live on the query string of the request URL. Figure 4.1 shows query string parameters for an example YouTube search, visible in the browser's address bar. In the Hacker Tracker application, a route and action for a similarly structured search URL could look like the following listing.

www.youtube.com/results?search_query=scalatra&oq=scalatra

Figure 4.1 A YouTube search with highlighted query string parameters

Listing 4.2 An action that reads query string params

```
get("/results") {
  val searchQuery = params("search_query")      ← Assigns the search_query
  val originalQuery = params("oq")          ←       parameter to a value
  println(searchQuery)             Assigns the oq
  println(originalQuery)           parameter to a value
  // Search for matching hackers
  // Display information about matching hackers
}
```

If the application is running locally, and you hit the URL http://localhost:8080/results?search_query=scalatra&oq=scalatra, Scalatra reads the incoming HTTP parameters from the request and makes them available in the `params` map. In this example, the value of `val searchQuery` will be the string `"scalatra"`.

4.3.2   *Path parameters*

Also called *route* parameters, path parameters are incorporated directly into the full path of the URL. If you've been programming for any length of time, you've almost certainly seen path parameters in action in the URLs of GitHub, the popular code-hosting service. Path parameters in a GitHub URL are highlighted in figure 4.2.

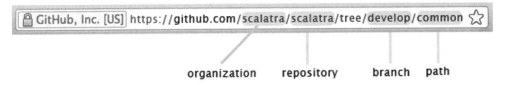

Figure 4.2   GitHub uses path parameters heavily in its repository browser.

The Hacker Tracker application already has a route with a path parameter in it. Let's make parameter handling more explicit by assigning the incoming :slug parameter to a value, as follows.

> **Listing 4.3   An action that reads a path parameter**

```
get("/hackers/:slug") {          Named path params form matchable
  val slug = params("slug")      parts of the URL's full path
  println(slug)
  // Retrieve info about this hacker, based on the slug
  // Display information about this hacker
}
```

Assigns the :slug path parameter to a value (annotation pointing to the code)

The route matcher here defines a path parameter called slug, which is denoted by the colon (:) in the route declaration. For each path parameter, Scalatra extracts the key and value of the path parameter from the URL's full path and makes it available to you in the params map.

Given the URL http://localhost:8080/hackers/ada-lovelace, val slug would equal "ada-lovelace".

4.3.3   *Form parameters*

Form parameters aren't carried around in the URL path or in the query string. Instead, they're part of the body of an HTTP request. They're often called *POST parameters*, because web programmers are used to thinking of HTTP POST requests as carrying this type of input, but it's worth noting that PUT and PATCH requests can also carry form parameters.

To try posting some form parameters to your application, you could either make an HTML form with its action set to an HTTP route in your application, or use the command line. The following listing shows a request to create a new hacker in the Hacker Tracker, which uses the curl command-line utility to send the parameters name and motto to the server.

Listing 4.4 Using the curl utility to add a hacker to the tracker

A form param with the key "motto"

A form param with the key "name"

```
curl \
--data-urlencode "name=Grace Hopper" \
--data-urlencode "motto=It is better to ask forgiveness \
than permission" \
http://localhost:8080/hackers
```

The URL to which the request should be posted

Assuming you've got a *nix terminal and have curl installed, you should be able to copy and paste that code into your terminal to send a request to a Scalatra application running on localhost. It will pack up the parameters name and motto and send them to your application.

> **TIP** Curl (pronounced "see url") is a command-line utility for making requests and inspecting responses. If you're using a Unix-based system, chances are you already have it. If you don't, you should seriously consider installing it, as it makes developing and experiencing RESTful APIs so much easier by exposing a command-line interface for everything that is HTTP. (Curl is also available on Windows through cygwin.)

Here's a route and action that can read the inbound name parameter.

Listing 4.5 An action that reads form params

Assigns the "motto" parameter to a value

Assigns the "name" parameter coming in on the POST body to a value

```
post("/hackers") {
  val name = params("name")
  val motto = params("motto")
  println(name)
  println(motto)
  // Create a new hacker with the incoming parameters
}
```

As with the other parameter types, form parameters are key-value pairs, and they become available inside your Scalatra actions in exactly the same way as path or query string parameters do: you use the params method to access incoming input. Note that although curl URL-encoded the value of name (so that it was sent as Grace%20Hopper), Scalatra automatically decodes incoming parameters so that val name contains the decoded string "Grace Hopper".

Query string, form, or route parameters?

Which parameter type you should use comes down to one question: how will you use the parameters? Here are some rules for deciding:

- If the parameter can be used to clearly identify a resource, it should be declared as route parameter. IDs are a fine example of parameters that fall into this category.

(continued)

- If the parameter controls things like a listing's sort column, or the sort order, the query string is an ideal place for it.
- If the parameter has a lot of content or is used to create a new resource, it should always go into the form parameters of the request body.

Last but not least, if putting the parameter in the route gets you cleaner URLs, by all means use route parameters. As an example, consider a listing of blog entries by date: `GET /entries/?date=2012-08-20` might work, but `GET /entries/2012/08/20` looks a lot nicer on the address bar.

4.3.4 *Params versus multiParams*

It's entirely possible to send multiple parameter values that share the same key. For instance, you might get query params on a request like the following.

Listing 4.6   A request with duplicate parameter keys

```
GET http://localhost:8080/tagged?tag=linguistic&tag=mustache
```

Note that the parameter key `tag` is in there twice. This is an entirely legal set of HTTP parameters, and indeed this sort of thing can be very useful if you want to build up arrays of parameters in some situation, such as tags or check box values.

Accessing these parameters in an action using `params("tag")` will retrieve only the first value. But there's another method, `multiParams("tag")`, that will retrieve all the available values of `tag` and return them in a Scala sequence. In Scala, a `Seq` is a kind of iterable that has a length and whose elements have fixed index positions, starting from 0.

Let's write a route and action that will read the incoming tag parameters from listing 4.6 and show what happens when you access them via both `params` and `multiParams`.

Listing 4.7   The difference between `params` and `multiParams`

```
get("/hackers/tagged") {
  println(params("tag"))
  for(x <- multiParams("tag")) {
    println(x)
  }
  val tags = multiParams("tag")
  // Retrieve hackers matching all the given tags
  // Display hackers matching all the given tags
}
```

Prints only "linguistic" → `println(params("tag"))`

But looping through multiParams ... ← `for(x <- multiParams("tag")) {`

... prints "linguistic" and then "mustache" → `println(x)`

Assigns the multiple tags parameters to a value ← `val tags = multiParams("tag")`

If you run the example, you'll see that printing `params` results in only the first value: `linguistic`. But when you loop through and print each element in the `multiParamsSeq`, you get all values matching the duplicate key: `linguistic` and `mustache`.

4.3.5 *Dealing with unexpected input*

Whenever you accept arbitrary input, you open up the possibility that a user, or another computer system, will send parameters that you don't expect. For example, in our previous examples of using HTTP parameters via the params method, there's no code to check either the existence or the type of incoming params.

In other words, it's possible that someone might hit the route and action in listing 4.8 with the properly formatted URL that you expect.

Listing 4.8 An accident waiting to happen

```
get("/results") {
  val searchQuery = params("search_query")   ⟵⎯┐  A missing :search_query param
  // Search for matching hackers                 │  will cause problems here.
  // Display information about matching hackers
}
```

The preceding code is expecting a request like this:

```
$ curl localhost:8080/results?search_query=larry
```

On the other hand, you might get a request like this:

```
$ curl localhost:8080/results
```

This time, the URL is missing the search_query query string parameter and the oq parameter. When it comes time to access the nonexistent search_query parameter key, Scalatra will throw an exception. If you attempt to view the page in a browser, you'll get a page like figure 4.3.

If you take a look at the stack trace, you'll notice that the culprit for the error is the innocent-looking call to params("search_query"). When you attempt to access a nonexistent key in the params map, Scala doesn't just return a null value, as might happen in some other languages. Instead, it throws an exception.

Why is Scala so strict in this respect? This is, in fact, one of the primary design goals of the Scala language (not just Scalatra).

AN INTRODUCTION TO PATTERN MATCHING USING THE OPTION TYPE

We're all used to those ugly moments when code that works just fine under some conditions gives back an unexpected error at runtime. This is often due to the program receiving some input it didn't expect.

In Java, this situation gives you the dreaded NullPointerException, or NPE for short. In C#, you might be told that your Object reference is not set to an instance of an object. Other languages have their own messages, but what they all have in common is that these errors happen *at runtime*, when it's possible that your users are actually trying to accomplish something.

Wouldn't it be nice if you could detect these problems at compile time instead?

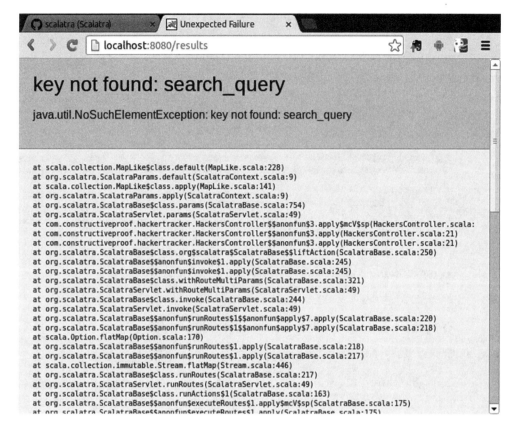

Figure 4.3   An exception resulting from bad input

Martin Odersky, the designer of Scala, thought so. He designed Scala's type system in a particularly clever (and elegant) way, allowing you to program in a style that means you may rarely see an NPE. One of the main ways of catching NPEs at compile time rather than runtime is by using the `Option` type.

> **NOTE**   Keep in mind that none of what follows is mandatory (as we've just proved by generating an NPE), but relying on Scala's type system will allow you to clean up your code dramatically and reduce your bug count. It's the recommended programming style in Scalatra.

You can think of `Option` as a simple truth value. It either is or isn't. Instead of `true` and `false`, though, `Option` has the subtypes `Some` and `None`. `Some` is a container for some value and `None` is the opposite: it's the container for *nothing* and is used when there's no `Some`.

The `Option` type and its subclasses `Some` and `None` give you an alternative to `null`s. Instead of confidently declaring that something has the type `String`, but with the unspoken understanding that sometimes you'll get back a live grenade instead, you can declare it to have a type of Option[String] and a value of either Some("wrapped value") or None.

If you use Option as a parameter type, it acts as an explicit signal to other coders (or your future self) that a return value of None is possible. In part, this is just a matter of properly communicating your intentions using the type system.

The biggest improvement Option offers over null, however, is that you can't forget to check for None, because it's part of the type system and can be checked at compile time. The compiler will force you to first check if you're dealing with Some, and if you are, to explicitly say what should happen with a None. Only after that does it allow you to access the contained value.

GETTING PARAMETERS AS OPTIONS

Currently, params("search_query") gives you the value you're after directly, but it contains the possibility of a runtime exception if it hits a null. To fix your action's handling of the search_query parameter, you'll need a way to access the params map that returns an Option.

What you want to use is params.get. This method, defined on Scala's Map class, has a return type of Option[String]. You then use Scala's pattern matching to check whether it's Some(string) or None.

Listing 4.9 Using `Option` to handle missing parameters

```
get("/results") {
  params.get("search_query") match {          ◁──── Starts pattern
    case Some(search_query) =>                        matching
      "You searched for: '" + search_query + "'"
    case None => "No search query, please provide one."  ◁──
  }
}
```

If there's Some search_query param, echoes it back ─▷ (annotation for the Some case)

Deals with the possibility of None, without using null (annotation for the None case)

The match starts pattern matching on an Option[String] returned from a call to params.get("search_query"). In the first case you match the actual value against the pattern Some(message). What that does is just match anything that is Some. By saying Some(search_query), you also tell the pattern to extract the value to search_query. The last line checks for the None case that sparked this discussion in the first place.

CHECKING THE CONTENTS

Although the preceding solution works just fine, it ignores one important thing: the data itself. The existence of the search_query parameter and whether there really is a search query in it are completely unrelated matters. The query might be an empty string. Or it might be whitespace.

You can reuse the same code from listing 4.9. Just add a guard on the Some case that checks the message, as in the following listing.

Listing 4.10   Adding a guard on pattern match

```
params.get("search_query") match {
  case Some(search_query) if search_query.trim.length > 0 =>     ◁──┐ Pattern
    "You searched for: '" + search_query + "'"                        matches can
                                                                      have conditions.
  case _ => "No search query, please provide one."     ◁──┐
}
                                Match all other patterns
                                with the _ placeholder.
```

First, the pattern matches against the type of the Some. Then, the safeguard (if) lets you make fine-grained decisions based on the value itself. In listing 4.10, the case statements effectively mean, *if there's a message and it's non-empty, then ...*

PROVIDING DEFAULT VALUES WITH GETORELSE

Often it's good enough to provide a default value. You could have fixed the error in the search service using params.getOrElse. Keep in mind that Scalatra's params are really just a standard Scala Map. This means that you can use the standard Scala getOrElse method on the Map class to good effect.

getOrElse tries to get a parameter value, and when it fails to do that, it uses a provided function to produce a default value. The following listing shows an example of how you might use it.

Listing 4.11   Giving parameters default values

```
get("/results") {
  "You searched for '" + params.getOrElse("search_query", "") + "'"
}
```

This is a lot shorter than what you saw in listing 4.9 and still manages to keep your code from throwing exceptions when your application doesn't receive a search_query parameter.

HALTING WITH GETORELSE

If you read carefully, you might have noticed that we said getOrElse takes a function to produce the default value. This function is called only if it's needed.

This means you can do interesting tricks with getOrElse. You could provide a function that logs the missing parameter to a debug log and after that returns a default value:

```
params.getOrElse("search_query", {
  log.debug("search query missing :( using default")
  ""
})
```

This is an interesting possibility, but something far more interesting is that you can throw exceptions from the default functions.

This might seem a bit crazy. Wasn't the original problem that your code could unexpectedly throw an exception? Well, yes. But it's a completely different thing when the exception in question is being explicitly thrown and you're forced by the type system to handle it properly.

What you can do is use `getOrElse` and `halt` together to stop your action whenever it finds a missing parameter. `halt` is a Scalatra method that throws a `HaltException`. When this happens, Scalatra renders a response according to the parameters given to the `halt` method call.

For example, if you wanted to replicate listing 4.9 in a more succinct way, you could rewrite it as follows.

Listing 4.12 Halting with `getOrElse`

```
get("/results") {
  val search_query =
    params.getOrElse("search_query",
    halt(200, "Please provide a search query"))

"You searched for '" + search_query + "'"
}
```

Now that you've seen how to do type-safe exception handling and halt execution, let's delve into type safety for HTTP parameters.

4.3.6 *Typed parameters*

So far we've only talked about `String` parameters. This has been enough for the simple search service, but in real-world applications you often need something a bit more fine-grained to satisfy the needs of type-safe libraries. Numbers need to be `Ints`, date strings should be converted to `Dates`, and decimals should be `Doubles` or `Floats`. You might also want to use your own custom types, such as `Name` or `PhoneNumber` instead of `String`.

Writing conversion logic for types can be boring, so Scalatra helps by giving you conversions to some of these primitive types for free, using the `params.getAs` method.

USING PARAMS.GETAS

You can use `params.getAs` like this:[1]

```
params.getAs[Double]("price") //=> Option(9.99)
```

Here, you give the type you want to convert to inside the brackets, and the parameter name like you would normally. The return value will be an `Option` of that type.

Let's say that you want to log a message when you're adding a new hacker to the Hacker Tracker. If the hacker was born before Unix, they're considered classical. The action should halt if it doesn't get properly formatted input. The following listing shows an example implementation.

---

[1] Yes, we're keenly aware that float arithmetic and money don't mix well, but it makes for a simple example.

Listing 4.13   Using `getAs` to get a parameter value with the desired type

```
post("/hackers") {
  val name = params.getAs[Name]("name").getOrElse(
      halt(BadRequest("Please provide a name")))

  val motto = params("motto")
  val birthYear =
    params.getAs[Int]("birth-year").getOrElse(
    halt(BadRequest("Please provide a year of birth.")))

  if(birthYear >= 1970) {
    println("Adding a hacker who was born \
        within the Unix epoch.")
  } else {
    println("Adding a classical hacker.")
  }

  // Create a new hacker with the incoming parameters
}
```

Attempts to get the birth year as an integer

Throws a BadRequest exception if the year of birth is missing or not an int

As before, you get the `name` and `motto` parameters as strings. The `birth-year` parameter gets pulled out of the incoming `params` map as an `Int`, and you prove it by using it to conditionally log the hacker's status (classical or Unix-era).

One nice thing about `getAs` is that it handles errors silently for you. If your action receives a value that doesn't look like an integer (such as `"nineteen seventy"`), calling `getAs[Int]("birth-year")` will still return `None`, just as if the parameter wasn't there to begin with.

By default, `getAs` supports conversions to the following types:

- *Integer types*—`Int`, `Long`, `Short`, `Byte`
- *Floating-point types*—`Float`, `Double`
- `Boolean`—The value of `true` converts to `Some(true)`, `false` to `Some(false)`, and everything else to `None`
- `java.util.Date`—Requires a format string to be set:

```
params.getAs[Date]("publishAt" -> "MM/dd/YYYY")
```

The date format string is explained in more detail in the JavaDocs of `SimpleDateFormat`, available from Oracle at http://mng.bz/itiM.

CUSTOM TYPES

Scalatra's type conversion mechanism is fully extensible. Let's look at an example.

Let's build a converter to convert name strings to `Name` instances. A name will be given in the format of `LastName, FirstName`, and the type converter's job will be to convert that string to an instance of the following case class:

```
case class Name(firstName: String, lastName: String)
```

Divide the work into three parts. The first part, parsing a `Name` out of a `String`, is just a matter of using `split` and doing some cleanup. You can pattern-match the returned `Array[String]` to extract the `lastName` and `firstName`:

```
def toName(str: String) = str.
  split(',').
  map(_.trim) match {
      case Array(lastName, firstName) =>
      Name(lastName, firstName)
}
```

`str.split(',').map(_.trim)` returns an `Array` of name parts. Using `map(_.trim)` applies the `String#trim()` method on each part to strip any surrounding whitespace from the parts.

What will ultimately reach the pattern match will be a two-element `Array` with the last and first names. For example, for the name `Doe, John`, the array would look like `Array(Doe, John)`. The pattern `Array(lastName, firstName)` will match that and extract `lastName` and `firstName` out for you.

Next, you need to define the type converter. A type converter is just a function that has the type of `TypeConverter[T]`. For this example, the type parameter `T` will be `Name`. With the `toName` method already defined, the code needed for the type converter is reduced to this:

```
val stringToName: TypeConverter[Name] = safe { str =>
  toName(str)
}
```

That `safe {` block will catch any exceptions resulting from bad casting attempts and return an `Option` instead.

In theory, you could stop here and start using the custom type conversion with `getAs`. But the code would be verbose, because you'd need to write `params.getAs[Name]("name")(stringToName)`.

To fix this, you can make `stringToName` an `implicit val`. A Scala `implicit` is like a compile-time decorator for doing type conversions. If you try to cast a variable from one type to another, and the compiler doesn't know what to do, it'll check in the current scope to see if there are any implicits defined that can handle the type conversion before it gives up and throws a compile-time exception.

Just add the keyword `implicit` to the definition, and you're ready:

```
implicit val stringToName: ...
```

With the converter in place, all that's left is utilizing the new converter. The following listing shows the current state of the controller (with print and logging statements taken out).

Listing 4.14 A Scalatra action with custom typed parameters

```scala
package com.constructiveproof.hackertracker

import org.scalatra._
import scalate.ScalateSupport
import org.scalatra.util.conversion.TypeConverter

class HackersController extends HackerTrackerStack {

  case class Name(
    lastName: String, firstName: String)

  def toName(str: String) = str.split(',').
    map(_.trim) match {
      case Array(lastName, firstName) =>
        Name(lastName, firstName)
  }

  implicit val stringToName:
    TypeConverter[String, Name] =
      safe { str =>
        toName(str)
      }

  post("/hackers") {
    val name = params.getAs[Name]("name").getOrElse(
      halt(BadRequest("Please provide a name")))

    val motto = params("motto")
    val birthYear = params.getAs[Int]("birth-year").getOrElse(
      halt(BadRequest("Please provide a year of birth.")))

    if (birthYear >= 1970) {
      println("Adding a hacker who was born within the Unix epoch.")
    } else {
      println("Adding a classical hacker.")
    }

    // Create a new hacker and redirect to /hackers/:slug
  }

  get("/hackers/:slug") {
    val slug = params("slug")
    // Retrieve and display info about this hacker
  }

  get("/results") {
    val searchQuery = params("search_query")
    // Search for and display matching hackers
  }

  get("/hackers/tagged") {
    val tags = multiParams("tag")
    // Retrieve and display hackers
    // matching all the given tags
  }
}
```

> ### Sharing your conversions
>
> If you want to use your custom converters across servlets, or if you have more than one of them, it might be a good idea to place them in a trait.
>
> Just extend `org.scalatra.util.conversion.TypeConverterSupport` from that trait, and you can then mix in the conversions to all servlets needing them.

This wraps up our discussion of parameter handling in Scalatra. Now that you've had an introduction to basic parameter handling, you should be able to confidently grab incoming input from the request.

Now let's turn our attention to the next parts of the request's lifespan: `before` and `after` filters, reading headers, reading and writing cookies, and writing out a response.

4.4   Filters

Just like its Sinatra forebear, Scalatra allows you to do selective processing before and after hitting the main body of a route action.

> ### Scalatra before/after filters are not servlet filters
>
> If you're coming from a Java background, you may be used to thinking of filters as *servlet filters*, which are a way of operating on the request at the servlet level.
>
> Although Scalatra classes can be filters in this sense, when we talk about filters in this section, we're talking about the equivalent of Sinatra's filters, which are (confusingly) called the same thing.

Let's say you've got a controller class that looks like the following listing.

Listing 4.15   Filters example

```
package com.constructiveproof.hackertracker

import org.scalatra._
import scalate.ScalateSupport
import org.scalatra.util.conversion.TypeConverter

class HackersController extends HackerTrackerStack {

  case class Name(lastName: String, firstName: String)

  def toName(str: String) = str.split(',').
    map(_.trim) match {
      case Array(lastName, firstName) =>
        Name(lastName, firstName)
  }
```

A before filter that runs before every route in this class

Connects to a (fake) database

Disconnects from the (fake) database

Sets a contentType before every request

An after filter that runs after the action

All action code runs between the before and after filters.

A fake database object to make the compiler happy

```scala
implicit val stringToName:
  TypeConverter[String, Name] =
    safe { str =>
      toName(str)
    }

before() {
  contentType="text/html"
  DataBase.connect
}

after() {
  DataBase.disconnect
}

post("/hackers") {
  val name = params.getAs[Name]("name").getOrElse(
    halt(BadRequest("Please provide a name"))
  )
  val motto = params("motto")
  val birthYear =
    params.getAs[Int]("birth-year").getOrElse(
      halt(BadRequest("Please provide a year of birth.")))
  // Create a new hacker and redirect to /hackers/:slug
}

get("/hackers/:slug") {
  val slug = params("slug")
  // Retrieve and display info about this hacker
}

get("/results") {
  val searchQuery = params("search_query")
  // Search for and display matching hackers
}

get("/hackers/tagged") {
  val tags = multiParams("tag")
  // Retrieve and display hackers
  // matching all the given tags
}
}

object DataBase {
  def connect = {
    println("Connecting to database.")
  }
  def disconnect = {
    println("Disconnecting from database.")
  }
  def insert(message: String) {
    println("Inserting '" + message +
        "' into the database")
  }
}
```

The code in the `before` filter will run before every matched route in `HackersCon-troller`. Keep in mind that the `before` filter will not be run if no matching routes are found; a request to /echo/foo/bar, for example, would not match any routes and the `before` filter would never run.

This `before` filter does two things:

- It sets a `contentType` on the response.
- It opens a fake database connection. You'll see real database connections in chapter 10. For now, you'll just stub them out.

Next, the action code runs. In this controller, multiple routes are defined: `post("/hack-ers")`, `get("/hackers/:slug")`, `get("/results")`, and `get("/hackers/tagged")`. If an incoming request maps to any of these routes, the `before` filter runs first, and then the route's action is run. Afterward, the `after` filter runs.

4.4.1 Selectively running filters

It's possible to define multiple filters at once, and to run filters selectively. If you wanted to set the content type before every request, but only open and close the database connection when it's in use on a specific route, you could set up your filters as follows.

Listing 4.16 Multiple and selective filters

```
before() {
  contentType="text/html"        ◁─────── Runs before all routes
  }

before("/hackers") {   ◁─────── Runs only before the post("/")
    DataBase.connect
}

after("/hackers") {   ◁─────── Runs only after the post("/")
    DataBase.disconnect
}
```

Listing 4.16 defines two `before` filters. The first one will set the `contentType` before every request.

The other filters defined here, `before("/hackers")` and `after("/hackers")`, will run *only* on the `post("/hackers")` route. The other routes will *not* trigger execution of these filters.

4.4.2 Filter conditions

It's also possible to run (or not run) filters based on fairly complex conditional code. For example, if you wanted to run a `before` filter for a specific route, but only on POST requests, you could do this:

```
before("/hackers", request.requestMethod == Post) {
  DataBase.connect;
}
```

The second argument to the `before` method is a Boolean condition that checks that the HTTP request verb is `POST`. It's possible to use any Boolean expression you can think of to conditionally run filters on your routes.

Filters are a great way to use the Don't Repeat Yourself (DRY) principle to clean up your code. Next, we'll look at several other handy helpers.

> **Skinny controllers, fat elsewhere**
>
> In Scalatra, you're free to structure your application in any way you like. Having said that, it pays to think of your action code as the place where you grab data off the incoming HTTP request and then quickly hand it off to other layers of your application that do the real work. If you do everything in your actions, you're probably not going to build the most modular, testable, and reusable code that you can. Put your controllers on a diet, and keep your action code thin.

4.5 Other kinds of user input

Besides HTTP parameters, there are several other kinds of information that you can read from a request, such as request headers and cookies.

4.5.1 Request headers

Sometimes you'll need to read headers off an incoming request. You can do this using the `request.getHeader()` method.

For example, if you want to know whether `text/html` is an acceptable content type for a given request, you can check by doing this:

```
request.getHeader("Accept").split(",").contains("text/html")
```

4.5.2 Cookies

You can easily read incoming cookies using the `cookies.get` method and write them using `cookies.update`, as shown in the following listing.

Listing 4.17 Reading and writing cookies

```
package org.scalatra.example

import org.scalatra._

class CookiesExample extends ScalatraServlet {      Reads the cookie using
  get("/") {                                        cookies.get("counter")
    val previous = cookies.get("counter") match {
      case Some(v) =>  v.toInt
      case None    => 0
    }                                               Writes to the cookie using
                                                    cookies.update("counter")
    cookies.update("counter", (previous+1).toString)
    <p>
       Hi, you have been on this page {previous} times already
    </p>
  }
}
```

Listing 4.17 shows the reading and writing of cookies. The cookies method is available in any of your actions.

The cookies method, like the params method, gives you access to a Scala Map containing available cookie keys and values. As with params, if you want to go back to using null values instead of Option and pattern matching, you can use cookies("counter") to get the value out directly.

4.6 Request helpers

Scalatra also includes some built-in helper methods to accomplish common HTTP-related tasks.

4.6.1 Halting

If you want to immediately stop execution within a filter or an action, you can call halt(). You can also supply an HTTP status, which will be sent back as part of the response: halt(403). Additionally, you can send back a status, a reason, whatever headers you want, and even a response body.

For convenience, you can used named arguments if you're sending back something complicated, as follows.

Listing 4.18   Halting

```
package com.example.app

import org.scalatra.ScalatraServlet

class GateController extends ScalatraServlet {

  before(){                                          If King Arthur is at the gate …
    if(params("name") == "Arthur") {                 Halts with a 403 forbidden HTTP status
      halt(status = 403,
        reason = "Forbidden",                        Gives a reason back to the client
        headers = Map("X-Your-Mother-Was-A" -> "hamster",   Sets some response headers
          "X-And-Your-Father-Smelt-Of" -> "Elderberries"),
        body = <h1>Go away or I shall taunt you a second time!</h1>)   Taunts the user in the returned response body
    }
  }

  get("/") {
    "the holy grail!"
  }
}
```

Almost anyone hitting the code in listing 4.18 will see the result shown in figure 4.4. But if your name is Arthur, execution will halt, as in figure 4.5.

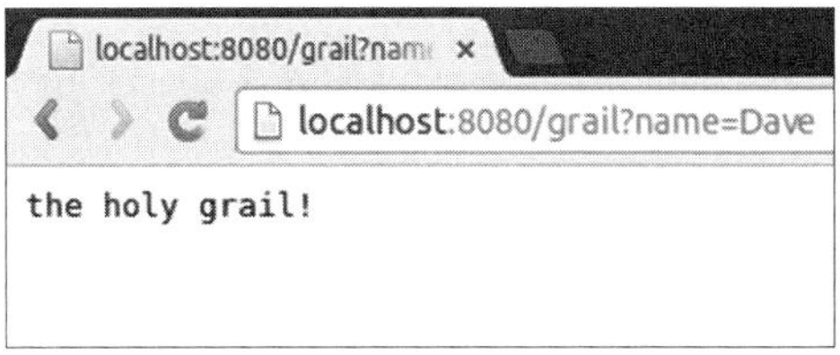

Figure 4.4   The holy grail

**Figure 4.5 Halt with
a response body**

As a creative exercise, feel free to combine this code with the cookie-counter example
from section 4.5.2 so you can detect when Arthur comes back for more.

4.6.2 Redirecting

Another common task in HTTP applications is issuing a redirect. To issue a temporary
(301) redirect, you can say `redirect("/someplace/else")` in any filter or action.

There are no built-in helpers for permanent redirects. If you want to issue a permanent redirect, your best bet is to do something like this:

```
halt(status = 301, headers = Map("Location" -> "http://example.org/"))
```

4.6.3 ActionResult

There's another way to issue HTTP responses (and potentially redirects). Scalatra
actions can return an `ActionResult`. An `ActionResult` is a conveniently named Scalatra type bundling up a specific HTTP response status, an optional redirect where appli-
cable, and headers.

An example is worth a thousand words. Let's rewrite listing 4.18 with an `Action-
Result` and include a nicer form of permanent 301 redirect.

Listing 4.19 `ActionResult` in action

```
package com.example.app

import org.scalatra.{Forbidden, ScalatraServlet}

class GateController extends ScalatraServlet {

  before(){
    if(params("name") == "Arthur") {          Forbidden object
      halt(Forbidden(             ◁──────────  is an ActionResult
        <h1>
          Go away or I shall taunt you a second time!
        </h1>,
        Map("X-Your-Mother-Was-A" -> "hamster",
          "X-And-Your-Father-Smelt-Of" -> "Elderberries"),
        "Forbidden"))
    }
  }

  get("/") {
    "the holy grail!"
```

```
  }

  get("/") {

  }

}
```

That `Forbidden` object is an `ActionResult` that's built into Scalatra. It will cause the framework to respond to the request with a 403 status.

There are several dozen other `ActionResult` objects in Scalatra, mapping to most HTTP status codes. `Ok` maps to a 200 response, `Created` maps to a 201, `BadRequest` maps to a 400, and `NotFound` maps to a 404. See the Scalatra source code at GitHub (https://github.com/scalatra/scalatra/blob/master/core/src/main/scala/org/scalatra/ActionResult.scala) for a full list.

`ActionResults` can make your intentions a lot clearer to readers of your code, especially when you return any of the lesser-known status codes.

4.7 *Summary*

- HTTP-based applications can accept input in a variety of ways, including form parameters, path parameters, and query parameters. Scalatra reads all of these types of parameters from incoming requests using the `params` function, which is part of the Scalatra DSL.

- The `params` function returns a Scala `Map` containing all incoming parameters. The map keys and values are strings.

- Scala's `Option` type is one of the language's key features. You can use it to check your code at compile time, guarding against runtime errors.

- You can execute code before any action in a servlet using the `before()` function. Combine it with conditional statements if you need to.

- Scalatra has built-in helpers for most HTTP-related tasks, including writing cookies, redirecting to alternate URLs, or halting execution.

- The `ActionResult` functions can be used when rendering a response. They return the proper HTTP status code for a given situation, and give an English-language explanation of your intentions, which can provide a useful explanation of what's going on to other programmers (or your future self).

Part 2

Common development tasks

The topics we'll discuss in this part of the book aren't necessarily part of the Scalatra core framework; you'll learn how to integrate with external libraries to extend Scalatra's core capabilities. Chapter 5 explores JSON handling, and chapter 6 shows you how to handle file uploads and serve files to clients. Chapter 7 looks at the details of HTML templating. Chapters 8 and 9 cover testing and application deployment, and chapter 10 discusses data storage and querying.

Handling JSON

This chapter covers

- Consuming and producing JSON using the Scalatra JSON module
- Handling heterogeneity when working with JSON
- Using JSONP

JSON is a common data interchange format for semistructured data. It's human-readable and supports primitive, array, and object values. Additionally, for web services it's the natural data format of the browser, due to its close relationship with JavaScript.

Scalatra offers a module that supports an application working with JSON. This chapter covers its use with practical examples taken from the food domain. Who knows, maybe you'll also learn a useful recipe!

5.1 Introducing JsonSupport

The Scalatra JSON module extends an application's request handling with two facets:

- An incoming JSON request is parsed to a JSON value.
- A JSON value is written to the response as JSON text, as a result of a route action.

Let's see how you can add JSON support to an application.

5.1.1   *Adding JSON support to an application*

Because Scalatra's JSON support is an optional module, it needs to be added as a
dependency to the sbt build definition:

```
libraryDependencies ++= Seq(
  "org.scalatra" %% "scalatra-json" % ScalatraVersion,
  "org.json4s"   %% "json4s-jackson" % "3.3.0")
```

Those dependencies pull in scalatra-json and Json4s. Json4s is a Scala JSON library;
scalatra-json is the actual JSON module that builds on top of Json4s, reusing its JSON-
handling methods and `JValue` data type. This chapter covers a fair amount of Json4s,
but for full documentation refer to the official website at http://json4s.org.

Let's look at what an application needs to do in order to handle JSON. Listing 5.1
shows a minimal example application defining two routes in a trait. You'll need to mix
these into a class in order to run them.

The `GET` route builds and returns a JSON document representing a delicious snack.
The `POST` route extracts a tuple out of a JSON request and prints it to the console.

Listing 5.1   A basic JSON example application

```
import org.scalatra._
import org.scalatra.json._

import org.json4s._                                               Mixes in the
import org.json4s.JsonDSL._                                  JacksonJsonSupport

trait MyJsonRoutes extends ScalatraBase with JacksonJsonSupport {    ◁─┘

  implicit val jsonFormats = DefaultFormats      ◁─────  Provides Json4s Formats

  get("/foods/foo_bar") {
    val productJson =                 ◁─────  Produces a JSON JValue
      ("label" -> "Foo bar") ~
      ("fairTrade" -> true) ~
      ("tags" -> List("bio", "chocolate"))

    productJson
  }
                                                       Reads a tuple from the
  post("/foods") {                                           JSON request

    def parseProduct(jv: JValue): (String, Boolean, List[String]) = {    ◁─┘
      val label = (jv \ "label").extract[String]
      val fairTrade = (jv \ "fairTrade").extract[Boolean]
      val tags = (jv \ "tags").extract[List[String]]

      (label, fairTrade, tags)
    }

    val product = parseProduct(parsedBody)      ◁─────  Invokes a simple parser
```

```
    println(product)
  }

}
```

Let's take a closer look at what happens in this listing. The `JacksonJsonSupport` trait is responsible for parsing an incoming JSON request to a `JValue` as well as for writing a result of type `JValue` as JSON text to a response. This is accomplished by hooking into Scalatra's request-response cycle.

The `GET` route returns a `JValue` as a result, which is written as JSON text to the response. Generally, if you intend to output JSON using Scalatra's JSON support, your JSON routes should always return a value of type `JValue`. When the route result is of type `JValue`, it's set implicitly to `application/json` by `JacksonJsonSupport`.

Because an HTTP request contains the JSON in textual form, `JacksonJsonSupport` provides the function `parsedBody`, which parses the JSON text and returns a value of type `JValue`. `parsedBody` does several things:

- Parses the JSON text from the HTTP request body and always returns a `JValue`.
- Returns `JNothing` if the JSON isn't well-formed.
- Returns `JNothing` if the HTTP request doesn't have the `Content-Type` header set to `application/json`.
- Parses once for each request, and caches the result. Subsequent calls return the cached result.

The request will be parsed eagerly before the route is invoked. With the JSON parsed from the request, the next logical step is usually to extract useful information from the JSON data. This can include the following:

- Selecting specific parts of a JSON document
- Extracting values of other types from a JSON primitive, array, or object
- Handling optional, missing, and null values

You may have noticed the implicit `jsonFormats` value. It holds serialization configuration telling Json4s how to handle specific cases when parsing and writing JSON. For instance, a JSON number can either be handled as a `Double` or a `BigDecimal`. The JSON support requires you to define this value.

The `Formats` type is explained in detail in section 5.3.1, and we'll look at constructing and working with JSON in more detail in section 5.2. For now we'll stay with the `DefaultFormats` settings. As a rule, you should always return a `JValue` from an action and use the `parsedBody` method to access the request's JSON.

Let's now take a closer look at the `JValue` type.

5.1.2   Introducing the JValue type

The `JValue` type represents a JSON intermediate model. You can think of a value of type `JValue` as the abstract representation of a JSON document, often called its *abstract syntax tree*. This simplifies further read and modify operations on that JSON data.

JSON is a typed language, so a `JValue` needs to support all types that may appear in a JSON document. Those are objects, arrays, and primitive values (such as string, number, Boolean, and null). For each JSON type, there's a counterpart in the intermediate model. Listing 5.2 shows the various types. Note that a `JValue` boxes a native Scala value—it acts as a container for a value of that type.

Listing 5.2 `JValue` type

```
sealed trait JValue
case class JString(s: String) extends JValue
case class JBool(value: Boolean) extends JValue

trait JNumber
case class JInt(num: BigInt) extends JValue with JNumber
case class JDouble(num: Double) extends JValue with JNumber
case class JDecimal(num: BigDecimal) extends JValue with JNumber

type JField = (String, JValue)
case class JObject(obj: List[JField]) extends JValue
case class JArray(arr: List[JValue]) extends JValue

case object JNothing extends JValue
case object JNull extends JValue
```

Let's look at how a JSON document is represented as a `JValue`. The following listing shows a sample JSON document.

Listing 5.3 A sample JSON document

```
{
  "label" : "Foo bar",
  "fairTrade" : true,
  "tags" : [ "bio", "chocolate" ]
}
```

Figure 5.1 shows how the document looks as a `JValue`. A JSON document forms a tree. The top-level object is a `JObject` containing a set of key-value pairs representing the JSON object. The keys (`label`, `tags`, and `fairTrade`) are of type `String`. The values are of type `JValue`.

A document tree can be arbitrarily deep. The array at the key `tags` is represented as a value of type `JArray`.

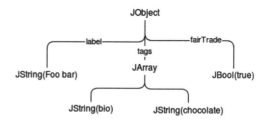

Figure 5.1   A JSON document as a `JValue`

Constructing this document from scratch using the `JValue` types is straightforward. Let's construct some objects and see what the resulting Scala types look like. You can play around with all of the JSON code in a Scala console. Result types are shown in comments below the assignment code.

```
val fooBar = JObject(
  "label" -> JString("Foo bar"),
  "fairTrade" -> JBool(true),
  "tags" -> JArray(List(JString("bio"), JString("chocolate"))))

// fooBar: org.json4s.JValue =
//   JObject(List((label,JString(Foo bar)), ...
```

The `JValue` can also be parsed from JSON text using the `parse` method, which is defined on the `JsonMethods` object:

```
import org.json4s.jackson.JsonMethods.parse

val txt =
  """{
    | "tags": ["bio","chocolate"],
    | "label": "Foo bar",
    | "fairTrade": true
    |}""".stripMargin

val parsed = parse(txt)
// parsed: org.json4s.JValue =
//   JObject(List((label,JString(Foo bar)), ...
```

When comparing the previously constructed value against the parsed value, they are equal. Note that the order of the fields in a `JObject` doesn't matter for equality:

```
fooBar == parsed
// res: Boolean = true
```

You should now have a basic understanding of the scope of Scalatra's JSON support. Remember that parsing and serialization is done by the JSON support transparently in a request-response cycle. Also note that it is easy to integrate another JSON library on your own, such as argonaut or play-json.

Now let's look at how you can work with JSON data.

5.2 Producing and consuming JSON

When receiving JSON, you'll probably want to be able to extract useful information. When sending JSON, you'll need to be able to construct it. Let's start with getting to know the JSON intermediate data model. We'll serialize a `Recipe` object instance as an example.

Applications use JSON to encode data that's delivered to the client, so the application needs to be able to create a JSON message. In this section, you'll learn a simple but effective DSL for constructing a JSON value that's then delivered to a client as the body of an HTTP response.

There are two ways to create JSON, which can also be combined:

- Construct it from scratch using the JValue types and the DSL.
- Decompose existing values to a JValue.

When your application receives a JSON request, it needs to be able to interpret the JSON contained in that request. This section will introduce you to the following:

- Parsing a JSON value from an HTTP request
- Navigating a JSON value to find the required information
- Extracting a value of a type from a JSON value
- Handling of extraction failures

The following listing shows a recipe for an Italian pasta dish as a JSON document. We'll use this JSON document to explain the concepts in this section.

Listing 5.4   Example recipe as JSON text

```
{
  "title": "Penne with cocktail tomatoes, Rucola and Goat cheese",
  "details": {
    "cuisine": "italian",
    "vegetarian": true
  },
  "ingredients": [{
      "label": "Penne",
      "quantity": "250g"
    }, {
      "label": "Cocktail tomatoes",
      "quantity": "300g"
    }, {
      "label": "Rucola",
      "quantity": "2 handful"
    }, {
      "label": "Goat cheese",
      "quantity": "200g"
    }, {
      "label": "Garlic cloves",
      "quantity": "2 tsps"
    }],
  "steps": [
    "Cook noodles until aldente.",
    "Quarter the tomatoes, wash the rucola, dice
      the goat's cheese and cut the garlic.",
    "Heat olive oil in a pan, add the garlic and the tomatoes and
      steam short (approx. for 5 minutes).",
    "Shortly before the noodles are ready add the rucola
      to the tomatoes.",
    "Drain the noodles and mix with the tomatoes,
      finally add the goat's cheese and serve."
  ]
}
```

Although it's possible to stick with the JValue types when processing JSON, it's often helpful or necessary to also employ classes. The JSON language features basic types, but classes give you additional expressivity and type safety. In addition, other third-party libraries, such as database-mapping layers, may require the use of classes.

The domain model consists of the types Recipe, RecipeDetails, and Ingredient-Line. The code is shown in the following listing.

Listing 5.5 Example recipe domain model

```
case class Recipe(title: String,
                  details: RecipeDetails,
                  ingredients: List[IngredientLine],
                  steps: List[String])

case class RecipeDetails(cuisine: String, vegetarian: Boolean,
                         diet: Option[String])

case class IngredientLine(label: String, quantity: String)
```

5.2.1 Producing JSON

There are three methods of creating a JValue in the Json4s library:

- Using the JValue types
- Using the JValue DSL
- Decomposing values to a JValue using a generic reflection-based method

Creating a JValue from scratch using the JValue types has the benefit that you can be explicit about the resulting JSON. But it's also the most verbose approach and can lead to cumbersome code. You saw this approach in section 5.1.2, so we'll employ the other two approaches here.

The DSL is based on a few simple operators and implicit conversion. In order to use the JSON DSL, it needs to be made available in the current scope by importing org.json4s.JsonDSL._. This enables conversion from primitive and collection types to a JValue by specifying the expected type for an expression:

```
val jsString: JValue = "italian"
// jsString: org.json4s.JValue = JString(italian)

val jsBool: JValue = true
// jsBool: org.json4s.JValue = JBool(true)
```

A JSON object is constructed from Tuple2[String, A], where A has an implicit view to JValue. The ~ operator combines multiple fields into a single JSON object. JSON arrays are created from Scala collections:

```
val detailsJson =
  ("cuisine" -> "italian") ~ ("vegetarian" -> true)
// detailsJson: org.json4s.JsonAST.JObject =
```

```
//    JObject(List((cuisine,JString(italian)),
//      (vegetarian,JBool(true))))

val tags: JValue = List("higher", "cuisine")
```

The next listing shows an example using nested objects, a list of primitives, and a list of nested objects, and constructs the JSON document from listing 5.4.

Listing 5.6　Producing a `JValue` with the DSL

```
val recipeJson =
  ("title"    ->
    "Penne with cocktail tomatoes, Rucola and Goat cheese") ~
  ("details" -> detailsJson) ~
  ("ingredients" -> List(
    ("label" ->   "Penne")                ~ ( "quantity" ->   "250g"),
    ("label" ->   "Cocktail tomatoes")   ~ ( "quantity" ->   "300g"),
    ("label" ->   "Rucola")               ~ ( "quantity" ->   "2 handful"),
    ("label" ->   "Goat cheese")          ~ ( "quantity" ->   "250g"),
    ("label" ->   "Garlic cloves")        ~ ( "quantity" ->   "250g"))) ~
  ("steps" -> List(
     "Cook noodles until aldente.",
     "Quarter the tomatoes, wash the rucola,
        dice the goat's cheese ...",
     "Heat olive oil in a pan, add the garlic and the tomatoes and ...",
     "Shortly before the noodles are ready add the rucola to the ...",
     "Drain the noodles and mix with the tomatoes,
        finally add the ...")))
```

One goal of the DSL is to construct a valid `JValue` with very little boilerplate code. Because the DSL is based on implicit conversion, this means a conversion function needs to be available for all values.

Say you want to support a class from the recipe domain model shown earlier, in listing 5.5. Assume that you want to convert a `RecipeDetails` value to a `JValue`. When trying to use a value of type `RecipeDetails` directly in the DSL, this won't work:

```
val jsObject: JValue =
  ("details" -> RecipeDetails("italian", true, None))
// <console>:23: error: No implicit view available
// from RecipeDetails => org.json4s.JsonAST.JValue.
```

The error tells you that no conversion function is available in the current scope. Now let's see how you can extend the DSL for your own types by providing one. The implicit function `details2jvalue` in the following listing takes a `RecipeDetails` and returns a `JValue`. This allows you to use a `RecipeDetails`.

Listing 5.7　Extending the DSL

```
implicit val formats = DefaultFormats

implicit def details2jvalue(rd: RecipeDetails): JValue =
  Extraction.decompose(rd)
```

```
val jsObject: JValue =
  ("details" -> RecipeDetails("italian", true, None))
// jsObject: org.json4s.JValue =
//   JObject(List(
//     (details,JObject(List((cuisine,JString(italian)),
//     (vegetarian,JBool(true)))))))
```

The function relies on decomposition to convert a `RecipeDetails` to a `JValue`. Decomposing is a generic reflection-based method. Depending on the concrete type of a value, either a `JObject`, a `JArray`, or a primitive value is constructed. It's exposed through the function `Extraction.decompose(a: Any): JValue`.

Generally, the following rules are used:

- A primitive value is converted to its matching JSON primitive (for example, a `String` will result in a `JString`).
- A collection value is converted to a JSON array, with the elements of the collection being converted recursively.
- An object is converted to a JSON object, with all constructor fields being converted recursively.

It's possible to override the default conversion behavior for a type by registering a custom serializer for that type. This is discussed in section 5.3.

The `JValue` DSL leads to concise code and allows you to produce JSON with little typing overhead. Decomposition doesn't involve writing any manual conversion code, and it's good for the average conversion case. It relies on general conventions that may not be suitable in all cases, so you may need to write a custom serializer.

Both approaches can be combined: decomposition can be used in the DSL, and the DSL can be used to write a custom serializer. Now let's move on and look at how to process JSON.

5.2.2 Consuming JSON

In this section, you'll learn how to traverse a JSON document and extract values from it. Let's say you're interested in a specific part of the JSON document, such as the title of the recipe in listing 5.4. In order to read this information, you need to be able to address that part of the document. Because a JSON object consists of nested key-value pairs, the keys can be used to perform a traversal trough the JSON document.

For example, selecting the value of the field with the name `"title"` works like this:

```
recipeJson \ "title"
// res: JString(Penne with cocktail tomatoes, Rucola and Goat cheese)
```

The function `\(nameToFind: String): JValue` represents a one-step select that tries to find a field with the given key in the current value. Multiple operations can be chained consecutively:

```
recipeJson \ "details" \ "cuisine"
// res: JString(italian)
```

This one-step selection process allows you to select values deep in nested objects. The syntax resembles XPath in the XML world, which is used to address parts of an XML document.

In an array, the select operation is applied to each contained value, and the results of these invocations are merged in a single JArray:

```
recipeJson \ "ingredients" \ "label"
// res: JArray(List(JString(Penne), JString(Cocktail tomatoes), ...))
```

In addition to simple selects, it's possible to do a recursive selection that searches all nested values. This is what the function \\(nameToFind: String): JValue does:

```
scala> recipeJson \\ "cuisine"
// res: org.json4s.JValue = JString(italian)
```

There are two special cases that we'll take a short look at now: one regarding missing values and the other regarding null values.

Missing values happen when a traversal can't find a suitable value in the JSON document. A missing value is represented by the JValue zero value, JNothing:

```
recipeJson \ "details" \ "prerequisites"
// res: JNothing
// there are no prerequisites, returns JNothing
```

Applying a select on a JNothing yields JNothing again.

A null value is often used to imply a missing value. It's represented as the unique value JNull.

Now that you know how to navigate through a JSON document, let's look at how you can extract a value of some arbitrary type, A, from a JValue. This is called *extraction*, and it's handled by the function extract[A], which is defined on a JValue.

The following types are valid targets to extract to:

- Case classes and classes
- Value types (Boolean, Int, Float, Double) or primitive reference types (String, Date)
- Standard collection types (List[T], Seq[T], Map[String, _], Set[T])
- Any type that has a configured custom deserializer (this is shown in section 5.3.3)

When extracting a value from a JValue, that JValue is checked for compatibility with the target type. When the two are compatible, an instance of the target type is constructed. Primitives and arrays are compatible with Scala's primitives and collections. For example, the title of the recipe can be extracted as a String by calling extract with String as the target type:

```
(recipeJson \ "title").extract[String]
// res: String = Penne with cocktail tomatoes, Rucola and Goat cheese
```

Collections are read from a JSON array. A list of preparation steps from the recipe can be extracted to a `List[String]`:

```
(recipeJson \ "steps").extract[List[String]]
// res: List[String] = List(Cook noodles until aldente., ...)
```

Class instances are extracted from JSON objects using a 1:1 mapping approach between a JSON object and a class. For each constructor parameter of the class type, a matching field in the object is required. This is similar to decomposition, described in section 5.2.2.

For example, the following code extracts a `RecipeDetails` value:

```
(recipeJson \ "details").extract[RecipeDetails]
// res: RecipeDetails = RecipeDetails(italian,true,None)
```

This is how extraction works. Note that because there is no `diet` in the JSON, a `None` is extracted.

The extraction fails at runtime when the JSON is incompatible with the type. For example, a `JBool` can't be extracted as a `String`, and a missing value is incompatible with every type. In this case an exception is raised:

```
JNothing.extract[String]
// MappingException:
// Did not find value which can be converted into java.lang.String
```

In the case where an extraction may fail, the value can optionally be extracted. This means the value is read into an instance of `Option[A]`. This is what `extractOpt[A] (json: JValue): Option[A]` does, with the following possible results:

- `Some(v)` —If the value can be extracted
- `None`—If the extraction fails
- `None`—If `extractOpt` is called on `JNull` or `JNothing`

The following code shows various examples of optional extraction. Note that `JNull` and `JNothing` are both handled as missing values:

```
JString("foo").extractOpt[String]
// res: Option[String] = Some(foo)

JString("foo").extractOpt[Boolean]
// res: Option[Boolean] = None

JNull.extractOpt[String]
// res: Option[String] = None

JNothing.extractOpt[String]
// res: Option[String] = None
```

The optional extraction can be combined with the \/ type from Scalaz (see https://github.com/scalaz/scalaz), resulting in a simple validation. Listing 5.8 shows how this can be done. The computation succeeds with an `Ok(..)` when all values are present. Otherwise, a `BadRequest()` is returned.

Listing 5.8   JSON validation using optional extraction and Scalaz's \/ type

```
trait MyJsonScalazRoutes extends ScalatraBase with JacksonJsonSupport {

  override def renderPipeline: RenderPipeline = ({          ◁───┐  Handles \/ as a return value
    case \/-(r) => r                                              by extending Scalatra's
    case -\/(l) => l                                              render pipeline and extracts
  }: RenderPipeline) orElse super.renderPipeline                  the value from the container

  post("/foods_alt") {                                         Short-circuits with BadRequest
                                                               when optional extraction fails
    for {
      label <- (parsedBody \ "label").extractOpt[String] \/> BadRequest()        ◁───┐
      fairTrade <- (parsedBody \ "fairTrade").extractOpt[Boolean] \/> BadRequest()
      tags <- (parsedBody \ "tags").extractOpt[List[String]] \/> BadRequest()
    } yield Ok((label, fairTrade, tags))        ◁───┐
                                                     Yields an Ok when all
  }                                                  previous steps succeed

}
```

This should give you some methods for extracting basic information from JSON. Let's now look at how to handle more-specific cases.

5.3   *Customizing JSON support and handling mismatches*

The conversion presented in the previous section is sufficient in cases where the structures of a class and a JSON object are very similar. In reality, there's often some form of discrepancy. This can be a simple variation in the naming of fields or a difference in the structures.

Sometimes you can adjust one side so that both match, but in some cases this may not be feasible. For example, when you're working with an existing data model, a code refactoring would be impossible due to dependencies. Similarly, when you're supporting a standardized JSON format, designing Scala classes to exactly match the JSON format can be impractical.

In these cases, a custom conversion function is a cheaper and more sensible alternative. This section covers common approaches for handling such cases.

5.3.1   *Customizing JSON support and using field serializers*

In Json4s, an implicit value of type `Formats` determines the concrete JSON handling. When mixing in the Scalatra JSON support, the implicit value needs to be defined, as shown earlier in listing 5.1.

There's an implementation with common default values in the `DefaultFormats` trait. The trait defines properties that can be overridden when the default behavior isn't sufficient. These are a few use cases where a custom `Formats` saves the day:

- When a date value should be read or written in a non-default date format
- When a JSON number should be read as a `BigDecimal` instead as a `Double`
- When there's a difference between a JSON object and some type, `A`, that requires specific conversion using a custom serializer or field serializer

Table 5.1 lists properties that can be overridden. For a full reference, see the official Json4s documentation at http://json4s.org.

Table 5.1   Properties of `Formats`

Formats property	Explanation	Default
`wantsBigDecimal:` `Boolean`	If `true`, a decimal value is read to JDecimal when decomposing. Otherwise, it's read to a JDouble.	`false`
`strictOptionParsing:` `Boolean`	If `true`, parsing to an `Option[T]` is strict. Incompatible values are then not mapped to None but throw an error.	`false`
`emptyValueStrategy:` `EmptyValueStrategy`	When set to `skip`, a None is skipped. `preserve` writes None as null.	`skip`
`dateFormatter:` `SimpleDateFormat`	Specifies the format used to parse and write dates.	`yyyy-MM-dd'T'` `HH:mm:ss'Z'`
`typeHints:` `TypeHints`	Specifies what type hints variant should be used.	`NoTypeHints`
`typeHintsFieldName:` `String`	Sets the name used as the key of the type hint field.	`jsonClass`
`customSerializers:` `List[Serializer[_]]`	Specifies a list of custom serializers.	Empty list
`customKeySerializers:` `List[KeySerializer[_]]`	Specifies a list of custom key serializers.	Empty list

`fieldSerializers:`
`List[(Class[_],`
`FieldSerializer[_])]`
	Specifies a list of field serializers.	Empty list

Let's see how the default formats handle dates. You'll define an implicit `Default-Formats` value and decompose a map with a `java.util.Date`. After that, you'll parse it again and extract the date. The date is written following the ISO 8601 standard.

Listing 5.9   Using the default `Formats`

```
import org.json4s._
import org.json4s.Extraction.decompose
import org.json4s.jackson.JsonMethods.{parse, compact}
import java.util.Date

implicit val formats = DefaultFormats

val txt = compact(decompose(Map("date" -> new Date())))
// txt: String = {"date":"2014-11-19T19:34:34Z"}

val date = (parse(txt) \ "date").extractOpt[Date]
// date: Option[java.util.Date] = Some(Wed Nov 19 20:34:34 CET 2014)
```

A custom `Formats` is most easily created by extending the `DefaultFormats` trait. As an exercise, you can create one that employs a custom date format, MM/dd/YYYY.

Listing 5.10   Creating a custom `Formats`

```
import java.text.SimpleDateFormat

implicit val formats = new DefaultFormats {
  override protected def dateFormatter: SimpleDateFormat = {
    new SimpleDateFormat("MM/dd/yyyy")
  }
}
val txt = compact(decompose(Map("date" -> new Date())))
// txt: String = {"date":"11/19/2014"}

val date = (parse(txt) \ "date").extractOpt[Date]
// date: Option[java.util.Date] = Some(Wed Nov 19 00:00:00 CET 2014)
```

A field serializer is useful when those fields that don't appear in a class constructor should be serialized. Assume you have a class, `Foo`, that you want to serialize with all its fields. The constructor has two parameters: x and y. Because y is prefixed by a val, there's also a y field. Additionally, there are a and b fields:

```
class Foo(x: String, val y: String) {
  private val a: String = "a"
  var b: String = "b"
}
```

With the default serialization, only the single field, y, that appears in the constructor is written to the JSON during serialization:

```
import org.json4s._
import org.json4s.JsonDSL._
import org.json4s.jackson.Serialization.write

implicit val formats = DefaultFormats
```

```
val foo = new Foo("x", "y")

val txt1 = write(foo)
// txt1: String = {"y":"y"}
```

In this example, you want all fields, y, a, and b, to appear. A field serializer does exactly that.

You can add a `FieldSerializer[Food]` using the + operator, resulting in a new `Formats`. Now all fields are taken into account:

```
import org.json4s._
import org.json4s.JsonDSL._
import org.json4s.jackson.Serialization

implicit val formats = DefaultFormats + new FieldSerializer[Foo]()

val foo = new Foo("x", "y")

val txt1 = Serialization.write(foo)
// txt1: String = {"y":"y","a":"a","b":"b"}
```

Section 5.3.3 shows how to further specialize the JSON handling for a type featuring custom serializers. Let's next look at how to employ type hints.

5.3.2 *Handling polymorphism with type hints*

In this section, we'll discuss how to use type hints, which are a way to work with polymorphic values. Let's assume that you need to work with the class hierarchy shown next. The `Measure` data type describes common measures that may appear in a recipe, and it improves the expressivity of the recipe model:

```
sealed trait Measure
case class Gram(value: Double) extends Measure
case class Teaspoon(value: Double) extends Measure
case class Tablespoon(value: Double) extends Measure
case class Handful(value: Double) extends Measure
case class Pieces(value: Double) extends Measure
case class Milliliter(value: Double) extends Measure
```

Let's further assume that you want to create a JSON array from a list of such values and read it back. This is the JSON that's generated by default:

```
val amounts = List(Handful(2), Gram(300), Teaspoon(2))
val amountsJson = Extraction.decompose(amounts)

[ {
  "value" : 2
}, {
  "value" : 300
}, {
  "value" : 2
} ]
```

Each element consists of a single field, v.

Note that by looking at the JSON representation, there's no clear way to determine what subtype of `Amount` a single element of this array represents. Consequently, it's not possible to read this array back to a `List[Amount]`. Instead, this results in the following exception:

```
amountsJson.extract[List[Measure]]
// MappingException:
// No constructor for type Measure, JObject(List((v,JInt(2))))
```

One way out of this dilemma is to use a synthetic field that holds type information. In Json4s, such a field is called a *type hint*. By default, the key is `jsonClass` and the value is equal to the name of the respective type. When a value is decomposed to a JSON object, a type hint field is added to it automatically, and when a value is extracted from a JSON object, the type hint is used to infer the actual type. In order to enable type hints, you can use the `withHints` method and provide a type hint configuration, as follows.

Listing 5.11   Using type hints

```
import org.json4s.Extraction.decompose
import org.json4s.jackson.JsonMethods.pretty

val hints = ShortTypeHints(List(
    classOf[Gram],
    classOf[Tablespoon],
    classOf[Teaspoon],
    classOf[Handful]))

implicit val formats = DefaultFormats.withHints(hints)

val amountsJson = decompose(amounts)

pretty(amountsJson)
// [ {
//   "jsonClass" : "Handful",
//   "v" : 2
// }, ...
// ]

amountsJson.extract[List[Measure]]
// res: List[Amount] = List(Handful(2), Gram(300), Teaspoon(2))
```

Here you use `ShortTypeHints` with a list of all classes where type hints should be enabled. The resulting JSON correctly interprets the objects, because there are no long ambiguities.

The format of the type hint field can also be customized. For example, there could already be a different naming convention for a type hint field other than `jsonClass`, or the class name could follow a special format. You can customize these two things.

Let's say you need to use the key _type. In order to define a non-default field name, the value `typeHintFieldName` can be overridden:

```
implicit val jsonFormats = new DefaultFormats {
  override val typeHintFieldName: String = "_type"
}
```

For the type hint value, there's an alternative implementation in the form of `Full-TypeHints` that uses the full class name.

The type hints can be overridden in the `Formats` as well:

```
implicit val jsonFormats = DefaultFormats.withHints(FullTypeHints(List(
    classOf[Gram],
    classOf[Tablespoon],
    classOf[Teaspoon],
    classOf[Handful])))
```

Type hints are a simple but effective approach to working with class hierarchies in polymorphic collections and fields. Let's now move on and look at how to work with custom serializers.

5.3.3 *Handling heterogeneity with custom serializers*

A custom serializer defines the JSON conversion for a specific type. In the case of a syntactical mismatch between JSON and a Scala type, a custom serializer can help you align the two formats through syntactical and structural transformations. In this section, we'll look at how you can make use of custom serializers.

Let's say your application wants to retrieve and send nutritional facts about food products, and the facts are represented as values of type `NutritionFacts`. Instead of typing the facts as primitives, they're represented as subtypes of `Fact`. This improves the expressivity of the model and prevents errors by early and strongly typing. The model is shown in the following listing.

Listing 5.12 Nutritional facts domain

```
sealed trait Fact
case class Energy(value: Int) extends Fact
case class Carbohydrate(value: Double) extends Fact
case class Fat(value: Double) extends Fact
case class Protein(value: Double) extends Fact

case class NutritionFacts(
    energy: Energy,
    carbohydrate: Carbohydrate,
    fat: Fat,
    protein: Protein)
```

The nutritional facts should be sent and received as JSON. The expected JSON format for the public API is defined as follows:

```
{
  "energy": 2050
  "fat": 33.9,
  "carbohydrate": 36.2,
  "protein": 7.9
}
```

Your goal is to be able to read and write a `NutritionFacts` value in exactly that format. Serializing a value to JSON using the default conversion yields the following:

```
val facts = NutritionFacts(
  Energy(2050),
  Carbohydrate(36.2),
  Fat(33.9),
  Protein(7.9))

pretty(decompose(facts))
// {
//    "energy": {
//      "value": 2050
//    },
//    ...
// }
```

This isn't exactly what you want. Each fact should be written as a JSON number and not as an object. Trying to read your expected JSON document also results in an extraction error:

```
val jsObj = parse("""
  { "energy": 2050,
    "carbohydrate": 36.2,
    "fat": 33.9,
    "protein": 7.9 }
""")

jsObj.extractOpt[NutritionFacts]
// None
```

In order to fix the mismatch between the two formats, you could adjust either your domain model or your public API. For example, you could primitively type the fact's values as `Double` instead.

But obviously this isn't always possible or preferable. Take as an example a big project employing a legacy data model or legacy API. Furthermore, adjusting a model just to overcome a technical problem is rarely an ideal solution.

What can you do instead? You can write a custom serializer. A custom serializer basically represents two partial functions: one function accepts a `JValue` and returns a `NutritionFacts`; the other function knows how to create a `NutritionFacts` from a JSON document.

The following listing shows how to define a custom serializer for the example. Note that you can use the full power of operations discussed in section 5.2.

Listing 5.13 Custom serializer for `NutritionFacts`

```
class NutritionFactsSerializer
  extends CustomSerializer[NutritionFacts](implicit formats => ({
    case jv: JValue =>
      val e = (jv \ "energy").extract[Int]
      val c = (jv \ "carbohydrate").extract[Double]
      val f = (jv \ "fat").extract[Double]
      val p = (jv \ "protein").extract[Double]

      NutritionFacts(
        Energy(e), Carbohydrate(c), Fat(f), Protein(p)) },
  {
    case facts: NutritionFacts =>
        ("energy" -> facts.energy.value) ~
        ("carbohydrate" -> facts.carbohydrate.value) ~
        ("fat" -> facts.fat.value) ~
        ("protein" -> facts.protein.value)
  }))
```

The custom serializer needs to be registered in the implicit `Formats` value. This can be achieved by using the + operator, which takes a `CustomSerializer` as an argument and returns a new `Formats`. The following listing shows an example with two routes using the custom serializer.

Listing 5.14 Using a custom serializer

```
trait FoodRoutes extends ScalatraBase with JacksonJsonSupport {

  implicit val jsonFormats = DefaultFormats +
    new NutritionFactsSerializer

  get("/foods/foo_bar/facts") {
    val facts = NutritionFacts(
      Energy(2050), Carbohydrate(36.2), Fat(33.9), Protein(7.9))

    val factsJson = Extraction.decompose(facts)

    factsJson
  }

  post("/foods/:name/facts") {
    val facts = parsedBody.extractOpt[NutritionFacts]
    println(f"updated facts: $facts")
  }

}
```

This should give you enough power to handle even major format mismatches.

5.4   *JSONP*

If you've already developed a browser-based web 2.0 application, you've probably heard of the same origin policy (SOP). This is a security measure that should prevent a resource from accessing resources located on a different host than the resource itself. It therefore prevents cross-site requests.

But sometimes you'll want your website to do exactly that, such as querying a web service located at another host using an Ajax request. With the SOP, this isn't possible without further ado. JSONP (JSON with Padding) allows you to work around SOP. It issues an HTTP request by inserting a `<script />` tag into the DOM instead of using Ajax. This works because the `src` attribute of a script isn't subject to SOP.

A JSONP request can be detected by the JSON module, and in the case of a JSONP request, the web service returns JavaScript source code instead of JSON. That JavaScript represents a function call passing the JSON data as argument. The name of the function is given as a query parameter.

A JSONP request is detected by comparing the request parameters against a pre-defined set of callback parameter names. Those parameters can be set by overriding the `jsonpCallbackParameterNames: Iterable[String]` method, as follows.

Listing 5.15 Supporting JSONP in an application

```
trait MyJsonpRoutes extends ScalatraBase with JacksonJsonSupport {

  override def jsonpCallbackParameterNames = Seq("jsonp")

  implicit val jsonFormats = DefaultFormats

  get("/foods/foo_bar") {
    val productJson =
      ("label" -> "Foo bar") ~
      ("fairTrade" -> true) ~
      ("tags" -> List("bio", "chocolate"))

    productJson
  }

}
```

The route can now be called with a query parameter, `jsonp`, that specifies the name of the local JavaScript method that should handle the response. The resulting JSON is returned as a JSONP response. Note that the content type of the response is text/javascript:

```
curl -v http://localhost:8080/foods/foo_bar\?jsonp\=handleResponse
> GET /foods/foo_bar?jsonp=handleResponse HTTP/1.1
> User-Agent: curl/7.37.1
> Host: localhost:8080
> Accept: */*
>
```

```
< HTTP/1.1 200 OK
< Date: Wed, 01 Jul 2015 12:05:00 GMT
< Content-Type: text/javascript; charset=UTF-8
< Content-Length: 84
<
/**/handleResponse({"label":"Foo bar","fairTrade":true,"tags":["bio","chocolate"]});
```

5.5 Summary

- The Scalatra JSON module integrates Json4s in Scalatra's request-response cycle and enables an application to handle JSON requests and answer with JSON responses.
- A JValue represents a JSON value. There is a DSL to create JSON as well as to navigate and extract information from it.
- A value can be converted to and from a JValue using automatic extraction and decomposition and by writing a custom serializer.
- JSONP enables a website to query JSON data from different sites in a browser.

Handling files
6

This chapter covers

- Serving files to a client via HTTP
- Receiving files from a client as an HTTP file upload

This chapter discusses how to implement file exchange over HTTP with Scalatra. As an example, you'll build a basic document store application that acts as an HTTP-based file server. It will serve documents from the filesystem, and new documents can be uploaded by a client. The user interface is depicted in figure 6.1.

Document Storage

Download a document   Create a new document

#	Name	Description	Download
0	strategy.jpg	bulletproof business strategy	download
1	manual.pdf	the manual about foos	download

File:

Choose File   No file chosen

Description:

Submit

Figure 6.1   User interface for the document store example

6.1 Serving files

First we'll discuss how to serve non-HTML files, such as text documents, web assets, and media files from a route. You'll also learn how to serve static resources and how to apply gzip compression to HTTP responses.

6.1.1 Serving files through a route

A route can serve a file by returning a file as a result. There's built-in support for the types `java.io.File`, `java.io.InputStream`, and `scala.Array[Byte]`.

When the type of a returned value is supported, that value is written to the HTTP response body. The file itself can be read by the route's action from various places, such as local or remote filesystems or databases:

```
get("/sample") {
  new File("images/cats.jpg")
}
```

When the file is written to the response, it ensures that a content type header is set. This header indicates the type of the file contained in the response body, and this information enables a client to appropriately interpret the response. Valid content types include `text/plain` for text, `image/jpeg` for JPEG images, and `application/octet-stream` for arbitrary binary data. When no content type is explicitly set by the route, the content type of the file is inferred. This is accomplished by a partial analysis of the file's data.

Let's build a file-server application as a more advanced example. The application should have a web API offering read and write access to documents in a document store. A `Document` represents the file's meta-information, including the file's ID, name, an optional content type, and a description. The `DocumentStore` will have methods to create, find, and list documents. A new document is stored as a map entry in an internal map, and the file content is written to the filesystem with the `Document` ID as the filename. The following listing shows the code.

Listing 6.1 Document and DocumentStore classes

```
case class Document(
  id: Long,
  name: String,
  contentType: Option[String],
  description: String)

case class DocumentStore(base: String) {

  private val fileNameIndex =
    collection.concurrent.TrieMap[Long, Document]()

  private val idCounter = new AtomicLong(0)
```

```
        def add(name: String,
          in: InputStream, contentType: Option[String],      ⟵──── Adds a new document
          description: String): Long = {
            copyStream(in, new FileOutputStream(getFile(id)))
            val id = idCounter.getAndIncrement
            fileNameIndex(id) = Document(id, name, contentType, description)
            id
        }

        def list: Seq[Document] = fileNameIndex.values.toSeq


        def findById(id: Long): Option[Document] = fileNameIndex.get(id)    ⟵

        def asFile(id: Long): File = new File(f"$base/$id")

        private def copyStream(input: InputStream, output: OutputStream) {    ⟵
          val buffer = Array.ofDim[Byte](1024)
          var bytesRead: Int = 0
          while (bytesRead != -1) {
            bytesRead = input.read(buffer)
            if (bytesRead > 0) output.write(buffer, 0, bytesRead)
          }
        }
      }
```

Returns a sequence of all documents ⟶

Returns a document for a given ID

Returns a file for a given ID ⟶

Writes an input stream to an output stream

Two optional response header fields can be useful when serving files: Content-Disposition and Content-Description. The Content-Disposition field contains information about the processing of the file contained in the response. If the disposition type is set to inline, then the document in the response should be displayed directly to the user. The disposition type defaults to attachment, which usually requires further action from the user to display a result (the browser usually presents the user with a Save As dialog box or just downloads the file in the background). Additionally, a filename parameter can be set in the Content-Disposition field. This provides the client with a default filename that can be used when storing the file in the filesystem. The Content-Description response header field can contain a short description about the request payload.

Listing 6.2 shows how to serve documents from the document store and how to include meta-information by setting the HTTP headers just discussed. A document can be queried by its ID. If it can be found, it's returned with the headers set; otherwise, a 404 error is returned.

Listing 6.2 Serving a file

```
class DocumentsApp(store: DocumentStore)
  extends ScalatraServlet with FileUploadSupport with ScalateSupport {

  get("/documents/:documentId") {
    val id = params.as[Long]("documentId")
```

```
    val doc = store.getDocument(id) getOrElse
      halt(404, reason = "could not find document")
    doc.contentType foreach { ct => contentType = ct }
    response.setHeader("Content-Disposition",
      f"""attachment; filename="${doc.name}"""")
    response.setHeader("Content-Description", doc.description)
    store.getFile(id)
  }
}
```

Let's turn to the document store now. The DocumentStore is created in the Scalatra-Bootstrap class when the application starts. You provide the DocumentStore to the application through constructor injection. Because the document store is initially empty, the following code adds some sample documents. (Adding documents to the store via an HTTP file upload is shown in section 6.2.)

```
import org.scalatra._
import javax.servlet.ServletContext
import org.scalatra.book.chapter05.{DocumentStore, DocumentsApp}

class ScalatraBootstrap extends LifeCycle {
  override def init(context: ServletContext) {
    val store = DocumentStore("data")
    store.add("strategy.jpg",
      new FileInputStream(new File("data/strategy.jpg")),
      Some("image/jpeg"),
      "bulletproof business strategy")
    store.add("manual.pdf",
      new FileInputStream(new File("data/manual.pdf")),
      Some("application/pdf"),
      "the manual about foos")

    val app = new DocumentsApp(store)
    context.mount(app, "/*")
  }
}
```

A request querying the sample document would query the URL http://localhost:8080/documents/0:

```
HTTP/1.1 200 OK
Content-Type: application/jpeg;charset=UTF-8
Content-Disposition: attachment; filename="strategy.jpg"
Content-Description: bulletproof business strategy

<<binary data>>
```

The response contains the stored document.

6.1.2 *Serving static resources*

A web application often consists of static web assets, like images, CSS, and HTML. They're usually located as static resources in the src/main/webapp source directory. Those resources can be served to a client in a generic way with the serveStatic-Resource method.

The serveStaticResource method resolves a resource from the request URL, and if one can be found, it's written to the response. Internally, the resource is resolved by using the ServletContext.getResource method.

If no action can be found for a URL, Scalatra tries to serve a static resource by invoking serveStaticResource. If no resource can be found, a 404 response is returned with the previously set content type removed. This default behavior is implemented in the notFound handler:

```
notFound {
  contentType = null
  serveStaticResource() getOrElse halt(404, <h1>Not found.</h1>)
}
```

If an application requires nonstandard handling of static resources, you can overwrite the notFound handler.

6.1.3 *Applying gzip compression to responses*

HTTP allows you to apply content encoding to the body of a response. In practice, this is often a compression algorithm that reduces the bandwidth used by a website.

Scalatra offers the option to encode outgoing responses with the gzip algorithm. In order to make use of it, the ContentEncodingSupport trait needs to be mixed into the application:

```
class DocumentsApp extends ScalatraServlet with ContentEncodingSupport {

  get("/sample") {
    new File("data/strategy.jpg")
  }

}
```

Now, when a client indicates that it's able to receive a response compressed with gzip (by sending an appropriate Accept-Encoding header), the response body is encoded and a Content-Encoding header is added to the response:

```
curl -H "Accept-Encoding: gzip" http://localhost:8080
```

6.2 *Receiving files*

A multipart request combines one or more different sets of data in a single message body. When your application receives a multipart request, Scalatra handles it as a multipart/form-data request, where each body part represents a form field consisting of the field's name and value. The value can be a simple string or binary data representing a document. Often a body part also contains a suggested filename and a description.

We'll start this section with a basic introduction to receiving files in an action. Then we'll discuss the possible configuration settings and how to handle errors during the upload. Along the way, we'll extend the document store code with a file upload.

6.2.1 *Supporting file uploads*

Scalatra's support for file uploads needs to be explicitly mixed into an application through the `FileUploadSupport` trait. When that trait is mixed in, and if a multipart request is detected, the body parts are extracted and made available to the application:

```
import org.scalatra.ScalatraServlet
import org.scalatra.servlet.FileUploadSupport
import org.scalatra.scalate.ScalateSupport

class DocumentsApp extends ScalatraServlet
  with FileUploadSupport with ScalateSupport {

}
```

Each form field with a specified filename is handled as a file; all other form fields are handled as standard parameters.

Each file is represented as an instance of `FileItem`. A `FileItem` describes the file's name, size, and original field name in the multipart request. The content type as well as the charset are available if they have been specified in the request; otherwise they are `None`. The `FileItem` fields and methods are listed in table 6.1.

Table 6.1 `FileItem` fields and methods

Name	Description
`size: Long`	Size of the file
`name: String`	Name of the file
`fieldName: String`	Name of the form field
`contentType: Option[String]`	Content type of the file
`charset: Option[String]`	Charset of the file
`write(file: java.io.File)`	Writes the data to the filesystem via a `java.io.File`
`write(fileName: String)`	Writes the data to the filesystem
`get: Array[Byte]`	Returns the data as a byte array
`getInputStream: java.io.InputStream`	Returns an `InputStream` to the data

A `FileItem` can be written to the filesystem, or the content can be retrieved as an `Array[Byte]` or `java.io.InputStream` for further processing. Parameters are merged with `GET` and `POST` parameters and can be accessed with either the `params` or `multi-Params` method, as discussed in chapter 4.

A `FileItem` can be retrieved with the method `fileParams(key: String)`. The key parameter is the name of the form field, which can contain multiple files. In that case, the `fileMultiParams(key: String)` method can be used, and it returns a `Seq[FileItem]`.

The following code performs a simple file-upload action:

```
post("/sample") {
  val file = fileParams("sample")
  val desc = params("description")
  <div>
    <h1>Received {file.getSize} bytes</h1>
    <p>Description: {desc}</p>
  </div>
}
```

This `POST` action expects a file with the name `sample` and a parameter with the name `description`. A sample `multipart/form-data` message conforming to those requirements is shown next.

Listing 6.3 Sample `multipart/form-data` message

```
--a93f5485f279c0
content-disposition: form-data; name="file"; filename="foobar.txt"

FOOBAZ
--a93f5485f279c0
content-disposition: form-data; name="description"

A document about foos.
--a93f5485f279c0--
```

You can send this message as an HTTP request via `curl`:

```
curl http://localhost:8080/sample \
  --data-binary @data/multipart-message.data \
  -X POST \
  -i -H "Content-Type: multipart/form-data; boundary=a93f5485f279c0"
```

You've now seen how to upload a document manually.

Next, let's extend the document store application with a file-upload form and functionality to receive uploads. The upload form is shown in the following listing. It's integrated in WEB-INF/templates/views/index.scaml and rendered with the main page.

Listing 6.4 A basic file-upload form

```
<div class="col-lg-3">
  <h4>Create a new document</h4>
  <form enctype="multipart/form-data" method="post" action="/documents">
    <div class="form-group">
      <label>File:</label>
```

```
      <input type="file" name="file">
    </div>
    <div class="form-group">
      <label>Description:</label>
      <input class="form-control"
        type="text" name="description" value="">
    </div>
    <input class="btn btn-default" type="submit">
  </form>
</div>
```

The next listing shows the upload handler.

```
post("/documents") {
  val file = fileParams.get("file") getOrElse
    halt(400, reason = "no file in request")
  val desc = params.get("description") getOrElse
    halt(400, reason = "no description given")
  val name = file.getName
  val in = file.getInputStream
  store.add(name, in, file.getContentType, desc)
  redirect("/")
}
```

First the input is validated, halting with a status code of 400 if a parameter is missing. The file is then added (with the given description) to the document store, and the client is redirected to the main page again.

6.2.2   *Configuring the upload support*

Having file-upload support in your application allows users to upload files to the server. But this means users can upload a lot of big files and consume your memory and disk space. It can therefore be useful to set certain limits on multipart request handling.

In listing 6.6, limits are applied to an application: a 30-MB maximum for a single file, and a 100-MB maximum for the entire request. When a request exceeds one of these limits, an exception is thrown, which you can handle as shown in section 6.2.3. The configuration is set by invoking the configureMultipartHandling method, providing a value of type MultipartConfig.

```
import org.scalatra.ScalatraServlet
import org.scalatra.servlet.FileUploadSupport
import org.scalatra.servlet.MultipartConfig
import org.scalatra.scalate.ScalateSupport

class DocumentsApp extends ScalatraServlet
```

```
with FileUploadSupport with ScalateSupport {

configureMultipartHandling(MultipartConfig(
  maxFileSize = Some(30 * 1024 * 1024),
  maxRequestSize = Some(100 * 1024 * 1024),
  ))

// ...

}
```

Table 6.2 lists the available fields of `MultipartConfig`, all of which are optional. If no field value is provided, the default value is used. Here a value of `-1` means *unlimited*, and in theory it could use all available memory. In reality, the concrete behavior also depends on the servlet container that's used. For example, some servlet containers ignore the `fileSizeThreshold` setting for body parts representing files, and write those to the disk by default.

Table 6.2 The fields of the `MultipartConfig` type

Name	Type	Default	Description
maxRequestSize	Option[Long]	Some(-1)	The maximum size allowed for a full multipart/form-data request
maxFileSize	Option[Long]	Some(-1)	The maximum size allowed for a single uploaded body part
location	Option[String]	" " (empty string)	The directory location where body parts that are cached to the file-system will be stored
fileSizeThreshold	Option[Int]	0	The size threshold after which a body part will be written to disk

Listing 6.6 showed the preferred approach to upload a configuration, but the web.xml deployment descriptor can also be used to configure upload support, as shown in listing 6.7. This can be useful when an application already makes substantial use of web.xml. It's possible because Scalatra's upload support builds on the Servlet 3.0 multipart API.

Listing 6.7 Configuration of upload support in web.xml

```
<servlet>
  <servlet-name>documents</servlet-name>
  <servlet-class>org.scalatra.book.chapter06.Documents</servlet-class>
  <multipart-config>
    <max-file-size>31457280</max-file-size>
    <max-request-size>104857600</max-request-size>
    <location>/tmp/uploads</location>
  </multipart-config>
</servlet>
```

This XML is functionally equivalent to the Scala code in listing 6.6.

6.2.3 *Handling upload errors*

When handling file uploads, errors can occur. For example, the file being uploaded may exceed the configured size limit, or there may not be enough space left on the filesystem. In such cases, an exception is thrown. By default, that exception is then shown to the user.

Listing 6.8 shows an error handler that handles two exceptions related to file uploads. A SizeConstraintExceededException is thrown when the uploaded file exceeds a file limit. An IOException implies that an I/O operation failed, such as when the permissions aren't sufficient to execute the operation.

> **Listing 6.8 Error handling for uploads**

```
error {
  case e: SizeConstraintExceededException =>     halt(500, "Too much!")
  case e: IOException =>     halt(500, "Server denied me my meal, thanks anyway.")
}
```

6.3 *Summary*

- Serving files through a route isn't as fast as serving files statically, but it can be useful if you want to apply some processing to files, serve a file from an arbitrary location, or construct an entirely new file in your response.
- Static file serving is useful when you want to quickly serve a file directly from the filesystem.
- Gzipping lets you compress your responses.

Server-side templating

In chapters 5 and 6, you saw how Scalatra can be used to build RESTful APIs by returning JSON and files directly from your controller actions. Scalatra excels at this architecture, but as an HTTP framework, it's also well suited to serving websites. In this chapter, we'll discuss what this means and look at how Scalatra can integrate various standalone templating systems to render the user interface.

7.1 Deciding whether server-side templating is right for you

Server-side templating will be a familiar topic to many readers. Many Scalatra users come from the Java world, where JSP and JavaServer Faces (JSF) are used to render websites. Others come from Ruby's Sinatra, which boasts integration with 20 templating systems.

Server-side templates have also been stigmatized as an outmoded design. The rise of web APIs has certainly led to some movement away from the technique. Still, there are certain types of Scalatra applications where they remain a great fit. Let's first examine whether server-side templates are right for you.

7.1.1 Websites

The distinction between websites and web applications is a bit fuzzy, but it's a topic worth considering as you build your architecture around Scalatra.

The term *website* doesn't mean *static*, but it does imply having a browser as a client. In these applications, the server generates the user interface in the form of HTML views. These are usually complemented by CSS and JavaScript. The client is a simple web browser. This architecture is sketched out in figure 7.1.

We'll assume the use of Scalate as a template engine for now. Scalate will be formally introduced in section 7.2. Let's follow the flow of a typical request in this architecture:

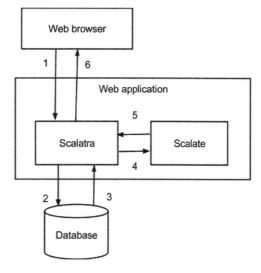

Figure 7.1 In a traditional website, the client is served directly by Scalatra.

1 The browser issues a request to Scalatra.
2 Scalatra queries the database.
3 The database responds with a result set.
4 Scalatra calls a Scalate template with the result set.
5 Scalate returns an HTML view.
6 Scalatra returns the HTML view to the client.

A site like Wikipedia is a great example of this architecture:

- It's document-oriented. Its primary purpose is to serve structured content to end users, and HTML is an ideal format.
- It doesn't require a sidebar with a streaming view of what one's friends are reading. It fits a simple request-response cycle.
- It needs to be easily indexed by search engines. There are ways to do this in other architectures, but none is as simple or as reliable as a simple HTML response at a stable URI.

Unsurprisingly, Wikipedia is built on server-side templates. This architecture won't add any buzzwords to your resume, but it's tried and true. But before diving in, let's consider an alternative view.

7.1.2 *Web APIs*

In recent years, many web applications have evolved into web APIs. There are several reasons for this:

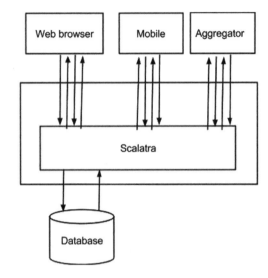

Figure 7.2   A RESTful API: a single Scalatra service serving disparate clients

- Browsers are as important as ever, but they now support richer user interfaces through single-page JavaScript apps, as opposed to regenerating the entire view on each trip to the server.
- Mobile applications are often built on UI toolkits that use HTTP for fetching and sending the data that drives them.
- Often, the client is actually another HTTP server, aggregating multiple services to provide new views into the data.

These apparently different use cases share one common trait: they have little use for server-generated HTML. Instead of responding with a user interface, the server responds with the data to drive an interface generated elsewhere. This decoupling of user interface from data allows a single API to serve a more diverse set of clients. This architecture is illustrated in figure 7.2.

There is a striking difference between figure 7.2 and figure 7.1: Scalate is gone. Relieved of the need to apply a standard HTML structure to the data, Scalate becomes superfluous in this style.

> **False dichotomy alert**
>
> As alluded to at the beginning of the section, it's a fuzzy line between website and web application.
>
> - Our canonical website example, Wikipedia, is not purely HTML. It implements autocomplete on search results via JSON.
> - A client-side application driven by RESTful endpoints may initialize itself from an HTML template.
> - A single Scalatra route might examine the request headers to determine whether the client wants an HTML view or a JSON view. This is called *content negotiation*, and it can result in a hybrid-style application.

In summary, server-side templating is far from dead, but it's also far from mandatory. If you're primarily interested in REST APIs, feel free to skim ahead to the next chapter. Otherwise, let's get our feet wet with Scalate.

7.2 Introducing Scalate

Scalate[1] is a fast and versatile server-side template system, directly supported by Scalatra as an optional module. A standout feature of Scalate is its support for multiple template dialects, which we'll cover in section 7.3.4. Other benefits of Scalate include these:

- Strongly typed templates[2]
- The ability to pass custom bindings
- Automatic template reloading and caching
- Error reporting with trace output and line numbers

We'll start by looking at Scalatra's dependencies file, project/build.scala, to ensure that Scalate is installed.

7.2.1 Installing Scalate in a Scalatra app

Scalatra comes with Scalate support by default when you create your project using giter8. You can see the relevant line in the `libraryDependencies` section of project/build.scala:

This line pulls in the Scalatra-Scalate integration and transitively pulls in a version of Scalate known to work with the selected version of Scalatra.

```
libraryDependencies ++= Seq(
    "org.scalatra" %% "scalatra" % ScalatraVersion,
    "org.scalatra" %% "scalatra-scalate" % ScalatraVersion,         ◁
    "org.scalatra" %% "scalatra-specs2" % ScalatraVersion % "test",
    "ch.qos.logback" % "logback-classic" % "1.1.3" % "runtime",
```

The giter8 template also creates a `WebAppStack` trait for customizing Scalatra's features across all of your servlets. If you look at the `WebAppStack` trait in src/main/scala, you'll see that the `ScalateSupport` trait is already included in the class declaration. Additionally, you'll see the default behavior of searching for templates and static resources. The exact location of your `WebAppStack` trait is determined by your package and application names, but you'll find it as the *WebAppStack.scala file in src/main/scala. Let's take a deeper look in the next listing.

Listing 7.1   The `WebAppStack` trait

```
package com.example.app        ◁   Your project's package. Replace the
                                   dots with slashes, prepend src/main/
import org.scalatra._              scala, and you'll find your trait.
import scalate.ScalateSupport

trait MyScalatraWebAppStack extends ScalatraServlet
    with ScalateSupport
```

Mixes in the Scalatra-Scalate integration

---

[1]   The core developers don't agree on whether it's two syllables or three, but all agree that the *te* stands for *template engine.*

[2]   True for each dialect except Mustache.

7.2.2 Scalate directory structure

Scalatra asks Scalate to look for layouts and views in a structure similar to Sinatra's. The major difference is that Scalatra templates go into a WEB-INF subdirectory. Let's look at the structure of a typical Scalatra application:

```
src/main/webapp
├── js
├── css
└── WEB-INF
    └── templates
        ├── layouts
        │   └── default.jade
        └── views
            └── hello-scalate.jade
```

You can see in the default Scalatra folder structure that the giter8 template provides an example layout and view template. We'll cover each of these in detail in the next section.

> **Why WEB-INF?**
>
> The WEB-INF convention comes from the servlet world. The src/main/webapp directory corresponds to the root of your web application. A GET request on /images/banner.png would map to src/main/webapp/images/banner.png if it falls through to serveStaticResource.
>
> The WEB-INF directory is special in that it's shielded from direct access. You wouldn't want serveStaticResource to find a scaml template, because it would render the template source instead of executing the template. Templates are inaccessible unless explicitly called because they're in a special directory.

Now that Scalate is installed, let's see it in action.

7.3   Serving content with the Scalate template system

Your first view will (not very cleverly) say hello to a user by name and offer some lucky numbers.

7.3.1 *Your first Scaml template*

You'll use Scaml for your first view. It's well-structured HTML, and it fits nicely with Scaml's strengths. Let's create the view in src/main/webapp/WEB-INF/templates/views/greeter.scaml, as shown in the following listing.

Listing 7.2 greeter.scaml

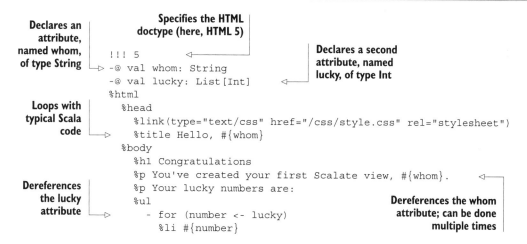

When you render the template, you get real HTML. If you squint at the template source, it even resembles HTML, but it's clearly different. Let's examine the Scaml code in more depth:

- *No HTML-style tags*—The familiar HTML tags are instead prefixed with a percent symbol (%).

- *No end tags*—Indentation is significant in Scaml. Nesting is inferred from the level of indentation.

- *Scala declarations*—At the top, you'll see some declarations that look like abstract Scala declarations.[3] A line beginning with -@ declares attributes for your template. Why? Keep reading.

- *A curious #{} syntax*—Code in this syntax is interpreted as Scala code and is rendered to the output. Because Scala is a static language, the code must type-check. By declaring a whom attribute, the #{whom} code compiles. #{who} would fail at compile time, because it's not declared.[4]

    Because #{whom} is declared as a String, you could use #{whom.toUpperCase} if you wanted to shout. #{lucky.toUpperCase} would fail at compile time because lucky is a list.

---

[3] You can also provide a default value by assigning the attribute in place: val whom: String = "Pete".

[4] Contrast this with more-dynamic templating languages, where such an error results in silently blank output or a literal null.

- *A for loop*—A line beginning with - also follows Scala code. Unlike the #{} syntax, it evaluates the code without emitting the result into the output. It's most commonly used to introduce looping constructs. Note that instead of an ad hoc looping syntax, Scaml reuses Scala's `for` comprehensions by reusing Scala itself. What good is code that emits no output in a template? There's one more thing.

- *Scaml code nested in Scala code*—Nested inside the `for` loop is a `%li` element. Just as you embedded Scala code in your Scaml, you can embed Scaml in your Scala code. Just as HTML nests tags, Scala nests blocks. It's all scoped in a Scaml template using the same indentation syntax. In listing 7.2, the `%li` element is part of the loop, so each lucky number in the list is rendered to the output.

   Notice that Scaml doesn't require any extra syntax for looping. It has a few simple ways of escaping to Scala, allowing you to harness the full power of Scala's `for` comprehensions to establish the looping logic.

Further views would proceed similarly, with similar HTML boilerplate. This should make any good developer uneasy. In the next discussion, we'll extract it into a layout.

7.3.2   Layouts

Don't Repeat Yourself (DRY) is a recurring principle in software development. In Scala code, you extract common code into helper functions. In a relational database, you normalize tables to reduce anomalies. Similarly, you can factor common code out of your templates. In Scalate, you use layouts.

When rendering your views, Scalate will look for a layout in the /WEB-INF/templates/layouts/default.{dialect} file, where `dialect` is one of the supported types.[5] There's no rule that the layout must be the same dialect as the template, though that's the most common case. Take a look at the example Scaml layout in the following listing.

Listing 7.3   default.scaml

```
!!! 5
-@ val body: String
-@ val title: String
%html
  %head
    %link(type="text/css" href="/css/style.css" rel="stylesheet")
    %title= title          ← Renders the title
  %body
    != body          ← Renders the body
```

The layout looks a lot like a view, but it introduces two new bits of Scaml syntax:

- `%title= title` creates an HTML element (that's the `%title` part) and fills it with the variable `title`. The syntax is shorthand for `%title #{title}`.

---

[5] Supported types are .scaml, .ssp, .jade, and .mustache.

- != is used to render the raw body variable. By default, interpolation sanitizes embedded HTML characters, turning < into < so that it displays literally instead of being interpreted as the start of a tag. Because you want the tags of a body to be treated as HTML, you need to turn off this escaping to render the body.

With the common HTML elements extracted to a layout, you can pull it out of greeter.scaml, and any other views. The amended greeter_dry.scaml is presented in the following listing.

Listing 7.4   greeter_dry.scaml for layout

```
-@ val whom: String
-@ val lucky: List[Int]
- attributes("title") = "Hello, "+whom          ⟵──┐ Passes an attribute
                                                      │ to the layout
%h1 Congratulations
%p You've created your first Scalate view, #{whom}.
%p Your lucky numbers are:
%ul
  - for (number <- lucky)
    %li #{number}
```

The most interesting thing in the slimmed-down greeter.scaml is the `attributes("title")` line. The layout requires a title, but in this case it's derived from the whom attribute. That line allows the template to provide the value of the attribute on the layout.

Recall that the layout in listing 7.3 declared a body attribute. body is a special name. The entire output of the view is passed to the layout as the body attribute, in the form of a `String`.

SELECTING AN ALTERNATE LAYOUT
body is one special attribute; the other is layout.

It's common for the authenticated portion of a website to require one layout, with navigation that applies to registered users, and for other pages to have a simplified layout for guests. A different layout can always be specified by setting the layout attribute:

```
- attributes("layout") = "/WEB-INF/templates/layouts/guest.scaml"
%h1 Welcome, guest
% This page will use the guest layout.
```

TIP You can even suppress the layout altogether by setting layout to the empty string.

Now that you have a template and a layout, let's see how to invoke it from Scalatra.

7.3.3   *Invoking your template*

Way back in listing 7.1, you saw an example of rendering a template with the layout-Template(path) command. That worked well in the notFound handler, but it didn't offer any opportunity to set template attributes. The signature is layout-Template(path: String, attributes: (String, Any)*).[6]

The attributes parameter allows you to specify a series of tuples to define the attributes. Let's create a simple servlet to invoke your greeter.

Listing 7.5   GreeterServlet

```
class GreeterServlet extends MyScalatraWebappStack {
  get("/greet/:whom") {
    val lucky =
      for (i <- (1 to 5).toList)
      yield util.Random.nextInt(48) + 1
    layoutTemplate("greeter.html",
      "whom" -> params("whom"),        Passes the attributes
       "lucky" -> lucky)               to the template.
  }
}
```

You name the template path "greeter". The layoutTemplate call uses the same logic as the findTemplate you used in the notFound handler to search for a template.

The conventions are as follows:

1 It first tries a direct match in the default directory: "greeter.html" -> "/WEB-INF/templates/views/greeter.html". This fails because your template has an extension of scaml.

2 It then tries appending the template suffix path: "greeter.html" -> "/WEB-INF/templates/views/greeter.html.scaml". Again, this fails.

3 Next, it tries replacing the path suffix with the template suffix: "greeter.html" -> "/WEB-INF/templates/views/greeter.scaml". This is a hit, and it's why your template renders.

4 Finally, it tries the same logic again with /index appended to the supplied path: "greeter.html" -> "/WEB-INF/templates/views/greeter.html/index". This is not useful here, but it's very useful for paths that represent directories.

After the path, you bind your attributes using Scala's convenient arrow syntax for Tuple2. You can specify attributes that aren't needed by the template, but any declared attribute without a default value must be passed.

> **TIP** layoutTemplate uses varargs syntax, which is great for a fixed number of attributes. If the attributes are dynamically generated, they're more likely to come in a Map. If your map is called attributeMap, you can invoke your template as layoutTemplate(path, attributeMap.toSeq: _*).

---

[6] There's also an implicit request and response, but don't worry about those. That's why they're implicit.

7.3.4   A comparison of dialects

As previously mentioned, Scalate also allows you to choose between a defined list of template dialects. We've focused on Scaml, which is concise and different enough from HTML to be interesting. But each dialect has benefits in its capabilities and formatting that you may already be familiar with. You should choose the template language that you are most comfortable with and that grants you the control you need.

There's no additional overhead to using more than one dialect in the same application, so it's reasonable to mix and match. The dialects are compared in table 7.1.

Table 7.1   A comparison of Scalate dialects

Dialect	Resembles	Notes
SSP	Java's Velocity, Java's JSP	Good for free-form markup with lots of mixed elements (such as a `<p>` tag interspersed with several anchors). Has even been used for non-HTML responses, such as CSV.
Scaml	Ruby's Haml	Depends on indentation instead of end tags to close HTML. Developers generally either love this or hate it. Good for highly structured content like tables, but awkward for rendering long blocks of content.
Jade	Node.js's Jade	Nearly identical to Haml. Loses the % before elements.
Mustache	Other Mustaches	Works inside the browser, so the front-end developer can develop without blocking on, or learning, anything about the server side. Of the Scalate dialects, it's the only one whose expressions aren't checked at compile time.

All of these dialects are covered in depth on the Scalate website (http://scalate.github .io/scalate/). If none of these satisfy, there's yet another option for server-side templating with Scalatra: Twirl.

7.4   Serving content with Twirl

Instead of integrating with Scalate, the Play Framework created its own template system. This was tightly coupled with the rest of the Play Framework, yet was attractive to other web frameworks. This prompted the Spray.io team to spin it off into a separate project called Twirl. Twirl templates are somewhat reminiscent of SSP in that they can generate free-form text rather than strict HTML structure. Like Scalate, Twirl templates are also compiled to catch as many errors as possible at compile time.

7.4.1   Configuring your project

Setting up a project for Twirl involves configuring a Simple Build Tool (SBT) plug-in rather than a simple library dependency. To add the Twirl SBT plugin, add a line to project/plugins.sbt, as follows:

```
addSbtPlugin("org.scalatra.sbt" % "scalatra-sbt" % "0.4.0")

addSbtPlugin("com.typesafe.sbt" % "sbt-twirl" % "1.0.4")
```

Adds the
Twirl plugin

TIP   The blank lines are important! *.sbt files are like *.scala files, but they require a blank line between each statement.

Finally, you need to add the Twirl settings to your project/build.scala, as in the following listing.

Listing 7.6   build.scala

```
import play.twirl.sbt.SbtTwirl                        ◁————————  Brings the Twirl
                                                                settings into scope
object Chapter07TwirlBuild extends Build {
  lazy val project = Project(
    Name,
    file("."),
    settings = Seq(
      organization := Organization,
      name := Name,
      version := Version,
      // and so on
    ).settings(ScalatraPlugin.scalatraSettings:_*)     ⎤  Configures this project
     .enablePlugins(SbtTwirl)                     ◁————⎦  to use Twirl
```

With that out of the way, it's time to see Twirl in action.

7.4.2   *Using Twirl*

It's important to recognize that Twirl is simply Scala mixed with text. The Twirl templates are compiled into standard Scala functions that can be called by the rest of the application.

All templates go into src/main/twirl. If you name your template src/main/twirl/greeting.scala.html, it will be available as a function named html.greeting. Note how the suffix, html, shifts to before the filename. Let's port the Scalate greeting to Twirl, as shown in the following listing.

Listing 7.7   greeting.scala.html

```
@(whom: String, lucky: List[Int])

<html>
  <head>
    <link type="text/css" href="/css/style.css" rel="stylesheet" />
    <title>Hello, @whom</title>
  </head>
  <body>
    <h1>Congratulations</h1>
    <p>You've created your first Twirl view, @whom.</p>
    <p>Your lucky numbers are:</p>
    <ul>
    @for(number <- lucky) {
      <li>@number</li>
```

```
    }
    </ul>
  </body>
</html>
```

This Twirl template takes the same two parameters, whom and lucky. That means the generated function will also take two parameters. To invoke the Twirl template, you call this function:

```
get("/greet/:whom") {
  contentType = "text/html"
  val lucky =
    for (i <- (1 to 5).toList)
    yield util.Random.nextInt(48) + 1
  html.greeting(params("whom"), lucky)        ⊲———— Twirl invocation
}
```

This looks substantially similar to the example in listing 7.5. You access the route parameter and generate the lucky numbers in the same fashion as with Scalate. Only the template call is different.

> **Twirl vs. Scalate**
>
> The function call interface of Twirl offers a huge advantage over Scalate. Recall that Scalate passes attributes to its templates as a `Map[String, Any]`. Although the template itself is checked at compile time, the call to the template isn't. In Twirl, it's a compile-time error to call a template with the wrong parameters.
>
> Does this mean Twirl should replace Scalate? Not necessarily. Scalate is more widely used, and it supports many more dialects.
>
> Both template engines have their strengths. In a better world, we'd have Scalate's wider dialect support merged with Twirl's API.

Twirl offers capabilities similar to Scalate for extracting layouts, escaping content, and so on. To learn more, please see the Twirl website (https://github.com/spray/twirl).

7.5 Summary

- Scalate is the mainstream templating system option, offering first-class integration with Scalatra.
- Twirl is the upstart contender that lacks formal support from the Scalatra team but is easy to integrate.

Testing 8

This chapter covers
- Integration testing with Specs2
- Unit testing with Specs2
- Testing with ScalaTest

By now, you've had a thorough introduction to the basic features of Scalatra. As good test-first developers, we feel a little guilty about waiting until now to introduce testing, but here we are.

Scalatra comes with a test DSL to simplify testing your application. The DSL follows the Scalatra philosophy of not being particularly opinionated. It works with both major Scala test frameworks, ScalaTest and Specs2. It's suited to both integration and unit testing. And if it doesn't fully suit your needs, it's easy to pull out the pieces that do. It's time to write your first test.

8.1 Integration testing with Specs2

Scalatra is built on the Java Servlet API. This design permits Scalatra to sit atop servers like Jetty and Tomcat, the most mature servers on the JVM. It also complicates testing for a few reasons:

- The central method of the Servlet API returns Unit.[1] With no return value to inspect, you have to intercept the response object.
- The API has a large surface area that's difficult to stub. In version 3.0 HttpServletRequest alone has 66 methods.
- Mocking a container is difficult because of the peculiar rules of the Servlet specification. Calling certain methods of HttpServletResponse is illegal at certain times, sendError throws an exception when called after the response is committed, and setHeader is ignored in the same state. You can't call getWriter and getOutputStream on the same response. Simulating these rules correctly would be as daunting as building a new container.

For these reasons, the servlet layer of an application is notoriously difficult to test and is therefore notoriously undertested. Talking directly to your Scalatra servlet isn't a viable approach.

Scalatra's test DSL takes a different tack: it embeds a live servlet container and speaks to it through an HTTP client. It sounds a bit bulky, but in the next section you'll see how simple it really is.

8.1.1 Getting started with Specs2

Like Scalate in chapter 7, Specs2 is integrated as a module. This involves an extra line in project/build.scala. Users of the giter8 template will find it already configured:

**Defines the scalatra-specs2
dependency in test scope.**

```
libraryDependencies ++= Seq(
  "org.scalatra" %% "scalatra-specs2" % ScalatraVersion % "test"    <┐
)
```

One important difference between scalatra-specs2 and other dependencies is the % "test" at the end of the dependency. This declares the dependency to be in *test* scope. Libraries in test scope are only available during test runs. Tests aren't meant to be deployed, so this separation enforces the divide and slims down the deployable artifact.

Also included in the giter8 template is a simple test named HelloWorldSpec. Tests are found in src/test/scala.[2]

Let's test a simple food servlet. It returns product information for potatoes, in JSON format. First, add the dependency to Json4s and Scalatra's JSON integration:

```
"org.scalatra" %% "scalatra-json"   % ScalatraVersion,
"org.json4s"   %% "json4s-jackson"  % "3.3.0",
```

Next, add the servlet, shown in the following listing.

---

[1] In Java, it's called void.

[2] Code in src/test/scala is compiled against the test scope described previously and is also excluded from the deployable artifact.

Listing 8.1   The `FoodServlet`

```
package org.scalatra.book.chapter08

import org.json4s.DefaultFormats
import org.json4s.JsonDSL._
import org.scalatra.ScalatraServlet
import org.scalatra.json._

class FoodServlet extends ScalatraServlet with JacksonJsonSupport {

  implicit lazy val jsonFormats = DefaultFormats

  get("/foods/potatoes") {
    val productJson =
      ("name" -> "potatoes") ~
        ("fairTrade" -> true) ~
        ("tags" -> List("vegetable", "tuber"))

    productJson
  }
}
```

Last, mount the `FoodServlet` in `ScalatraBootstrap`:

```
context.mount(new FoodServlet, "/*")
```

Rename `HelloWorldSpec` to `FoodServletSpec`, and make it look like the next listing.

Listing 8.2   Immutable Specs2 test

Base trait enables the Scalatra integration of the Specs2 DSL

Brings ScalatraSpec into scope

Specs2 syntax describes what will be asserted

Describes the test

Ties the test description to the method that implements it

Mounts the servlet to the root path so it can be called

Issues a GET request to the specified path

Asserts that the status of response was 200 (OK)

```
package org.scalatra.book.chapter08

import org.scalatra.test.specs2._

class FoodServletSpec extends ScalatraSpec {
    def is = s2"""

  GET /foods/potatoes on FoodServlet
    should return status 200
        $potatoesOk
  """

  addServlet(classOf[FoodServlet], "/*")

  def potatoesOk =
    get("/foods/potatoes") {
        status must_== 200
    }
}
```

There's a lot going on here in a relatively small amount of code. The first thing to notice is that you define a class that extends `ScalatraSpec`. Just as `ScalatraServlet` enables the DSL for your application, `ScalatraSpec` enables the DSL for your test.

After that comes an `is` method with some curious syntax. A Specs2 acceptance test is a literate specification: the text on the left declares the intent in a format you can discuss with your non-technical product manager to agree on the specification, and the bindings to the code that implement the test are swept off to the right. It's a foreign syntax to those coming from the xUnit family of test frameworks, and it seems like overkill with a single assertion, but as a specification grows larger, the syntax keeps front and center exactly what you're trying to accomplish.

> ### Specs2 string interpolation
>
> The `s2` syntax uses Scala's customizable string-interpolation features to cleanly separate the descriptions from the code. The `s` interpolator in the standard library is common in Scala code. A string literal prefixed with `s` may embed Scala expressions with `${}` syntax. For example, `s"Byte.MaxValue == ${Byte.MaxValue}"` results in `String"ByteMaxValue == 127"`. The interpolated code is typechecked just like any other Scala code, preventing silly runtime mistakes.
>
> Scala goes one step further, allowing libraries to provide custom `String` interpolators. Specs2's `is` method doesn't return a `String` but a special Specs2 data structure called `Fragments` to describe the test. The `s2` syntax converts the `String` literal, with embedded code, into the necessary `Fragments`. More on the motivation for using this syntax can be found in Eric Torreborre's article "Specs2 2.0 - Interpolated" on his blog (http://mng.bz/0AOC).

Next, you add your servlet. It's as simple as providing the class reference and the path to mount it to. The path specification is identical to what you find in `ScalatraBootstrap`.

Finally, we get to the test. The `get("/foods/potatoes")` block is designed to resemble the corresponding Scalatra route that matches it. But the separate purposes of the core framework and test framework give rise to separate rules:

- Path parameters aren't supported. You can specify a query string, which you'll see later. The intent is not to define a broad matcher like a route, but rather an exact path for a single test case.
- Similarly, Boolean guards and regular expressions aren't supported. Neither of these fit with the idea of specifying a single path for a request.

Inside the `get` block is the assertion of your test—that the status must equal 200. Review the code from listing 8.2 again, and read it out loud: `status must_== 200`. The code reads exactly as you'd describe the test. This is another example of Specs2's philosophy of literate specifications.

The status code is just one part of a response. In the next specification, you'll enhance the test to cover all the basics of the response.

8.1.2 Asserting over the entire response

An HTTP response can be thought of as being composed of three main parts:

- The status
- The headers
- The body

You've already seen how to assert the correct status code. Let's now enhance the test to test the other two parts.

Listing 8.3   Testing headers and the body

```
class FoodServletSpec extends ScalatraSpec { def is = s2"""
GET /foods/potatoes on FoodServlet
  should return status 200                    $potatoesOk
  should be JSON                              $potatoesJson
  should contain name potatoes               $potatoesName
"""

  addServlet(classOf[FoodServlet], "/*")

  def potatoesOk = get("/foods/potatoes") {
    status must_== 200
  }

  def potatoesJson = get("/foods/potatoes") {
    header("Content-Type") must startWith ("application/json;")
  }

  def potatoesName = get("/foods/potatoes") {
    body must contain("""{name: "potatos"}""")
  }
}
```

Asserts that the Content-Type header specifies a JSON response

Asserts that the media type is correct for JSON

These examples hardly require any explanation, but they're useful to see in action. The literate style is easy to read, but because Scala isn't a natural language parser, it does require some knowledge to write correctly.

> **TIP**   We discussed triple-quoted string literals in section 3.3.2. Specs2 descriptions like the one in listing 8.3 frequently contain characters like quotation marks that benefit from the same escaping rules as regular expressions. We recommend using the """ syntax in s2.

One interesting note is the use of Specs2's matchers. You've already seen must_==. This example introduces startsWith and contain. You could write everything as an equality check, but you're not particularly interested in the charset of the content type nor the rest of the response body. Overspecification makes tests brittle. The rich matcher vocabulary lets you say exactly what you mean, and no more.

The test is still a bit unsatisfying. The body is JSON, but you're testing it as a `String`. Even with the `contain` matcher, the test could fail for whitespace issues on structurally equivalent JSON. In the next section, you'll test the JSON directly.

8.1.3 Testing as JValues

The Json4s object model was introduced in chapter 5. It would be nice to use that model directly. The following listing parses the body to a `JValue` and specifies the test in terms of JSON instead of a `JValue`.

Listing 8.4 Testing headers and the body as *JValues*

```
import org.json4s._                                    Imports the JSON parse and
 import org.json4s.jackson.JsonMethods                 query methods from Json4s

class FoodServletSpec extends ScalatraSpec {

  def potatoesName = get("/foods/potatoes") {
    val json = JsonMethods.parse(body)                 Parses the response
    json \ "name" must_== JString("potatos")           body to a JValue
  }
                      Tests the name in terms of a JValue
}
```

This is much nicer. Instead of making assertions about the output string, you make assertions about the JSON. The \ character is an operator provided by Json4s to find the child element of a JSON object. You could instead use \\ to recursively search `json` for a key named `name`, but in this case you expect it to be a child of the root.

The result of \ is another `JValue`. In this case, you expect a `String`, which is represented in Json4s as a `JString`. So you assert that the name equals `JString("potatos")`.

For a service that returns JSON, the `JsonMethods.parse(body)` will be repeated often. Let's DRY that up with a helper trait to mix into all the tests.

Listing 8.5 Testing headers and the body with a helper trait

```
import org.json4s.JValue
import org.json4s.jackson.JsonMethods
                                                       Requires that children
trait JsonBodySupport { self: ScalatraTests =>         are Scalatra tests
  def jsonBody: JValue = JsonMethods.parse(body)
}
                                                       Enables the jsonBody syntax
class FoodServletSpec extends ScalatraSpec with JsonBodySupport {

  def potatoesName = get("/foods/potatoes") {
    jsonBody \ "name" must_== JString("potatos")       Asserts against the
  }                                                    parsed JSON body
}
```

The `JsonBodySupport` takes advantage of a Scala feature called *self-types*. You specify that any class that extends `JsonBodySupport` must also be a subtype of `ScalatraTests`. This gives your trait access to all the members of `ScalatraTests`, such as body.

> ### ScalatraTests vs. ScalatraSpec
>
> `ScalatraSpec` is a subtype of `ScalatraTests`, and it could be used just as well in the subtype. But by using the more abstract `ScalatraTests`, your helper can also be mixed into ScalaTest suites, which we'll introduce in section 8.3. The `self` type allows your `JsonBodySupport` to refer to members of `ScalatraTests`, such as body.

Your new `JsonBodySupport` can now be mixed into any Scalatra test for easy testing of a JSON service. Similar techniques can be used to support XML, HTML, or whatever other text-based format may be prevalent in your service.

> **TIP**   Most responses are some form of text, but you may wish to test a binary output format, such as a protocol buffer, an image, or a compressed response. `bodyBytes`, built into `ScalatraTests`, is the equivalent of body, but returns an `Array[Byte]`.

In the next section, you'll learn to run your tests, and we'll also bring relief to any astute readers who caught the typo intentionally propagated through this section.

8.1.4   *Running your tests*

You've already seen how sbt compiles your code, and you'll learn in chapter 9 how it packages your code for deployment. It's also a great way to run tests. Just run `sbt test` from the command line.

The output is shown in the next listing. Framework logging is omitted for brevity.

Listing 8.6   A successful sbt test run

```
[info]  FoodServletSpec
[info]  GET /foods/potatoes on FoodServlet
[info]    + should return status 200
[info]    + should be JSON
[info]    x should contain name potatoes
[error]  'JString(potatoes)' is not equal to 'JString(potatos)'
           (FoodServletSpec.scala:26)
[info]
[info]
[info]  Total for specification FoodServletSpec
[info]  Finished in 797 ms
[info]  3 examples, 1 failure, 0 error
[info]  ScalaTest
[info]  Run completed in 1 second, 702 milliseconds.
```

The output contains the description of each test extracted from the code.

\+ indicates success.

x indicates failure.

Shows what failed and where

```
[info] Total number of tests run: 0
[info] Suites: completed 0, aborted 0
[info] Tests: succeeded 0, failed 0, canceled 0, ignored 0, pending 0
[info] No tests were executed.
[error] Failed: Total 3, Failed 1, Errors 0, Passed 2
[error] Failed tests:
[error]     org.scalatra.book.chapter07.FoodServletSpec
[error] (test:testOnly) sbt.TestsFailedException: Tests unsuccessful
[error] Total time: 7 s, completed Aug 18, 2014 2:39:56 AM
```

One bad apple spoils the bunch.

You have your first test and, not unexpectedly, your first test failure. Cheer up: this is a good thing! It's good practice to write the test, see it fail, and then implement (or fix) the main code. Seeing the test switch from failing to passing with a change to the main code serves as a sort of test of the tests, warding off false positives.

Now you need to make the test pass. The sample output shows that you have been expecting *potatos* when the correct output is *potatoes*. You can fix the assertion:

```
def potatoesName = get("/foods/potatoes") {
  val json = JsonMethods.parse(body)
  json \ "name" must_== JString("potatoes")
}
```

Now run sbt test from the console again, and you should see the following output:

```
[info] FoodServletSpec
[info] GET /foods/potatoes on FoodServlet
[info]    + should return status 200
[info]    + should be JSON
[info]    + should contain name potatoes
[info]
[info] Total for specification FoodServletSpec
[info] Finished in 665 ms
[info] 3 examples, 0 failure, 0 error
[info] ScalaTest
[info] Run completed in 1 second, 305 milliseconds.
[info] Total number of tests run: 0
[info] Suites: completed 0, aborted 0
[info] Tests: succeeded 0, failed 0, canceled 0, ignored 0, pending 0
[info] No tests were executed.
[info] Passed: Total 3, Failed 0, Errors 0, Passed 3
[success] Total time: 5 s, completed Aug 18, 2014 2:48:13 AM
```

Indicates all the tests passed. In most terminals, this is highlighted in green.

The tests pass. Celebrate with the beverage of your choice, and then we'll talk about white-box testing.

8.2   Unit testing with Specs2

The tests in the previous section were black-box tests. The specification considers only the inputs (requests) and outputs (responses) without any regard to implementation. The route could be a simple XML literal, or it could cheat and make a system call to spin up a Sinatra server and proxy the result. As long as the response matches the specification, the tests pass. This is a useful mode of operation for integration testing, when you want to test the behavior of the entire application. It's not so good for unit testing.

Unit tests are so named because they test a single unit of the code, rather than the entire application. Why is this advantageous?

- *They're easier to write.* Working with a single unit requires less setup.
- *They're easier to deploy.* If your tests don't hit the live database, you don't need to worry about granting your test box access to the live database.
- *They run faster.* It's faster to go through one layer than all the layers.

Let's look at a unit-testing example by building a new service that launches nukes.

8.2.1   *Testing with stubbed dependencies*

You may be concerned that the sample application will result in the extinction of humankind as soon as you submit a successful request to launch the nukes. Worry not, because you're going to stub out the dependency. First you need the *business logic*, shown in the following listing.

Listing 8.7   Stubbed dependencies

```scala
trait NukeLauncher {          Pulling out a
  def launch(): Unit          trait makes it
}                             more testable.
                                                  This object would be used
                                                  in the production setup.
object RealNukeLauncher extends NukeLauncher {
  def launch(): Unit = ???
  }                             Implementation left as an exercise
                                for you. Note that the use of ??? is
                                perfectly legal in Scala.
class StubNukeLauncher extends NukeLauncher {
  var isLaunched = false
  def launch(): Unit = isLaunched = true
}
```

Whether it's a database, a message queue, or a nuclear missile silo, it can be difficult to set up the external resources an integration test needs. Verifying a successful launch via the setting of a var will be a much more pleasant developer experience than inspecting a mushroom cloud. This is an ideal time for a unit test.

The danger of public vars

On top of the inherent dangers in handling nuclear warheads, astute observers will note that we also left a public var on the trait. This is generally not good design in Scala. Mutable state is hard to reason about, and the object isn't thread-safe for a concurrent environment.

We stand by it here. This stub implementation isn't going to be subject to a highly concurrent environment. It needs to be trivially verifiable when accessed by a single thread in a unit test, so you can concentrate on your real business problem, such as the nuke.

Next, you'll create a servlet to provide an HTTP interface to conveniently launch the nukes from a safe, remote location.

8.2.2 *Injecting dependencies into a servlet*

In order to unit test your servlet, you need to be able to swap in different implementations of the nuke launcher. The simplest way to do this is through constructor injection. Your servlet will take a single constructor parameter, as shown in the following listing.

Listing 8.8 Nuke launcher servlet

```
class NukeLauncherServlet(launcher: NukeLauncher )          ◁─── Constructor parameter
  extends ScalatraServlet {                                       accepts the trait
  val NuclearCode = "password123"

  post("/launch") {
    if (params("code") == NuclearCode)
      launcher.launch()
    else
      Forbidden()
  }
}
```

Accepting an instance of the NukeLauncher trait makes it simple to configure this servlet for either test or production. First, here's an example production ScalatraBootstrap file with the live launcher.

Listing 8.9 Example *ScalatraBootstrap* with live dependency

```
class ScalatraBootstrap extends LifeCycle {
  override def init(context: ServletContext) {
    context.mount(new NukeLauncherServlet(RealNukeLauncher), "/nuke/*")     ◁──┐
  }                                                                            │
}                                       Production implementation of the trait ┘
```

Because this is a white-box test, you can assume that the servlet delegates to a NukeLauncher. As such, it's fair to swap in a stub instance for testing, as shown in listing 8.10. This test will introduce the unit test syntax of Specs2.

Listing 8.10 A unit specification for the Nuke launcher

```
import org.scalatra.test.specs2._                           Uses the
import org.specs2.mutable.After                             mutable
                                                            Specs2 style
class NukeLauncherSpec extends MutableScalatraSpec with After {  ◁──
  sequential                              ◁───────────────────┐
                                                              │  Runs the tests sequentially
  val stubLauncher = new StubNukeLauncher │ because the stub is stateful
  addServlet(new NukeLauncherServlet(stubLauncher), "/*")
```

```
def after: Any = stubLauncher.isLaunched = false          ⊲——   Cleans up the state
                                                                 between test runs
def launch[A](code: String)(f: => A): A =        ⊲——   Factors out common logic
  post("/launch", "code" -> code) { f }  ⊲
                                                  Invokes the post with a
"The wrong pass code" should {                    form-encoded parameter
  "respond with forbidden" in {
    launch("wrong") {
      status must_== 403
    }
  }

  "not launch the nukes" in {
    launch("wrong") {
      stubLauncher.isLaunched must_== false
    }
  }
}

"The right pass code" should {
  "launch the nukes" in {
    launch("password123") {
      stubLauncher.isLaunched must_== true
    }
  }
}
}
```

The post call is the first time you've submitted parameters. post takes a variable argument list of String->String tuples and passes them as parameters in the form body. get has a similar signature for query parameters. In fact, all the HTTP methods take several overloads to handle the common use cases of parameters, headers, and bodies. These are best learned by looking at the Scaladoc.

Because the same post to /launch appears three times in the test, it's extracted to a launch helper. A broken test is a broken build, so test code needs to be maintained as surely as production code. Factoring out the duplicate code, even in tests, will tend to save time in the long run.

The other new feature in listing 8.10 is the sequential declaration. By default, Specs2 runs each test in a spec in parallel. This can speed up test runs when all code under test is immutable. But when an object under test, like the StubNukeLauncher, is mutable, this parallelism results in non-deterministic test failures. The right passcode may be submitted in a different thread while the wrong passcode is being asserted. In cases where it's impossible or awkward to write in a pure functional style, the sequential declaration offers a simple way out. Because sbt can run separate specs in parallel, as long as no state is shared between specs, sequential may not even add significantly to test time.

You can now run your unit test. The stub successfully isolates your tidy API from its burdensome dependency to allow more thorough tests than you otherwise might have written.

> ### Specs2 acceptance vs. unit test syntax
>
> The Specs2 documentation calls the two forms of testing *acceptance* and *unit* tests. The acceptance tests are immutable and require a single matcher result to be returned. The unit tests run in a mutable context and are more flexible about where matching is done.
>
> A thorough examination of the differences is included in the official Specs2 documentation. We follow the convention here to demonstrate both. In practice, people tend to pick the syntax they like better and stick to it.

Having seen the major features of Specs2, we'll now take a look at ScalaTest.

8.3 *Testing with ScalaTest*

ScalaTest is an alternative test framework to Specs2. Both are mature, both are flexible, and both are maintained by highly responsive developers. The differences are more a matter of taste than of substance.

> ### Scalatra's own preference
>
> Scalatra is tested with its own DSL and employs a mix of ScalaTest and Specs2. Scalatra has multiple contributors, and different ones prefer different frameworks. The tests run together in a single report, which is a testament to sbt's abstract test interface.
>
> Although using both is supported, it's not recommended. It's good for Scalatra's internals, because it helps test the test integrations. But for your project, look at both, learn one well, and know that you can't go wrong.

8.3.1 *Setting up Scalatra's ScalaTest*

Setting up Scalatra's ScalaTest integration requires minimal changes from the giter8 project. It's as easy as changing a single line in the library dependencies from `scalatra-specs2` to `scalatra-scalatest`.

Open project/build.scala and make sure `libraryDependencies` contains the following line:

```
libraryDependencies ++= Seq(
  "org.scalatra" %% "scalatra-scalatest" % ScalatraVersion % "test"   <─┐
)
```
Defines the scalatra-scalatest dependency in test scope

That's all the setup required. The next time you reload your sbt project, it will fetch ScalaTest and the scalatra-scalatest integration library. The next thing you need to do is port the existing Specs2 test to ScalaTest.

8.3.2 *Your first ScalaTest*

Open your ScalatraServletSpec file from listing 8.2, and compare it to the ScalaTest port in the following listing.

Listing 8.11 A ScalaTest `WordSpec`

```
package org.scalatra.book.chapter07

import org.json4s.JString                          Replace specs2
import org.scalatra.test.scalatest._      ◁──────  with scalatest.

class FoodServletWordSpec extends ScalatraWordSpec
  with JsonBodySupport {

  addServlet(classOf[FoodServlet], "/*")

  "GET /foods/potatoes on FoodServlet" must {
    "return status 200" in {
      get("/foods/potatoes") {                      Compare to Specs2's
        status should equal(200)          ◁──────   must_== .
      }
    }

    "be JSON" in {
      get("/foods/potatoes") {
        header("Content-Type") should startWith("application/json;")   ◁──┐
      }                                                                    │
    }                                                           This matcher is the
                                                                same as Specs2's.
    "should have name potatoes" in {
      get("/foods/potatoes") {
        jsonBody \ "name" should equal(JString("potatoes"))
      }
    }
  }
}
```

The `WordSpec` of ScalaTest and the mutable specification of Specs2 are similar in how they intermingle the descriptions with the implementations. This is just one of the many syntaxes that ScalaTest supports. Another worth looking at is `ScalatraFun-Suite`, where developers coming from xUnit will feel at home.

Some matchers, like the equality test, changed from Specs2. Others, like `startsWith`, did not. Like Specs2, ScalaTest comes with an expressive, literate library of matchers. But, again, Scala is a compiled language, not a natural language, so you have to learn the precise vocabulary of the test framework you choose.[3]

Two very important things didn't change in this port: the `get` blocks that define the request, and the references to the parts of the response inside the header. These

---

[3] Matcher differences are the greatest source of confusion when one works in both Specs2 and ScalaTest on a regular basis; hence, our recommendation to pick just one for your organization.

come from the abstract Scalatra test framework and operate in exactly the same fashion in both ScalaTest and Specs2.

That was easy. Now it's time to run your ScalaTest.

8.3.3 *Running ScalaTest tests*

Once again, run `sbt test`. Just as Scalatra abstracts over the test frameworks, so does sbt. The same command works for both.

An example run follows:

```
[info] FoodServletWordSpec:
[info] GET /foods/potatoes on FoodServlet
[info] - must return status 200
[info] - must be JSON
[info] - must should have name potatoes
[info] ScalaTest
[info] Run completed in 1 second, 187 milliseconds.
[info] Total number of tests run: 3
[info] Suites: completed 1, aborted 0
[info] Tests: succeeded 3, failed 0, canceled 0, ignored 0, pending 0
[info] All tests passed.
[info] Passed: Total 3, Failed 0, Errors 0, Passed 3
[success] Total time: 1 s, completed Aug 18, 2014 3:03:00 AM
```

The formatting of the test descriptions differs a bit from what you saw in listing 8.6, but the test counts and success lines are the same as in Specs2. From a tooling perspective, it matters little.

8.4 *Summary*

- Scalatra's test DSL is similar to the main DSL you use in your application code. This makes it easy for any Scalatra developer to write tests.
- Scalatra offers first-class support for both of Scala's major test libraries, ScalaTest and Specs2. You can use a wide variety of testing styles.
- Run your application inside the embedded container to integration-test your application easily.
- Alternatively, wiring up your Scalatra servlets with stub dependencies via constructor injection allows you to isolate your HTTP logic with unit tests.

Configuration,
build, and deployment

9

This chapter covers

- Application configuration and environments
- sbt builds and working with plugins
- Deploying as a web archive
- Deploying as a standalone distribution
- Running a Scalatra application as a Docker container

This chapter discusses topics related to configuring, building, and running an application. In section 9.1 you'll learn how to provide configuration to an application and how to work with application environments. Section 9.2 covers defining the sbt build and employing sbt plugins.

Once you've built your application, you'll need to know how to deploy it and make it available to the public. The next two sections provide a gentle introduction to the mysteries of JVM deployments, suitable for people coming from other backgrounds. Section 9.3 discusses the web archive (WAR) file, which is a typical deployment method for servlet-based web applications. Section 9.4 builds a standalone application, which embeds a servlet container. Section 9.5 then shows how to use Scalatra with Docker. We'll start with configuration.

9.1 Configuring a Scalatra application

An application's configuration is how you tell the application about the environment it runs in. It's the context that allows an application to adapt itself to different environments. For example, one setting might hold the directory on the filesystem that's used to store file uploads.

The configuration allows an application to expose different behavior depending on the context the application runs in. As an example, the logging output in a development environment can be more chatty than it is in a production environment.

9.1.1 Working with application environments

Usually, when you're developing an application, there are several environments it can run in. A programmer develops the application in the *development* environment. In the *production* environment, the application is served to the public. There can be other environments as well. For example, before shipping an application to production, the application can be tested on a staging site. In the *staging* environment, the application behaves similar to the production environment, but it runs in a non-public area.

Scalatra has built-in support for simple `String`-based application environments. The current environment in which a Scalatra application runs can be read using the `environment` method defined on `ScalatraBase`. If no environment is set, the environment defaults to `"DEVELOPMENT"`:

```
get("/me") {
  environment match {
    case "DEVELOPMENT" =>
      println("oh hai")

    case "PRODUCTION" =>
    case _ =>
  }
}
```

The method `isDevelopment` returns `true` when the application runs in a development environment. In a development environment, the Scalatra kernel sends more-detailed error information to the developer, which may be useful when debugging a problem. This information includes the stacktrace in the case of an uncaught exception on the server side, and a list of all available routes if no route can be found to answer a request.

You can also use the `isDevelopment` method in your application:

```
get("/me") {
  if (isDevelopment) {
    //
  } else {
    //
  }
}
```

The application environment is set through the `org.scalatra.environment` key either as a system property or using the web.xml file, found at src/main/webapp/ WEB-INF/web.xml. For example, a system property can be set through a command-line parameter: `-Dorg.scalatra.environment=production`. The web.xml file sets the parameter as a context parameter, as shown in the following listing.

Listing 9.1   web.xml setting the application environment

```xml
<?xml version="1.0" encoding="UTF-8"?>
<web-app xmlns:xsi="http://www.w3.org/2001/XMLSchema-instance"
      xmlns="http://java.sun.com/xml/ns/javaee"
      xmlns:web="http://java.sun.com/xml/ns/javaee/web-app_3_0.xsd"
      xsi:schemaLocation="http://java.sun.com/xml/ns/javaee
      http://java.sun.com/xml/ns/javaee/web-app_3_0.xsd"
      id="WebApp_ID" version="3.0>

  <context-param>
    <param-name>org.scalatra.environment</param-name>
    <param-value>production</param-value>
  </context-param>

  <listener>
    <listener-class>
      org.scalatra.servlet.ScalatraListener
    </listener-class>
  </listener>
</web-app>
```

Application environments provide the option to modify the runtime behavior of the application based on what environment the application currently runs in.

In the next section, we'll take a look at how to provide configuration to an application. You'll also see a more formalized way of expressing application environments.

9.1.2   *Using a type-safe application configuration*

An application configuration collects all the variable settings of that application in a single place. In this section, we'll show you how to use the typesafe config library (https://github.com/typesafehub/config); it offers typed access to configurations written in HOCON, which is a JSON-based language.

You'll need to add a dependency to the library in the project build definition, project/build.scala:

```
libraryDependencies += "com.typesafe" % "config" % "1.2.1"
```

A sample application configuration is shown in the next listing. It contains typical settings, such as the public URL of the application, the application environment, and an email account.

Listing 9.2   A sample application.conf

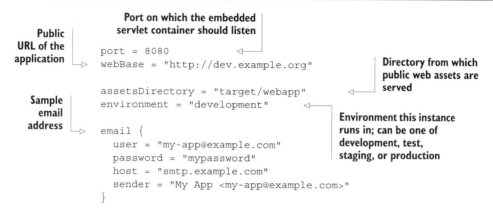

The public web assets directory (assetsDirectory) and embedded servlet container port (port) are useful when embedding a servlet container in your application (see sections 9.4 and 9.5). assetsDirectory is usually set to target/webapp (section 9.2.2) or target/web/stage (section 9.2.3). In a production environment, it might be a relative path such as ./webapp or an absolute path such as /app/webapp. webBase defines the public URL of the application as seen from the user agent. The AppConfig type shown in the following listing holds the configuration values.

Listing 9.3   AppConfig and MailConfig types

```
case class AppConfig(
  port: Int,
  webBase: String,
  assetsDirectory: String,
  env: AppEnvironment,
  mailConfig: MailConfig) {

  def isProduction = env == Production
  def isDevelopment = env == Development
}

case class MailConfig(
  user: String,
  password: String,
  host: String,
  sender: String)
```

The AppEnvironment type in listing 9.4 represents all possible application environments, as alternatives to the simple string-based application environments. The conversion between String and AppEnvironment exists as two functions in the AppEnvironment trait's companion object (also called AppEnvironment).

Listing 9.4   Application environment types

```
sealed trait AppEnvironment
case object Development extends AppEnvironment
case object Staging extends AppEnvironment
case object Test extends AppEnvironment
case object Production extends AppEnvironment

object AppEnvironment {
  def fromString(s: String): AppEnvironment = {
    s match {
      case "development" => Development
      case "staging" => Staging
      case "test" => Test
      case "production" => Production
    }
  }

  def asString(s: AppEnvironment): String = {
    s match {
      case Development => "development"
      case Staging => "staging"
      case Test => "test"
      case Production => "production"
    }
  }
}
```

The configuration is stored in src/main/resources/application.conf, which makes it available on the JVM classpath. The application.conf file is loaded by the Config-Factory and represented as a value of type Config, which allows read access to the configuration. The following code loads the configuration, reads the webBase setting, and prints it to stdout:

```
import com.typesafe.config.ConfigFactory

val cfg = ConfigFactory.load
val webBase = cfg.getString("webBase")

println(webBase)
```

Listing 9.5 shows a configuration reader from Config to your AppConfig type. Any error in the configuration throws an exception at runtime, which allows your application to fail fast during startup in the case of syntactically invalid configuration.

Listing 9.5   A simple configuration factory

```
object AppConfig {
  def load: AppConfig = {
    val cfg = ConfigFactory.load

    val assetsDirectory = cfg.getString("assetsDirectory")
```

```
val webBase = cfg.getString("webBase")
val port = cfg.getInt("port")
val env = AppEnvironment.fromString(cfg.getString("environment"))
val mailConfig = MailConfig(
  cfg.getString("email.user"),
  cfg.getString("email.password"),
  cfg.getString("email.host"),
  cfg.getString("email.sender"))

AppConfig(port, webBase, assetsDirectory, env, mailConfig)
  }
}
```

The configuration can now be used throughout the application. The servlet declares its dependency to AppConfig through a constructor parameter. For example, you can use the value of webBase to create a hypothetical URL shortener:

```
class Chapter09(appConfig: AppConfig) extends ScalatraServlet {
  get("/shorten-url") {
    val token = UrlShortener.nextFreeToken
    f"${appConfig.webBase}/$token"
  }
}
```

The configuration is loaded in the application's LifeCycle, ScalatraBootstrap. This is shown in the following listing. Note that you read the Scalatra application environment from the configuration.

Listing 9.6 Loading an application-specific configuration in a LifeCycle

```
import org.scalatra.book.chapter09._
import org.scalatra._
import javax.servlet.ServletContext

class ScalatraBootstrap extends LifeCycle {        Creates the environment-
  override def init(context: ServletContext) {     specific application
    val conf = AppConfig.load          ◁────────── configuration
    sys.props(org.scalatra.EnvironmentKey) = conf.env.asString

    val app = new Chapter09(conf)
    context.mount(app, "/*")      ◁───────┐
  }                              Creates the handler of the
}                                application and mounts it
```

The application.conf can also be provided from the classpath by specifying a system property when starting the JVM:

```
-Dconfig.file=/opt/instances/production/application.conf
```

For more details, see the official documentation of the config library.

9.2   *Building a Scalatra application*

During the development of an application, common tasks are executed on a regular basis. For example, after you make changes to the source code, the code is compiled, and related tests can be executed. Before you release an application, a distributable package of the application must be created. A build tool helps you automate these tasks, leading to repeatable and reliable builds.

sbt (Simple Build Tool) is a build tool for Scala. It can be used to build a Scalatra application, and you should already be familiar with it, having used it in the previous chapter. This section will look at some of the details of developing a Scalatra application with sbt.

9.2.1   *A Scalatra application as an sbt project*

When you're using the giter8 (g8) template, a Scalatra application is built around an sbt project. This means there's an sbt build definition, and the project layout follows the standard sbt structure and conventions. As a result, you can let sbt manage the dependencies and use it to build the application, and reuse the wealth of functionality wrapped in sbt extensions.

The project layout was introduced in chapter 2; we'll briefly recap the structure here. Note that all paths are relative to the base directory:

```
.
├── build.sbt
├── project
│   ├── build.properties
│   ├── Build.scala
│   └── plugins.sbt
├── src
│   ├── main
│   │   ├── resources
│   │   ├── scala
│   │   └── webapp
│   └── test
│       └── scala
└── target
```

The application sources and resources are usually found in the src folder. The src/main/scala folder contains the main Scala sources. The src/main/resources folder contains application resources, which are available on the application's classpath during runtime. The src/main/webapp folder contains web resources that are available to the public. A similar structure exists in src/test, but it's specifically for tests and doesn't appear in a distributable application package. Those defaults have been inspired by other build tools and have proven their usefulness in practice. The target folder contains all the resources generated during a build.

The project folder holds sbt-specific resources. The project/plugins.sbt file specifies which sbt plugins the build uses. The project/build.properties file usually sets the sbt version that's used when building the project. The build definition of an application is defined in the build.sbt file or in project/Build.scala.

A build definition describes how to build an application. It consists of one or more projects. Each project holds a list of `Settings`. When sbt loads the build definition, all the settings of a project are evaluated, resulting in an immutable map that is the internal representation of that project. The following listing shows a sample build definition with a single project, taken from the file project/Build.scala.

Listing 9.7 Sample build definition

```
import sbt._                          ◁──────┐  Declares required imports, such
import Keys._                                 │  as built-in and plugin keys
import org.scalatra.sbt._
import org.scalatra.sbt.PluginKeys._
import com.earldouglas.xwp.JettyPlugin
import com.mojolly.scalate._
import com.mojolly.scalate.ScalatePlugin._
import com.mojolly.scalate.ScalatePlugin.ScalateKeys._


object Chapter09Build extends Build {    ◁────── Build definition
  val Organization = "org.scalatra"
  val Name = "chapter09"
  val Version = "0.1.0-SNAPSHOT"
  val ScalaVersion = "2.11.6"
  val ScalatraVersion = "2.4.0"

  val mySettings =
    ScalatraPlugin.scalatraSettings ++
    Seq(
      organization := Organization,
      name := Name,
      version := Version,
      scalaVersion := ScalaVersion,
      resolvers += Classpaths.typesafeReleases,
      libraryDependencies ++= Seq(
        "org.scalatra" %% "scalatra" % ScalatraVersion,
        "org.scalatra" %% "scalatra-scalate" % ScalatraVersion,
        "org.scalatra" %% "scalatra-specs2" % ScalatraVersion % "test",
        "ch.qos.logback" % "logback-classic" % "1.1.3" % "runtime",
        "javax.servlet" % "javax.servlet-api" % "3.1.0" % "provided"
      )
    )
                                          ┌─── Creates an instance
  lazy val project = Project(Name, file(".")) ◁──┘   of a Project ...
    .enablePlugins(JettyPlugin)
    .settings(mySettings:_*)      ◁────┐  ... and provides the previously
}                                       │  defined settings for it
```

The build definition is represented by the `Chapter09Build` object extending the `Build` trait. A sequence of settings is collected in the `mySettings` value and used to construct a value of type `Project`. The settings here provide general information about a project (organization, name, version), the Scala version used to compile the sources, an additional resolver (which is a repository for dependencies), and the dependencies of the project. Using constants makes the build definition more maintainable; for example, the Scala and Scalatra versions are defined here as constants.

> **TIP** There are several project templates that can be used to create an sbt project. These templates contain the required build definition and basic application resources, so you don't need to start from scratch. You can find a template for a simple Scalatra application at https://github.com/scalatra/scalatra-sbt.g8.

Let's take a closer look at the settings. A `Setting` maps a key to some value. Using sbt's `:=` operator, you can construct a setting that, when evaluated, sets a value in the project's internal map. For example, the following code represents an assignment to the keys `organization` and `name`, describing the publisher of the project and the project's name, respectively:

```
organization := "org.scalatra"
name := "chapter09"
```

sbt has built-in keys that are imported from `sbt.Keys._`. Plugins often define their own keys, which can be imported as well.

The dependencies of a project are represented by the key `libraryDependencies`. For example, you can add a dependency to `scalatra-specs2` like this:

```
libraryDependencies +=
    "org.scalatra" %% "scalatra-specs2" % "2.4.0" % "test"
    _____/  _____/  \_____/  \____/
          |                 |               |       |
       groupId          artifactId       version  scope
```

Here the `+=` method results in a `Setting` that adds the dependency to the existing values instead of replacing that value in the map. A dependency is specified through its `groupId`, `artifactId`, and `version`. There can be additional specifiers, such as a `scope` in which the dependency is valid, or an exclusion for specific transitive dependencies. In this example, the dependency is scoped to `test`, which makes it available only when running the tests.

Reusable functionality is often packaged in a plugin. The file project/plugins.sbt contains a list of the sbt plugins that should be added to an sbt build. To take one example, the Scalatra developers have built an sbt plugin called scalatra-sbt. A dependency to it is contained in the default g8 template:

```
addSbtPlugin("org.scalatra.sbt" % "scalatra-sbt" % "0.4.0")
```

The scalatra-sbt plugin adds a servlet container that can be used during development. It also supports building deployable web archive (WAR) packages of an application.

The settings from scalatra-sbt are combined with other settings in your application's build file, found at project/build.scala, by accessing `ScalatraPlugin.scalatra-Settings` like this:

```
lazy val project = Project("chapter09", file("."))
    .enablePlugins(JettyPlugin)
    .settings(myProjectSettings: _*)
    .settings(ScalatraPlugin.scalatraSettings)
```

The next section presents some background information about xsbt-web-plugin. Sections 9.3 and 9.4 show how to build a deployable package of an application.

9.2.2 Working with the xsbt-web-plugin

xsbt-web-plugin is an extension to sbt that integrates a servlet-based web application into an sbt build. The scalatra-sbt plugin depends on it.

xsbt-web-plugin, in turn, consists of three other plugins: WebappPlugin, ContainerPlugin, and WarPlugin. In this section, we'll take a look at WebappPlugin and ContainerPlugin. WarPlugin's job is to package the web application as a WAR file in order to deploy it to an external servlet container. This is discussed in section 9.3.

WebappPlugin integrates a web application layout in an sbt build. The web application resource directory contains the static resources of a web application. It's represented by the key `sourceDirectory` in `webappPrepare` and defaults to src/main/webapp. The web application destination directory is where those resources, together with the dependencies, are copied during a build. It's represented by the key `target` in `webappPrepare` and defaults to target/webapp. For example, the servlet container serves the web application from here:

```
sourceDirectory in webappPrepare := (sourceDirectory in Compile).value / "webapp"
target in webappPrepare         := (target in Compile).value / "webapp"
```

Following the servlet standard, the WEB-INF directory—which is not publicly accessible—contains the web.xml deployment descriptor and the dependency JARs in WEB-INF/lib. WebappPlugin provides the base on which both ContainerPlugin and WarPlugin build.

ContainerPlugin integrates a servlet container into sbt that can be used to host the web application on the developer's local machine. The servlet container serves the web application from the web application destination directory. Two specific plugins, JettyPlugin and ContainerPlugin, use Jetty and Tomcat, respectively, as the underlying servlet container. We stick with JettyPlugin here. JettyPlugin needs to be enabled via `enablePlugins(JettyPlugin)`.

The `jetty:start` task starts a servlet container in a forked JVM process that hosts the web application. Before the server is started, any running container process is stopped. The server can be stopped with the `jetty:stop` task.

The webappPrepare task copies the web application resources from the web application's source directory to the target directory. You can use it to watch changes and mirror those by prefixing it with ~:

```
> jetty:start
[info] starting server ...
INFO: Started ServerConnector@5598f84b{HTTP/1.1}{0.0.0.0:8080}
2015-02-08 16:11:05.137:INFO:oejs.Server:main: Started @6438ms
[success] Total time: 0 s, completed 08.02.2015 16:10:58

> ~webappPrepare
[success] Total time: 0 s, completed 08.02.2015 16:11:40
1. Waiting for source changes... (press enter to interrupt)
```

If you're using the servlet container for development, there may be situations where you want to change the default configuration. Let's look at an example.

The servlet container listens to http://localhost:8080 by default. The port can be set through the containerPort in Jetty setting in case a different port needs to be chosen. This is useful for avoiding conflicts with other applications. The following changes the port to 8090:

```
import com.earldouglas.xwp.JettyPlugin.autoImport._
import com.earldouglas.xwp.ContainerPlugin.autoImport._

val mySettings = Seq(
    // ...
    containerPort in Jetty := 8090
)

lazy val project = Project("chapter09", file("."))
    .enablePlugins(JettyPlugin)
    .settings(mySettings: _*)
```

The servlet container runs in a forked JVM. You can configure the forked JVM process through a ForkOptions value. The following snippet sets the maximum heap size of the forked JVM to 8 GB:

```
val mySettings = Seq(
    containerForkOptions in Jetty :=
      new ForkOptions(runJVMOptions = Seq("-Xmx8g"))
)
```

You can check the plugin documentation for further details. Next, we'll look at another plugin: sbt-web.

9.2.3   *Using sbt-web to simplify working with web assets*

The sbt-web plugin adds the notion of web assets and introduces an incremental build pipeline to an sbt build. Assets are resources that are served by a web server, such as JavaScript or CSS files. The asset pipeline produces assets from asset sources and asset resources. Sbt-web provides a common base on which assets-related plugins can be built. There's a wealth of such plugins for different technologies (for example, Sass/ Less, UglifyJS, and gzip).

Asset sources exist in src/main/assets, and the asset pipeline produces assets from those sources. The final product is written to the target/web/stage directory.

A simple pipeline consisting of two steps can, for example, compile a Sass file to CSS and then fingerprint the CSS file with an MD5 checksum, which enables aggressive browser caching. Asset resources are copied to the staging directory as is. They're found in src/main/public. The following listing shows a sample layout.

Listing 9.8   sbt-web project layout

```
.
├── project
├── src
│   ├── main
│   │   ├── assets
│   │   │   └── css/main.less
│   │   ├── public
│   │   │   └── WEB-INF/web.xml
│   │   ├── resources
│   │   └── scala
│   └── test
└── target
    ├── stage
    └── web/stage
```

The actual functionality is realized by specific sbt plugins. Let's look at an example that uses sbt-less and sbt-filter. sbt-less integrates the Less CSS preprocessor in an sbt build. sbt-filter allows you to filter resources from the final product.

Let's add the plugins to the build via project/plugins.sbt:

```
addSbtPlugin("com.typesafe.sbt" % "sbt-less" % "1.0.6")

addSbtPlugin("com.slidingautonomy.sbt" % "sbt-filter" % "1.0.1")
```

The sbt-web plugin is enabled through `enablePlugins(SbtWeb)`, which includes default settings for all the plugins. The asset pipeline is run with the `web-stage` task, which produces the assets to target/web/stage.

The sbt-less plugin is a generator that generates CSS assets from Less asset sources. It's enabled by default.

The sbt-filter plugin runs as an asset task in the asset pipeline. It receives the assets from a previous stage and filters out all the Less source files (*.less). It needs to be added to the `pipelineStage`.

You can integrate xsbt-web-plugin and sbt-web by telling xsbt-web-plugin that the public web application resources are found in src/main/public instead of src/main/webapp and that the servlet container should serve the application from target/web/

stage. In addition, the `test` and `jetty:start` tasks each depend on the `web-stage` task. The next listing shows the build definition.

Listing 9.9   Build definition using sbt-web

```
import com.earldouglas.xwp.JettyPlugin
import com.earldouglas.xwp.WebappPlugin.autoImport._
import com.earldouglas.xwp.JettyPlugin.autoImport._
import com.earldouglas.xwp.ContainerPlugin.start
import com.slidingautonomy.sbt.filter.Import._

val webSettings = Seq(
  pipelineStages := Seq(filter),
  includeFilter in filter := "*.less" || "*.css.map"
  webappSrc in webapp := (resourceDirectory in Assets).value,
  webappDest in webapp := (stagingDirectory in Assets).value,
  webappPrepare <<= webappPrepare dependsOn (stage in Assets),
  (test in Test) <<= (test in Test) dependsOn (stage in Assets)
)

lazy val project = Project("chapter09", file("."))
  .settings(mySettings:_*)
  .settings(webSettings:_*)
  .enablePlugins(SbtWeb, JettyPlugin)
```

Defines settings for sbt-web → `val webSettings = Seq(`

Runs the filter stage in the asset pipeline

Filters out Less sources and source maps

sbt-web and xsbt-web-plugin integration

Makes test and webappPrepare depend on web-stage task

Enables sbt-web plugins ← `.enablePlugins(SbtWeb, JettyPlugin)`

Now you can start the servlet container using `jetty:start` and then run the asset pipeline:

```
> jetty:start
[info] LESS compiling on 1 source(s)
[info] starting server ...
[success] Total time: 0 s, completed 08.02.2015 00:48:29

> ~web-stage
[success] Total time: 1 s, completed 08.02.2015 00:49:14
1. Waiting for source changes... (press enter to interrupt)
```

When you visit http://localhost:8080/css/main.css with a browser, you should be able to see the generated CSS.

When your application grows, running the asset pipeline can take time. It can be useful to run a more lightweight asset pipeline during development, leading to shorter turnaround times. The development asset pipeline can emit additional resources, such as source maps. A simple way to achieve this is by using a system property:

```
val devSettings = Seq()

val prodSettings = Seq(
  pipelineStages := Seq(filter),
  includeFilter in filter := "*.less" || "*.css.map"
)
```

```
val stage = sys.props.getOrElse("stage", "production")
val webSettings = {
  if (stage == "dev") devSettings
  else prodSettings
}
```

When sbt is started with sbt -Dstage=dev, the filter stage is omitted and the CSS source maps will be available to the browser.

That was a quick introduction to the sbt-web plugin. Let's now look at precompiling Scalate templates.

9.2.4 *Precompiling Scalate templates with the scalate-generator plugin*

The xsbt-scalate-generator plugin integrates the Scalate template library into sbt. Basically, it enables you to precompile Scalate templates during the normal compilation process. This speeds up the availability of an application and ensures the validity of all templates. Runtime errors related to syntax errors are detected during compile time.

The plugin is added to project/plugins.sbt:

```
addSbtPlugin("com.mojolly.scalate" %
        "xsbt-scalate-generator" % "0.5.0")
```

A collection of templates for an application is configured by a TemplateConfig value, which represents the location of the templates, default imports, variable bindings, and a package name. Listing 9.10 shows how a TemplateConfig for a simple Scalatra application is assigned to scalateTemplateConfig in Compile. The default settings are combined in the value ScalatePlugin.scalateSettings. For more-detailed documentation, we again refer you to the official xsbt-scalate-generate website at https://github.com/backchatio/xsbt-scalate-generate.

> **Listing 9.10 Configuring the scalate-generator plugin**

```
import com.mojolly.scalate._
import com.mojolly.scalate.ScalatePlugin._
import com.mojolly.scalate.ScalatePlugin.ScalateKeys._

val myScalateSettings = ScalatePlugin.scalateSettings ++ Seq(
  scalateTemplateConfig in Compile := Seq(
    TemplateConfig(
      (sourceDirectory in Compile).value /
        "webapp" / "WEB-INF" / "templates",        ◁────  Defines a
      Seq.empty, /* default imports should be added here */  configuration for a
      Seq.empty, /* add extra bindings here */               template location that
      Some("templates")                                       takes templates from
    )                                                          src/main/webapp/
  )                                                            WEB-INF/templates
)                                                              and precompiles them
                                                               using a "templates"
lazy val project = Project("chapter09", file("."))            package prefix
  .enablePlugins(JettyPlugin)
```

```
.settings(myProjectSettings: _*)
.settings(ScalatraPlugin.scalatraSettings: _*)          Uses the settings
.settings(myScalateSettings: _*)           ◁───────     in the project
```

The templates are compiled with the `compile` task. During development mode, the template sources additionally need to be synchronized to the target folder using the `webappPrepare` task:

```
> ~webappPrepare
[info] Compiling Templates in Template Directory: \
  /home/stefan/Code/funk/black-coffee/src/main/webapp/WEB-INF/templates
[success] Total time: 0 s, completed 08.02.2015 02:06:02
1. Waiting for source changes... (press enter to interrupt)
```

Now you know the basics of using sbt and sbt plugins. The next two sections will discuss creating deployable packages.

9.3   *Deploying as a web archive*

Web application archive (WAR) files are a typical way to deploy an application to a servlet container.

A WAR file corresponds to a self-contained version of a servlet-based web application. Like a JAR file, a WAR file is in zip format but has a .war suffix. It contains the resources required to run a web application. A servlet container is able to receive a WAR file and host the contained web application.

Listing 9.11 shows the structure of a simple WAR file. The servlet container serves the web application from the base directory, and public resources are at the base directory. The folders WEB-INF and META-INF are inaccessible via HTTP. The .jar libraries are contained in the /WEB-INF/lib directory. Any .class files and resources are contained in /WEB-INF/classes. Those two directories also constitute the classpath of the web application.

> **Listing 9.11   Sample WAR archive structure**

```
.
├── META-INF
│   └── MANIFEST.MF
└── WEB-INF
    ├── lib
    │   ├── chapter-9_2.11-0.1.0-SNAPSHOT.jar
    │   ├── scala-compiler-2.11.0.jar
    │   ├── scala-library-2.11.6.jar
    │   ├── scalatra_2.11-2.4.0.jar
    │   └── slf4j-api-1.7.10.jar
    ├── templates
    │   ├── layouts
    │   │   └── default.jade
    │   └── views
    │       └── hello-scalate.jade
    └── web.xml
```

A WAR file is created with the `package` task from WarPlugin (of xsbt-web-plugin). When you create a WAR file, the various project resources are fused into a single package. The file is written to the `target` folder:

```
> package
[info] Packaging
  .../target/scala-2.11/chapter09_2.11-0.1.0-SNAPSHOT.war.
[info] Done packaging.
```

This file can now be deployed to a servlet container. There's a wide range of servlet containers to choose from. Configuring a servlet container is a complex problem on its own; luckily, here we'll use the Apache Tomcat servlet container with the default configuration. If you need to install it, download the binary distribution of Tomcat from http://tomcat.apache.org/ and unpack it to the filesystem. The server can be started with the start script in the apache-tomcat-[version]/bin directory.

Now that Tomcat is running, you can deploy the web application. A simple way to do this is by copying the WAR file to the apache-tomcat-[version]/webapps folder. During the deployment of the web application, the lifecycle is initialized, which sets up the Scalatra application. By default, the servlet container uses the name of the WAR file as the context path. For example, if the WAR file is named chapter09_2.11-0.1.0-SNAPSHOT.war, the web application will be available under http://host:port/chapter09_2.11-0.1.0-SNAPSHOT/.

The web application is now deployed to a servlet container and ready to use. A new version of the application can be deployed by copying the new WAR file to the apache-tomcat-[version]/webapps folder.

WAR deployment depends on an external servlet container and creates the additional overhead of configuration and maintenance. In some cases, a standalone distribution of the application is more feasible. We'll present a way to achieve this in the next section.

9.4   *Deploying as a standalone distribution*

In this section, we'll present a way of embedding a servlet container in an application. This is in contrast to having an external servlet container that manages the application.

We'll also show how you can create a standalone distribution of an application with DistPlugin from scalatra-sbt. A standalone distribution consists of the application classes, resources, and runtime libraries, packaged as a zip archive.

9.4.1   *Embedding a servlet container in an application*

You're going to embed Jetty. Jetty is a lightweight servlet container that can easily be embedded in an application.

Let's start by adding a dependency to Jetty in the file project/build.scala:

```
"org.eclipse.jetty" % "jetty-webapp" % "9.2.10.v20150310"
```

Next, listing 9.12 shows a sample launcher, which starts a Jetty servlet container with a Scalatra application registered on it. You set up the server with a single connector that receives incoming HTTP connections. A `WebAppContext` for the Scalatra application is registered. After the servlet container is started, the `ScalatraListener` invokes the application's `LifeCycle` where the usual initialization takes place.

Listing 9.12 A basic standalone launcher

```
import org.scalatra.book.chapter09.AppConfig

import org.eclipse.jetty.server._
import org.eclipse.jetty.webapp.WebAppContext
import org.scalatra.servlet.ScalatraListener

object ScalatraLauncher extends App {

  val conf = AppConfig.load          ◁—— Loads the configuration

  val server = new Server            ◁┐  Creates an embedded Jetty that
  server.setStopTimeout(5000)         │  listens on the configured host/port
  server.setStopAtShutdown(true)      ┘

  val connector = new ServerConnector(server)
  connector.setHost("127.0.0.1")
  connector.setPort(conf.port)
                                        Creates the web application context:
  server.addConnector(connector)        sets the context path, resource
                                        base, and context listener
  val webAppContext = new WebAppContext    ◁——
  webAppContext.setContextPath("/")
  webAppContext.setResourceBase(conf.assetsDirectory)
  webAppContext.setEventListeners(Array(new ScalatraListener))
  server.setHandler(webAppContext)

  server.start          ◁—— Starts the server
  server.join

}
```

The `port` and the `assetsDirectory` are configured in application.conf. This was discussed in section 9.1.2.

9.4.2 *Building a distribution package*

Now we'll look at the standalone distribution structure. The folder structure is shown in listing 9.13. The /lib folder constitutes the application's classpath. It contains the compiled application classes, the third-party libraries as .jar files, and the classpath resources. The /bin folder contains a shell script that starts the JVM and runs the launcher. The /webapp folder contains all the web resources. Log files will be written to the /logs folder.

Listing 9.13 Structure of a standalone distribution

```
.
├── bin
│   └── chapter09
├── lib
│   ├── chapter09-standalone_2.11-0.1.0-SNAPSHOT.jar
│   ├── jetty-webapp-9.2.10.v20150310.jar
│   ├── scala-compiler-2.11.0.jar
│   └── scala-library-2.11.6.jar
├── logs
└── webapp
    └── WEB-INF
```

The distribution is built using DistPlugin. This plugin provides the `stage` and `dist` tasks. The former task stages the application to target/dist, and the latter creates a zip package from those resources.

The plugin's settings are included in the build definition, such as project/build.scala:

```
lazy val project = Project("chapter09-standalone", file("."))
  .settings(mySettings: _*)
  .settings(DistPlugin.distSettings:_*)
```

When you stage an application, a launcher script is also generated. The launcher script essentially sets the classpath, defines JVM settings, and then runs the standalone launcher class. A typical launcher script looks like this:

```
#!/bin/env bash

export CLASSPATH="lib:lib/scala-library.jar:lib/...
export JAVA_OPTS="-Xms2g -Xmx2g -XX:PermSize=256m -XX:MaxPermSize=256m"
export LC_CTYPE=en_US.UTF-8
export LC_ALL=en_US.utf-8

java $JAVA_OPTS -cp $CLASSPATH ScalatraLauncher
```

The script can be configured through several settings, as illustrated in the following listing. This example creates a `Seq[Setting]` consisting of `DistPlugin.distSettings` and the custom settings.

Listing 9.14 Customizing the default scalatra-sbt `dist` task

mainClass sets the launcher class name.

memSetting sets maximum and initial heap sizes.

```
val myDistSettings =
  DistPlugin.distSettings ++ Seq(
    exportJars := true,
    mainClass in Dist := Some("ScalatraLauncher"),
    memSetting in Dist := "2g",
    permGenSetting in Dist := "256m",
```

Packages the .class files and resources as a JAR file before exporting to the classpath

permMemSetting sets PermGen size.

envExports values will be exported when starting the JVM.

```
    envExports in Dist := Seq("LC_CTYPE=en_US.UTF-8",
                              "LC_ALL=en_US.utf-8"),
    javaOptions in Dist ++= Seq("-Xss4m",
      "-Dfile.encoding=UTF-8",
      "-Dlogback.configurationFile=logback.production.xml",
      "-Dorg.scalatra.environment=production")
  )

lazy val project = Project("chapter09-standalone", file("."))
  .settings(mySettings: _*)
  .settings(myDistSettings: _*)
```

javaOptions lists additional parameters that will be supplied to the JVM.

You can now create the standalone distribution using sbt. webappPrepare (or web-stage when using sbt-web) stages the web application to target/web. The stage task prepares the distribution in the target/dist directory. From those resources, the dist task creates a zip package. The tasks are prefixed with the dist scope:

```
> webappPrepare
[success] Total time: 0 s, completed 11.02.2015 23:01:45

> dist:stage
[success] Total time: 7 s, completed 11.02.2015 23:01:57

> dist:dist
[success] Total time: 2 s, completed 11.02.2015 23:02:20
```

The zip can now be distributed to other systems, unpacked, and executed:

```
# cp ./target/chapter09-standalone-0.1.0-SNAPSHOT.zip .
# unzip chapter09-standalone-0.1.0-SNAPSHOT.zip
Archive:  chapter09-standalone-0.1.0-SNAPSHOT.zip
   creating: chapter09-standalone/
   creating: chapter09-standalone/bin/
   creating: chapter09-standalone/lib/
   ...
# cd chapter09-standalone
# chmod +x bin/chapter09-standalone
# bin/chapter09-standalone
INFO  org.eclipse.jetty.util.log - Logging initialized @922ms
INFO  org.eclipse.jetty.server.Server - jetty-9.2.10.v20150310
INFO  o.scalatra.servlet.ScalatraListener -
      The cycle class name from the config: ScalatraBootstrap
INFO  o.scalatra.servlet.ScalatraListener -
      Initializing life cycle class: ScalatraBootstrap
INFO  o.e.jetty.server.ServerConnector -
      Started ServerConnector@6b12eaa3{HTTP/1.1}{localhost:8080}
INFO  org.eclipse.jetty.server.Server - Started @2257ms
```

9.5 *Running Scalatra as a Docker container*

Docker allows you to bundle a service as an image. The Docker image is basically an immutable template from which one or more containers can be run. A container represents a running service and is isolated from the host system it runs in, comparable to a virtual machine. In this section, we'll show how you can use sbt-docker with Scalatra.

The sbt-docker plugin (https://github.com/marcuslonnberg/sbt-docker) integrates the building of a Docker image into an sbt build. It offers a task to build the image and a DSL to express a Dockerfile, which is the specification from which a Docker image is created. A Docker image for a Scalatra application might, for example, consist of an Ubuntu base system, a Java JDK, and the compiled web application.

A prototypical structure of a Scalatra application is shown in listing 9.15. The application lives in the /app directory. The configuration for the application and the logging are stored in /app/conf. The /app/data folder holds working data, such as log files, user uploads, or a database. The compiled application and the libraries reside as .jar files in the /app/lib directory. The public web assets are served from /app/webapp.

Listing 9.15 Scalatra application structure

```
app
|-- conf
|   |-- application.conf
|   `-- logback.xml
|-- data
|   `-- logs
|-- lib
|   |-- chapter09-docker_2.11-0.1.0-SNAPSHOT.jar
|   |-- ...
|   `-- slf4j-api-1.7.10.jar
`-- webapp
    |-- WEB-INF
    `-- static.txt
```

The sbt-docker plugin expects the Dockerfile definition to be in the `dockerfile in docker` setting. Listing 9.16 shows an excerpt from the sbt build. On top of an Ubuntu base image, a JDK and the Scalatra application are installed. The compiled application and all dependencies are copied as .jar files to /app/lib, and all the web assets are copied to /app/webapp.

Listing 9.16 Dockerizing a Scalatra application

```
val myDockerSettings = Seq(
  mainClass := Some("ScalatraLauncher"),     <─── Defines a main class
  exportJars := true,                        <─── Packages the .class files and resources as a
                                                  JAR file before exporting to the classpath
  docker <<= docker.dependsOn(`package`),    <─── Makes the docker task
                                                  depend on the package task
  imageNames in docker := Seq(ImageName("org.scalatra/chapter09-docker")),  <─── Defines a name for
                                                                                 the Docker image

  dockerfile in docker := {                  <─── Defines a Dockerfile
```

```
    val webappDir = (webappDest in webapp).value
    val mainclass = mainClass.value.getOrElse(sys.error("No main class"))
    val classpath = (fullClasspath in Runtime).value
    val classpathString =
      classpath.files.map("/app/lib/" + _.getName).mkString(":")

  new Dockerfile {                          ◁─────  Uses an Ubuntu
    from("ubuntu:14.04")   ◁────────                base image

    runRaw("apt-get update")                      ◁──────   Updates and
    runRaw("apt-get install -y vim curl wget unzip")        installs packages

    runRaw("mkdir -p /usr/lib/jvm")        ◁─────── Installs Oracle JDK 1.8
    runRaw(
      "wget --header \"Cookie: oraclelicense=accept-securebackup-cookie\"" +
      " -O /usr/lib/jvm/jdk-8u51.tar.gz http://download.oracle.com/" +
      "otn-pub/java/jdk/8u51-b16/jdk-8u51-linux-x64.tar.gz")
    runRaw("tar xzf /usr/lib/jvm/jdk-8u51.tar.gz --directory /usr/lib/jvm")
    runRaw("update-alternatives --install /usr/bin/java java" +
      " /usr/lib/jvm/jdk1.8.0_51/bin/java 100")
    runRaw("update-alternatives --install /usr/bin/javac javac" +
      " /usr/lib/jvm/jdk1.8.0_51/bin/javac 100")
                                                   Adds all .jar files
                                                   to /app/lib
    add(classpath.files, "/app/lib/")    ◁─────┘

    add(webappDir, "/app/webapp")        ◁───── Adds all webapp files (from webappPrepare
    runRaw("rm -rf /app/webapp/WEB-INF/lib")     task) to /app/webapp, and removes the .jar
                                                 libs from WEB-INF/lib

    volume("/app/conf")         ◁───┐
    volume("/app/data")             │    Declares volumes, ports,
    expose(80)                      │    and working directory
    workDir("/app")

    cmdRaw(            ◁──────   Defines the default command
      f"java " +               of the container
        f"-Xmx4g" +
        f"-Dlogback.configurationFile=/app/conf/logback.xml " +
        f"-Dconfig.file=/app/conf/application.conf " +
        f"-cp $classpathString $mainclass")
  }
 }
)

lazy val project = Project("chapter09-docker", file("."))
  .enablePlugins(DockerPlugin)
  .settings(mySettings: _*)
  .settings(myScalateSettings: _*)            Includes settings
  .settings(myDockerSettings: _*)    ◁─────   in the project
```

The Docker image is tagged as `org.scalatra/chapter09-docker` with the `image-Names in docker` setting. When running a container from that image, it can be referenced by that name. With this specification, the `docker` task is able to create a Docker image:

```
> docker
[info] Compiling Templates
[info] Compiling Scala sources
[info] Packaging
[info] Done packaging.
[info] Sending build context to Docker daemon
[info] Step 0 : FROM ubuntu:14.04
[info]  ---> 8251da35e7a7
[info] Step 1 : RUN apt-get update
[info]  ---> Using cache
[info]  ---> f6ab6f8cec44
[info] ...
[info] Removing intermediate container 81f7377e71ed
[info] Successfully built 4e28509888f8
[info] Tagging image 4e28509888f8 with name: org.scalatra/chapter09-docker
[success] Total time: 28 s
>
```

Note that when building the image, Docker may use intermediate images from the cache and not rerun the full Dockerfile. The caching strategy can be tuned with the buildOptions in docker setting. See the plugin documentation for more details.

In order to start and stop the container, you can use the two shell scripts shown in listings 9.17 and 9.18.

Listing 9.17　Start script for container

```
#!/bin/bash

BASE=$(dirname $(readlink -f $0))

docker run -d \
  -v $BASE/data:/app/data \
  -v $BASE/conf:/app/conf:ro \
  -p 8080:80 \
  --name chapter09-standalone \
  org.scalatra/chapter09-docker
```

Listing 9.18　Stop script for container

```
#!/bin/bash

docker stop chapter09-standalone

docker rm chapter09-standalone
```

Now you're ready to run containers from this image.

The shell script start.sh starts a container from the image that runs in detached mode in the background. The container's port 80 is forwarded to port 8080 on the host system. The docker ps command shows a list of all running containers. The output of the application is shown with docker logs. The container can be stopped with a stop.sh script:

```
$ ./start.sh
11416efae5543b69e909c65eca6368e55528befe40a2250fbaf405b314071103

$ docker ps
CONTAINER ID        IMAGE                           COMMAND
   CREATED               STATUS          PORTS                   NAMES

11416efae554        org.scalatra/chapter09-docker   "/bin/sh -c 'java
➥ -X    2 seconds ago
   Up 2 seconds          0.0.0.0:8080->80/tcp    chapter09-standalone

$ docker logs chapter09-standalone
org.eclipse.jetty.util.log - Logging initialized @809ms
org.eclipse.jetty.server.Server - jetty-9.2.10.v20150310
o.scalatra.servlet.ScalatraListener -
      The cycle class name from the config: ScalatraBootstrap
o.scalatra.servlet.ScalatraListener
➥ - Initializing life cycle class: ScalatraBootstrap
o.e.jetty.server.ServerConnector
➥ - Started ServerConnector@d737b89{HTTP/1.1}{0.0.0.0:80}
org.eclipse.jetty.server.Server - Started @1519ms

$ ./stop.sh
```

The data directories are mounted from the host system (/app/conf and /app/data). Because the container just holds the application binaries, no data is lost when the container is replaced, such as when a newer version is available. The lifecycle of the application container and the data are separate. As a rule of thumb, containers should be immutable and disposable.

A Docker image is usually distributed to and run on other machines. Distribution can be achieved by publishing the image to a public or private Docker registry. Alternatively, the image can be copied via the filesystem and network. The command docker save writes the image to the filesystem:

```
$ docker save -o chapter09-docker.tar.gz org.scalatra/chapter09-docker
$ ls chapter09-docker.tar.gz
-rw-rw-r-- 1 user user  817M Sep 22 22:24 chapter09-docker.tar.gz
```

The image can then be copied (via SSH, for example) and imported using the docker load command:

```
$ docker load -i chapter09-docker.tar.gz
$ ./start.sh
```

This concludes your introduction to using Docker with sbt and Scalatra.

9.6 *Summary*

- A Scalatra application is usually built with sbt and has a sbt build definition. sbt is a modern build tool, with simple and effective concepts, based on tasks and settings.

- Configuration and environments allow for adapting an application to different situations.

- sbt plugins represent reusable logic in the form of tasks and settings. They deal with common build-related use cases. A multitude of plugins have been developed by the community.

- xsbt-web-plugin adds support for packaging servlet-based web applications as well as running an application in a servlet container during development.

- sbt-web introduces an asset pipeline for a web application, supporting a range of tools and standards. Usually, an asset pipeline consists of a sequence of compilation and transformation steps. Each step passes its results to the following steps.

- scalate-generator precompiles Scalate templates as .class files. This improves the application loading time and provides additional compile-time safety. Errors in a template appear during compilation and make a build either fail or succeed.

- scalatra-sbt generates a standalone zip distribution of an application, consisting of the embedded HTTP server, dependencies, and assets. The zip file can be downloaded and installed on another system.

- sbt-docker creates Docker containers for a Scala application. A container is similar to a standalone distribution but also contains at minimum the operating system and a Java Runtime Environment. That way, it can be run on another system with minimal prerequisites.

Working with a database

10

This chapter covers

- Working with persistent data in a Scalatra application

- Introducing the Slick library and integrating it into a Scalatra application

- Creating a persistence layer using Slick's table models, queries, and DBIO actions

In this chapter, you'll work with persistent data in a Scalatra application and use the Slick library. Slick integrates relational databases in the Scala language, providing a type-safe query language.

10.1 Working with a relational database and example scenario

A database is typically used by an application to store persistent data. That way, the data can be efficiently queried, loss of data can be minimized, and scaling the database is possible. The application doesn't talk to the database directly, but uses a database library that provides methods for querying and updating the database.

Scalatra has no built-in support or preference for a specific database system or database library. In principle, all databases that provide a connector library for the JVM can be used.

This chapter shows how you can integrate the Slick library in a Scalatra web application and includes a tutorial on using Slick. Interaction with the database is often abstracted away in the application architecture and encapsulated in a persistence layer. This is shown in figure 10.1.

Slick makes it possible to use a relational database from the Scala language in a type-safe way without writing SQL. A database table is described as a `Table` model, and Slick maps a database table to a Scala type. From a `Table` model, a `Query` can be derived, which can be further specialized and composed with other queries. A query can be turned into a DBIO action, which represents an interaction with the database. DBIO actions can be composed and are eventually executed on a `Database` object.

We'll start with the integration of the Slick library and then progress to more-advanced Slick concepts. Presenting the full details is beyond the scope of this book, but you can find them in the official documentation (http://slick.typesafe.com/docs/).

Slick tries to mirror the relational model in the Scala language. As a result, Slick allows you to stay close to the relational database model while supporting type-safe interaction with it. This is sometimes called *functional-relational mapping*, in contrast to *object-relational mapping*. Being able to work with simple and composable queries can lead to good reasoning about the actual database interaction and the resulting performance.

The sample application you'll build in this section is a website dedicated to sharing climbing routes in different areas of the world. The relational database consists of two tables for areas and routes. Each table defines typical columns such as ID, name, and

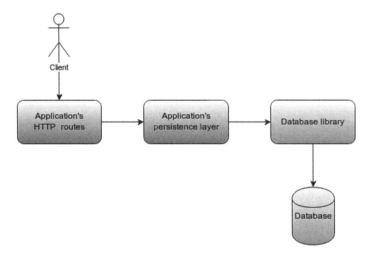

Figure 10.1   Components involved in the database interaction

description. A route belongs to exactly one area. In Scala, this model is represented as two classes: Area and Route.

Listing 10.1   Example domain: `Area` and `Route`

```
case class Area(
  id: Int,
  name: String,
  location: String,
  latitude: Double,
  longitude: Double,
  description: String)

case class Route(
  id: Int,
  areaId: Int,
  mountainName: Option[String],
  routeName: String,
  latitude: Double,
  longitude: Double,
  description: String)
```

10.2   *Integrating Slick and working with a DBIO action*

Let's start with integrating Slick. You're going to do the following:

- Add Slick to the application build
- Set up and configure a Database object
- Create and run DBIO actions

Slick needs to be added to the dependencies in the application's build definition in project/Build.scala. You'll also need to add a dependency to the database system you want to use. Slick has support for a wide range of database systems; here you'll use the H2 embedded database, which can easily be embedded and has acceptable performance for this sample application:

```
libraryDependencies ++= Seq(
  "com.typesafe.slick" %% "slick" % "3.0.0",
  "com.h2database" % "h2" % "1.4.187")
```

All the types, values, and implicit conversions that Slick requires to build queries and execute DBIO actions are bundled as members of the driver's api value and can be imported from there. Further, because Slick is fully asynchronous, an Execution-Context needs to be available. The following snippet imports from the H2Driver and relies on Scala's default ExecutionContext:

```
import slick.driver.H2Driver.api._

import scala.concurrent.ExecutionContext.Implicits.global
```

In order to talk to the database, the `Driver` helps by translating Slick queries to database-specific SQL. There's a driver for each supported database system. For example, the driver for MySQL is called `MySQLDriver`, and for H2 it's `H2Driver`. Most drivers extend `JdbcDriver`, which is a generic driver for relational databases using JDBC. It knows enough to be able to execute plain SQL statements.

A `Database` object represents the database and is responsible for running database actions in the form of values of type `DBIO[T]`. This object usually is created early in the application lifecycle. There are several factory methods. In this example, you call the `forURL` method, which accepts the JDBC driver's classname as well as a connection URI and returns a `Database` object:

```
val jdbcUrl = "jdbc:h2:mem:chapter09;DB_CLOSE_DELAY=-1"
val jdbcDriverClass = "org.h2.Driver"
val db = Database.forURL(jdbcUrl, driver = jdbcDriverClass)
```

Each interaction with the database is encapsulated in a `DBIO[T]` action, where `T` is the return type of that action. A DBIO action is defined at some place in the application and can be executed using the `run` method of the `Database` object. The method returns a `Future[T]` as the result, and Slick runs the action fully asynchronously, meaning the execution doesn't block the current thread.

A simple way to construct an action is by formulating a plain SQL query using the string interpolation operators `sql` and `sqlu`. The following example creates an action running a single SQL statement, which creates a table called `foo`. You use Scala's `Await` to wait for the query to finish and the result to be available:

```
val createAction: DBIO[Int] = sqlu"create table foo(name varchar)"
val run: Future[Int] = db.run(createAction)
Await.result(run, Duration(5, "seconds"))
```

The `sqlu` interpolator yields a DBIO action giving the number of modified rows as an `Int`. The `sql` interpolator declares its return type using the `as[T]` method. The DBIO action yields a `Seq[T]`. A query can contain variables, and each embedded variable reference is converted to a bind variable in the resulting query.

Multiple actions can be composed together to form a new action running all the statements of the single actions. One way to do this is to use the `DBIO.seq` method, which accepts a variable number of DBIO actions. The following listing shows an example of how to construct and run actions.

Listing 10.2   Creating, composing, and running DBIO actions

```
import scala.concurrent.Future            ⟵┐  Imports scala.concurrent and
import scala.concurrent.Await                │  Slick result conversion types
import scala.concurrent.duration.Duration    │
import slick.jdbc.GetResult._               ⟵┘                    Creates
                                                                  DBIO actions
                                                                  using sqlu
val createFoo: DBIO[Int] = sqlu"create table foo(name varchar)"  ⟵ interpolator
```

```
val dropFoo: DBIO[Int] = sqlu"drop table foo"

def insertFoo(name: String): DBIO[Int] = sqlu"insert into foo values ($name)"

val selectFoo: DBIO[Seq[String]] = sql"select name from foo".as[String]

val composedAction: DBIO[Unit] = DBIO.seq(
  createFoo,
  insertFoo("air"),
  insertFoo("water"),
  selectFoo map { xs => xs foreach println },
  dropFoo
)

val run: Future[Unit] = db.run(composedAction)

Await.result(run, Duration(5, "seconds"))
```

> **Uses variables with SQL string interpolation**

> **Queries data from the database**

> **Creates a composed action from other actions**

> **Runs all statements of the composed action in a single transaction and waits for the result**

Note that the preceding composed action involves the side effect of printing the results of the action. In the following example, you'll see another way to chain multiple actions using `flatMap`. Here the `composedAction` returns the results of the `selectAction` and prints them later to stdout:

```
val composedAction: DBIO[Seq[String]] = for {
  _ <- createAction
  _ <- insertAction("air")
  _ <- insertAction("water")
  xs <- selectAction
  _ <- dropAction
} yield xs

db.run(composedAction) foreach { xs => println(xs) }
// Vector(air, water)
```

By default, all statements are executed in auto-commit mode. That means when one statement fails, the following statements aren't executed, possibly leaving the database in an inconsistent state. In order to avoid this, multiple statements can be grouped in a transaction, guaranteeing that either all statements are applied as an atomic group, or none are. In the case of a failure, no changes are applied, leaving the database always in a consistent state.

A transactional DBIO action can be built by invoking `transactionally` on an action. The following example runs all the statements of `composedAction` in a single transaction:

```
db.run(composedAction.transactionally)
```

The actual initialization happens in the application's `LifeCycle`, as shown in the next listing. The `Database` object is provided to the `Chapter10App` via the constructor. The database schema and sample data are created during initialization using the `DbSetup` object.

Listing 10.3   Integration of Slick in the application's `LifeCycle`

```
import org.scalatra.book.chapter10.{DbSetup, Chapter10App}

import org.scalatra._
import javax.servlet.ServletContext

import slick.driver.H2Driver.api._
import scala.concurrent.Await
import scala.concurrent.duration.Duration

class ScalatraBootstrap extends LifeCycle {

  val jdbcUrl = "jdbc:h2:mem:chapter10;DB_CLOSE_DELAY=-1"
  val jdbcDriverClass = "org.h2.Driver"
  val db = Database.forURL(jdbcUrl, driver = jdbcDriverClass)

  val app = new Chapter10App(db)

  override def init(context: ServletContext): Unit = {
    val res = db.run(DbSetup.createDatabase)

    Await.result(res, Duration(5, "seconds"))

    context.mount(app, "/*")
  }

  override def destroy(context: ServletContext): Unit = {
    db.close()
  }

}
```

JDBC URL, JDBC driver class, and Slick driver class

Builds the Database object

Creates the database schema if it doesn't exist

Blocks here

Mounts the application to /*

At the end of the application lifecycle, closes the database

This section demonstrated the integration of Slick in an application and working with DBIO actions. You've seen how to compose DBIO actions either with DBIO.seq or by using a for comprehension.

Plain SQL queries can be useful, but they aren't statically typed and checked by the compiler. In the next section, we'll show you how to define types for your tables.

10.3   *Defining table models and working with a TableQuery*

In Slick, a database table is described as a Table in Scala code. This allows it to formulate statically typed queries against that table without having to write SQL.

A table is described with a few methods and types. The columns of the table appear as def methods invoking the column[T] method. The type parameter, T, is the Scala type of the column, and the name of the column is given as an argument. You use Option[T] to indicate that a column is nullable. You mark the primary key of a table with O.PrimaryKey, and an auto-increment column can be annotated with O.AutoInc. You can explicitly specify a relation to another table using the foreignKey method.

Each table definition needs to define a default projection, *, constituting the default selection on that table. The result type of * must be aligned to the type parameter, T, of the table definition. For example, Table[(Int, String)] has a default projection of type (Rep[Int], Rep[String]). Rep[T] lifts a T into the Slick DSL:

```
class Foos(tag: Tag) extends Table[(Int, String)](tag, "FOOS") {
  def id = column[Int]("INT", O.PrimaryKey, O.AutoInc)
  def name = column[String]("NAME")

  def * = (id, name)
}
```

The following listing shows table definitions for two tables: Area and Route. When you map a table row to a custom entity type, you need to define a bidirectional mapping function between the column types and the entity type using the <> operator. For example, the default projection of Areas provides a mapping between a single row and Area.

Listing 10.4   Table definitions for the Area and Route tables

**Defines a Table type
for the areas relation**

**Sets primary
key and auto-
increment
attributes for
the id column**

**Defines all required columns
with their names and types**

**Defines
the default
projection
for queries
to the table**

**A mountain name
is optional and is
therefore mapped
to the type
Option[String].**

```
object Tables {
  class Areas(tag: Tag) extends Table[Area](tag, "AREAS") {
    def id          = column[Int]("ID", O.PrimaryKey, O.AutoInc)
    def name        = column[String]("NAME")
    def location    = column[String]("LOCATION")
    def latitude    = column[Double]("LATITUDE")
    def longitude   = column[Double]("LONGITUDE")
    def description = column[String]("DESCRIPTION")

    def * = (id, name, location, longitude, latitude, description)
        <> (Area.tupled, Area.unapply)
  }

  class Routes(tag: Tag) extends Table[Route](tag, "ROUTES") {
    def id          = column[Int]("ID", O.PrimaryKey, O.AutoInc)
    def areaId      = column[Int]("AREAID")
    def mountainName = column[Option[String]]("MOUNTAINNAME")
    def routeName   = column[String]("ROUTENAME")
    def description = column[String]("DESCRIPTION")
    def latitude    = column[Double]("LATITUDE")
    def longitude   = column[Double]("LONGITUDE")

    def * = columns <> (Route.tupled, Route.unapply)

    def area = foreignKey("FK_ROUTE_AREA", areaId, areas)(_.id)
  }

  val areas = TableQuery[Areas]
  val routes = TableQuery[Routes]

}
```

**Defines a Table type
for the routes relation**

**Specifies table queries
for both tables**

A `TableQuery[E <: AbstractTable[_]]` represents a `Query` on the table `E` using the table's default projection. A `TableQuery` can, for example, select all rows of that table. Further, it can be used to insert new rows, manage the database schema, and act as a starting point for building more specific queries (this is shown in greater detail in section 10.4). Listing 10.4 defines a `TableQuery` value for each table.

Let's see how to manage the database schema with Slick. A `TableQuery` has a `schema` method yielding a `SchemaDescription` that describes that table. The `create` method from a schema definition yields a DBIO action that runs the SQL statements required to create the schema for that table. The `drop` method drops the table from the database schema. Multiple schemas can be combined with the ++ method. You can define a create and drop action for the example tables like this:

```
import Tables.{routes, areas}

val createTables: DBIO[Unit] = (routes.schema ++ areas.schema).create

val dropTables: DBIO[Unit] = (routes.schema ++ areas.schema).drop
```

Now let's look at querying data from a table. A `Query` represents a specific multiset of tuples from the database. The `result` method returns a `DBIO[Seq[T]]` representing an I/O action, which runs the query on a database connection and gives the result. Invoking `headOption` on an action restricts the action on only the first row as a `DBIO[Option[T]]`, whereas `head` gives the first row as a `DBIO[T]`. You can invoke the `result` method on the `TableQuery`:

```
val allRoutes: DBIO[Seq[Route]] = routes.result

val firstOpt: DBIO[Option[Route]] = routes.result.headOption

val first: DBIO[Route] = routes.result.head
```

New rows can be inserted with the += and ++= methods, similar to Scala collections. The difference is that here a DBIO action is returned. The += method inserts a single row, and ++= inserts a sequence of rows. A new area can be inserted like this:

```
val insertArea: DBIO[Int] = {
  areas += Area(0, "Magic Wood", "Switzerland, Europe", 46.3347, 9.2612,
    "Hidden in the forest of the Avers valley there are some of the ...")
}
```

By default, an insert returns the number of affected rows. When the table has an auto-increment column, that column is ignored when inserting a new row. Here it's set to 0.

You can also use an `Option[Int]` to represent an ID type. Instead of returning the number of affected rows, it's also possible to return the generated ID. This can be achieved by fusing the insert query and a select query that returns the ID with the `returning` method, as shown here:

```
val insertAreaReturnId: DBIO[Int] = {
  val area = Area(0, "Magic Wood", "Switzerland, Europe", 46.3347, 9.2612,
    "Hidden in the forest of the Avers valley there are some of the ...")

  (areas returning areas.map(_.id)) += area
}
```

The next listing shows how to insert data into multiple tables by combining two insert
actions. The `insertRoutes` action references the ID of the newly inserted area in the
first action.

Listing 10.5   Inserting sample data

```
def insertRoutes(areaId: Int): DBIO[Option[Int]] = {     ◁─── Defines an action that
  routes ++= Seq(                                               inserts multiple routes
    Route(0, areaId, None, "Downunder", 46.3347, 9.2612, "Boulder, 7C+ at ..."),
    Route(0, areaId, None, "The Wizard", 46.3347, 9.2612, "Boulder, 7C at ..."),
    Route(0, areaId, None, "Master of a cow", 46.3347, 9.2612, "Boulder, 7C+ ...")
  )
}

val insertSampleData: DBIO[Int] = for {          ◁─── An action that inserts
  areaId <- insertAreaReturnId                        an area and then inserts
  _      <- insertRoutes(areaId)                       multiple routes
} yield areaId

val res: Future[Int] = db.run(insertSampleData)     ◁─── Runs the
res foreach println                                        DBIO action
```

When you run a DBIO action in a Scalatra action, a `Future` is typically returned (either
directly or in the form of an `AsyncResult`). When returning a `Future`, you need
ensure that `FutureSupport` is mixed into your application in order to enable asynchronous request processing (see chapter 12 for more details).

Listing 10.6 shows a sample application defining two actions for the /areas route.
A GET action loads a list of all areas from the database and renders that list in a tem-
plate. The POST action creates a new area in the database and returns an HTTP 302
Found status code with the URL to the new area resource. Both actions return a
Future. Note that the code maps over the result of a single DBIO action.

Listing 10.6   Using Slick DBIO actions in Scalatra actions

```
class Chapter10App extends ScalatraServlet with ScalateSupport with FutureSupport { ◁─┐
  override protected implicit def executor = scala.concurrent.ExecutionContext.global │
                                                                        Mixes in the
  before("/*") {                                                     FutureSupport trait
    contentType = "text/html"                                      and defines an implicit
  }                                   GET action                    ExecutionContext for
                                      shows all areas               handling the Futures
  get("/areas") {         ◁───────────┘
    new AsyncResult {
```

```
    val is = {                              Runs a DBIO action and
                                            maps to a template
      db.run(allAreas) map { areas =>   ◁──
        jade("areas.jade", "areas" -> areas)
      }

    }
  }
}                               POST action creates
                                a new area
post("/areas") {             ◁──
  val name         = params.get("name") getOrElse halt(BadRequest())
  val location     = params.get("location") getOrElse halt(BadRequest())
  val latitude     = params.getAs[Double]("latitude") getOrElse halt(BadRequest())
  val longitude    = params.getAs[Double]("longitude") getOrElse halt(BadRequest())
  val description  = params.get("description") getOrElse halt(BadRequest())

  db.run(createArea(name, location, latitude, longitude, description)) map { area =>
    Found(f"/areas/${area.id}")    ◁──
  }                                    Runs a DBIO action and
}                                      maps to an HTTP 302 Found
}
```

Defining a table model for database tables is straightforward and allows you to define type-safe queries. Now let's look at some more-challenging queries.

10.4 Using the query language

In this section, we'll look at defining queries using the query language. A query is represented as a value of type Query, which is eventually translated by the Slick query compiler to an SQL statement.

10.4.1 Defining queries

One fundamental Query is TableQuery, which represents the default projection of the table. It's often used as a starting point for building more-specific queries with the operators of the query language method:

```
val areas = TableQuery[Areas]
val routes = TableQuery[Routes]
```

A new query can be derived from an existing one. For example, the filter method filters a result set using a predicate. The map method projects each result tuple to a subset of its attributes. These methods are similar to those of the Scala collection types. Because a Query object is immutable, an operation always creates a new query, and the original Query on the left side stays unmodified.

For example, you can select all routes in the area with ID 2 and project the resulting tuples to the route's id and name. You start with a TableQuery that will return all rows, and build a new Query object using filter and map:

```
val routesQuery =
  routes.filter(_.areaId === 2).map(r => (r.id, r.routeName))
```

Note that the comparison in the filter predicate is realized using the === method. This clause translates to a WHERE expression in the generated SQL query.

For each column type, there are operators similar to the SQL operators for that datatype. Table 10.1 shows a list of datatypes and operators.

Table 10.1 Operators for column types

Column types	Operators
All columns	===, =!=, <, <=, >, >=, in, inSet, inSetBind, between, ifNull
Optional columns	getOrElse, get, isEmpty, isDefined
Numeric columns	+, -, -, *, /, %, abs, ceil, floor, sign
Boolean columns	&&, ||, unary_!
String columns	length, like, startsWith, endsWith, toUpperCase, toLowerCase, ltrim, rtrim, trim, reverseString, substring, substring, take, drop, replace, indexOf
Single columns	min, max, sum, avg, length, exists

Alternatively, you can build a query using a for comprehension, which may lead to more-readable and concise code. The previous routesQuery expressed as a for comprehension looks like this:

```
val routesQuery = for {
  route <- routes
  if route.areaId === 2
} yield (route.id, route.routeName)
```

In the routesQuery, the left sides of the clauses in the for comprehension extend Rep[T]. For example, route is a value of type Table[Route], and route.id is a value of type Rep[Int].

You can turn the Query into a DBIO action by using the result method, as shown in section 10.3. The following listing shows a complete example, defining a Table-Query, a Query, and a DBIO action. The action is run, and you wait for the result by blocking on the Future. After that, you print the result to stdout.

Listing 10.7 TableQuery, Query, and DBIO action

```
val routes = TableQuery[Routes]       ◁——— Defines a TableQuery

val routesQuery = routes.filter(_.areaId === 2).map(r => (r.id, r.routeName))  ◁—┐
```

Defines a Query that selects all routes in a specific area and projects all resulting rows to the id and routeName columns, yielding a Tuple2[Int, String]

```
val routesAction: DBIO[Option[(Int, String)]] = routesQuery.result.headOption
```

Defines an Action that returns only the first result as an Option[(Int, String)]

```
val action: DBIO[Option[(Int, String)]] = for {
  _ <- DbSetup.createDatabase
  x <- routesAction
  _ <- DbSetup.dropDatabase
} yield x

val res = Await.result(db.run(action), Duration(5, "seconds"))
```

Runs a composed action and blocks for the result

```
println(res)
// Some((2,Bobcat-Houlihan))
```

There are other methods in addition to `filter` and `map`. A specific range in a result set can be selected with the `take` and `drop` methods, leading to a `LIMIT` SQL clause:

```
val lessRoutes = routes.drop(3).take(10)
```

You can sort a result set with the `sortBy` method, which accepts a sort criterion. The methods `asc` and `desc` allow you to specify the sort order for each single column:

```
val sortById = routes.sortBy(_.id.desc)
val sortByIdName = routes.sortBy(r => (r.areaId.asc, r.routeName))
```

There are several methods you can use to aggregate a result set. The methods `min`, `max`, `sum`, `avg`, `length`, and `exists` aggregate a single column of a result set. The `groupBy` method aggregates a result set by a column and projects each aggregated result set to a flat tuple.

For example, the following query groups routes by the `areaId` and creates statistics consisting of the number of routes and the coordinate boundaries of that area, based on the routes in that area:

```
val statistics = routes
  .groupBy(_.areaId)
  .map { case (areaId, rs) =>
    (areaId,
    rs.length,
    rs.map(_.longitude).min,
    rs.map(_.longitude).max,
    rs.map(_.latitude).min,
    rs.map(_.latitude).max)
  }
```

It's possible to compose queries that let you reuse and modularize queries. For example, you can fetch all areas where the ID appears in a set of other IDs by fusing a subquery using the `in` operator. In the following snippet, the subquery queries all distinct area IDs where the area has at least one route with the route name matching a suffix test:

```
def bySuffix(str: String) = {
    query.filter(_.routeName.toLowerCase like f"%%${str.toLowerCase}")
    .groupBy(_.areaId).map(_._1)
}

val areasWithTrails = areas.filter(_.id in bySuffix("trails"))
```

10.4.2 Defining joins

A join can be expressed either as an applicative join or as a monadic join. Let's first take a look at applicative joins.

There are Slick methods for each SQL join method: join for cross or inner joins, and leftJoin, rightJoin, and outerJoin. Each join operator fuses two queries into a single one, returning a tuple of the single result types. You can give a join condition using an on clause.

The following snippet shows examples for cross, inner, and left joins using applicative join syntax:

```
val crossJoin = areas join routes
val innerJoin = routes join areas on (_.areaId === _.id)
val leftJoin = areas joinLeft routes on (_.id === _.areaId)
```

The monadic join style uses flatMap to construct joins. For example, an inner join has a filter specifying the join condition:

```
val innerJoinMonadic = for {
  r <- routes
  a <- areas if r.areaId === a.id
} yield (r, a)
```

The foreign key declaration in the table definition (see listing 10.4) can be used to navigate from the source to the target table:

```
val trailAreasQuery = for {
  route <- routes
  if (route.routeName.toLowerCase like "%trail")
  area <- route.area
} yield area
```

10.4.3 Using update and delete statements

You've now seen how to insert and query data from the database. Let's look at how you can update and delete rows.

The update operation is defined for a Query and updates all tuples of the projection to the given values. An update can be invoked on the default projection or a subset of the columns. Values for nullable columns can be omitted.

You can update the description of a specific route as follows:

```
routes.byName("Midnight Lightning")
  .map(r => r.description)
  .update("Midnight Lightning is a problem on the Columbia Boulder.")
```

The delete operation deletes all rows that a query would yield:

```
routes.byName("Midnight Lightning").delete
```

10.4.4 Organizing queries as extension methods

If you have a lot of queries, it can be useful to organize them a bit. The next listing shows how to extend the Query[Routes, Route, Seq] type with the queries from sections 10.4.1 and 10.4.2 using an implicit class.

Listing 10.8 Organizing queries as extension methods

```
implicit class RoutesQueryExtensions(query: Query[Routes, Route, Seq]) {    ⊲┐

  val lessRoutes = query.drop(3).take(10)                    Defines a few useful queries as
                                                             extension methods to a Query
  val sortById = query.sortBy(_.id.desc)
  val sortByIdName = query.sortBy(r => (r.areaId.asc, r.routeName))

  val statistics = query
    .groupBy(_.areaId)
    .map { case (areaId, rs) =>      (areaId,
      rs.length,
      rs.map(_.longitude).min,
      rs.map(_.longitude).max,
      rs.map(_.latitude).min,
      rs.map(_.latitude).max)
  }

  def byId(id: Int) = query.filter(_.id === id)
  def byName(name: String) = query.filter(_.routeName === name)

  def bySuffix(str: String) =
    query.filter(_.routeName.toLowerCase like f"%%${str.toLowerCase}")

  val distinctAreaIds = query.groupBy(_.areaId).map(_._1)

}
                                            A helper function that
def log(title: String)(xs: Seq[Any]): Unit = {    ⊲───   prints results to stdout
  println(f"$title")
  xs foreach { x => println(f"--$x") }
  println
}
                                                       Composes
                                                       a query using the
val trailAreaIds = routes.bySuffix("trails").distinctAreaIds   ⊲───  extension methods
val areasWithTrails = areas.filter(_.id in trailAreaIds)
```

```
val action = for {                    ⊲──── Builds a few more queries
  _ <- DbSetup.createDatabase
  _ <- routes.lessRoutes.result map log("limited routes")
  _ <- routes.sortById.result map log("sorted routes (id)")
  _ <- routes.sortByIdName.result map log("sorted routes (id, name)")
  _ <- routes.statistics.result map log("area statistics")
  _ <- DbSetup.dropDatabase
} yield ()
```

As you can see from the example of the `areasWithTrails` query, you can improve the readability of a query by reusing a few basic predefined queries.

10.5   *Summary*

- Slick allows you to work with a relational database in a functional way. It can easily be integrated into a Scalatra application.
- Table models define Scala types for database tables. They let you safely refer to table names and columns in queries.
- Queries are written in a language similar to relational algebra so that you can retain Scala's type safety while still staying close to the SQL database.
- A DBIO action represents a composable database read and write operation and usually consists of one or more queries.

Part 3

Advanced topics

The final part of this book explores several types of advanced subject matter. Chapter 11 discusses how you can secure your application using HTTP sessions and authentication strategies. Chapter 12 covers asynchronous programming and using Scala's advanced support for concurrent programming. Chapter 13 shows you how to build, secure, and document APIs using the Swagger framework.

Authentication 11

This chapter covers

- Stateful vs. stateless authentication
- The Scentry authentication framework
- HTTP Basic authentication
- Session handling in Scalatra
- Form-based login with a username and password
- Remembering a user with a cookie
- Defining multiple authentication strategies for a single application

Authentication, the act of confirming that somebody is who you think they are, is something you'll do over and over when constructing HTTP applications. To illustrate how authentication works in Scalatra, you'll protect parts of the Hacker Tracker application from chapter 4. You'll change it so that only logged-in users can add, remove, or edit hackers.

It's worth understanding right at the start that typically there are big differences between web applications and HTTP APIs when it comes to authentication. Web applications usually require a user to log in once, and then they hold on to that authentication state across multiple requests: they are *stateful*. APIs usually require that each request is authenticated independently of all other requests: they are *stateless*.

We'll take a look at web application security using stateful authentication in this chapter. If you're interested in protecting your APIs, there are many ways to accomplish that—OAuth2 and HMACs are the most popular. OAuth2 is beyond the scope of this chapter. HMAC is shown in chapter 13.

11.1   *A new, improved Hacker Tracker*

In the code samples for this chapter, you'll find two versions of the Hacker Tracker application. The first, chapter11/hacker-tracker-unprotected, is a more advanced version of the Hacker Tracker from chapter 4. The version in chapter 4 demonstrated routes, actions, and parameters, but it didn't actually save anything. This new version has a web form for creating new hackers and the ability to save them using an embedded H2 database.

To see it in action, start Scalatra:

```
cd chapter11/hacker-tracker-unprotected
chmod +x sbt
./sbt
~jetty:start
```

Let's look at what's been added since the last time you saw the project. Open it in your editor or IDE. You'll see that there are two new folders in src/main/scala/com/constructiveproof/hackertracker. In the init folder, there's a bunch of database initializer code; and in the models folder is a persistence system for hackers that uses the Squeryl object-relational mapper. The functionality of HackersController has been expanded so that it can save hackers to the database. There's also a new controller, DatabaseSetupController, which can create or drop a database for you, set up the database schema, and print out the database schema to the console.

Let's try setting up a new database. Open your browser and hit the URL http://localhost:8080/database/create. Several things will happen:

- Scalatra will tell Squeryl to create an H2 database storage file on disk.
- Squeryl will attempt to create the file in your home directory, at the path ~/db/hackertracker.db.
- You'll be redirected to a hacker-creation form.

The hacker-creation form looks like figure 11.1 (note that there are a lot of problems with this form from a security perspective).

There's also a route allowing you to drop the database, at http://localhost:8080/database/drop. Hit that route, and you'll destroy the database. You'll see output as shown in figure 11.2.

If you're a security specialist, you'll have noted the problem: most web applications don't allow anonymous web users to create, drop, and re-create the data store. In fact, most don't expose these operations via HTTP. Let's put the second objection

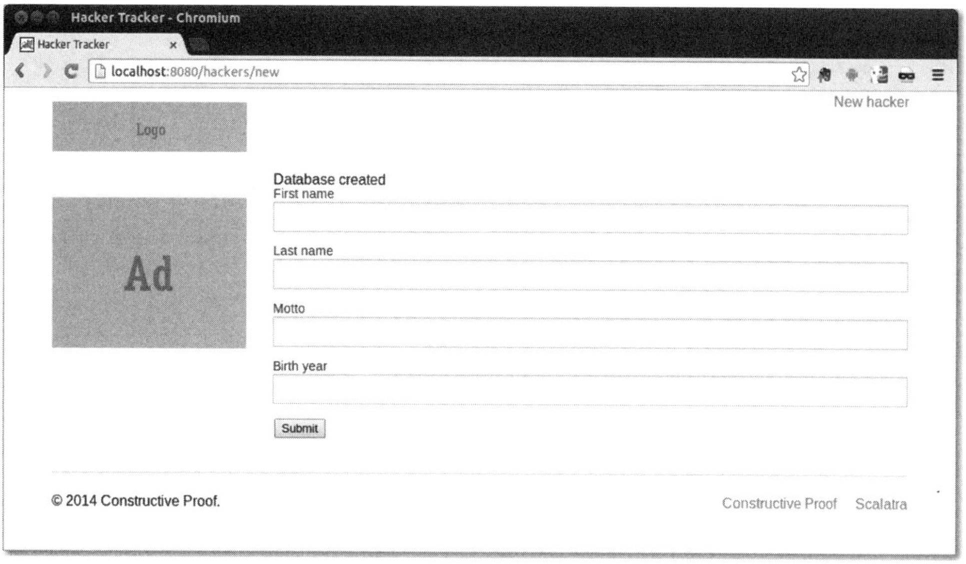

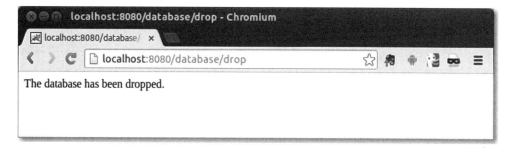

Figure 11.1　The hacker-creation form

Figure 11.2　Dropping the database

aside and assume that you want routes for database creation and destruction, but that only properly authenticated users should be allowed to do these things. How can you enforce this?

There are many ways to do it. If you're an old Java servlet hand and can deal with the stench of XML configuration, you can use native servlet security configuration to protect your routes. After all, Scalatra runs inside a normal Java servlet container; all the 2003-era options are available to you, if you want them.

Another option is Apache Shiro. Again, because Shiro is designed for servlet applications, and Scalatra is a servlet-based framework, this will work just fine. The good thing about Shiro is that you get not only authentication support (is this user who they say they are?), you also get authorization support (what is this user allowed to do?). But in this chapter, we'll focus on what Scalatra provides natively.

11.2   *An introduction to Scentry*

Scalatra includes its own authentication framework called Scentry. It's a version of Ruby's Warden authentication framework that has been ported to Scala.

Like Warden, Scentry is structured around the concept of authentication *strategies*. A strategy is a self-contained piece of logic for checking whether an authentication attempt should succeed or fail. Strategies can run additional code after authentication or logout takes place, allowing you to take care of things like giving the user a session or destroying cookies on logout.

You can protect your application in whatever ways you'd like, but these are some common strategies:

- A `BasicAuthStrategy` that prevents a user from seeing a web page without the proper credentials.
- A `UserPasswordStrategy` that allows a user to log in from a web form.
- A `RememberMeStrategy` that remembers the user for a week after they've logged in, so that they don't need to enter their credentials every time they visit the site.

Another way in which Scentry is like Warden is that it requires a session. Let's take a quick detour and look at session handling in Scalatra.

11.2.1   *Session handling in Scalatra*

Most of the stateful authentication methods we'll be looking at involve using server-side session mechanisms to remember a user's identity between requests. Because session-handling mechanisms underpin so much of the stateful security model, it's a good idea to understand how sessions work in Scalatra.

Like many other frameworks, Scalatra needs to use some tricks to remember anything about a given user between requests. In reality, every HTTP request is independent of every other HTTP request; all HTTP applications are naturally stateless. To get around this, Scalatra can be configured to set a session cookie in a user's browser during a request. When the user later makes another request, the session cookie is sent back to the server. The server has a bit of RAM put aside to remember the information inside the user's session cookie. This allows the server to differentiate between users and provide a decent illusion of statefulness between requests.

Scalatra is a servlet-based framework, and the Java servlet specification dictates how sessions are implemented by whatever container (such as Jetty, Tomcat, JBoss, WebSphere, GlassFish) your application is running in.

By default, Scalatra controller classes don't set up sessions. Leaving session functionality out of your application reduces RAM consumption and data transfer, so it makes sense to leave sessions off if you're building a stateless application, such as an API. But when you need them, you need them.

Sessions are a core part of Scalatra, and you can start a session in one of several ways. The most explicit way to trigger a session is to mix Scalatra's `SessionSupport` trait into one or more of your controllers. This will cause Scalatra to set a session cookie and remember a user between successive requests. Mixing in `FlashMapSupport`, which allows you to "flash" short amounts of information to a user between requests, will also trigger a session. This is why `FlashMapSupport` isn't turned on by default.

Let's use Scentry to protect the Hacker Tracker. You'll start simply and use Scentry to protect the database creation and destruction routes using HTTP Basic authentication.

HTTP Basic authentication will be familiar if you've been around on the web for a while: it pops up an ugly-looking login box that's part of the browser, and it requires a username and password in order to proceed.

11.2.2 *Scentry setup*

Setting up Scentry is fairly simple. First, add the Scentry dependency to your project/build.scala file in the `libraryDependencies` section:

```
"org.scalatra" %% "scalatra-auth" % ScalatraVersion,
```

Make sure you restart sbt to pick up the dependency.

Now you have access to all of Scentry's authentication methods in your application, and you've had a basic introduction to sessions in Scalatra. Let's look at how you can protect routes using Scentry.

There are a variety of ways to protect routes but still give access to logged-in users:

- HTTP Basic authentication
- Forms authentication with a username and password
- A Remember Me cookie

We'll look at each of these over the next several sections.

11.3 *Protecting routes with HTTP Basic authentication*

Giving anonymous users on the web the ability to drop your database is a little dangerous. Now that Scentry is installed, you can fix that hole. You'll need to write two pieces of code:

- An authentication strategy
- A trait that you can mix into the controller you want to protect

You'll write a `BasicAuthStrategy` and a `BasicAuthSupport` trait to mix into the `DatabaseSetupController` to protect it.

11.3.1 *The simplest possible Scentry strategy*

The anatomy of any Scentry strategy is fairly simple. Strategies are just regular Scala classes that inherit from `ScentryStrategy`. They must implement two methods: a way to retrieve a user for authentication purposes, and a way to authenticate that the user is who they say they are.

The simplest possible strategy would look something like the following code. Don't add this code to your application—it's just an example to explain what a very simple strategy should look like. You'll write a working one in a moment:

Gives your strategy class a name

```
class YourStrategy()
    extends ScentryStrategy[YourUserClass] {
    def authenticate()
        (implicit request: HttpServletRequest,
        response: HttpServletResponse):
        Option[YourUserClass] = {
        // authentication logic goes here
    }
}
```

Extends ScentryStrategy and says what your User class is

The authenticate() method is where your authentication logic goes.

Returns an Option[YourUserClass]

Note that you're obliged to carry an implicit request and response around with you when defining strategies. This is ugly, but it's needed in order to make asynchronous requests work in a safe way.

When defining a strategy, you need to tell Scentry what your User class is. In most cases, it will probably be called something like User or Account. In security speak, this is the *security subject*—the thing that you're trying to authenticate. In the previous example code, the subject is YourUserClass.

The only method you *must* include is authenticate(). If authentication succeeds, this method should return Some(user). If authentication fails, it should return None.

Strategies are flexible, and you can define a lot of extra things about them. For instance, you can conditionally determine whether an authentication strategy should be run, or trigger actions at quite a few different points in the authentication lifecycle. You'll see some of these in this chapter.

11.3.2 *A basic auth strategy*

Enough of the theory. Let's define a real strategy.

First, you need to define a User class. Put the following code into models/Models.scala:

```
case class User(id:String)
```

This defines a User model that you can use as an authentication subject. It's a Scala case class that takes a single string parameter as an id. It won't persist to disk using Squeryl, but it's enough to show authentication in action.

You need a place to keep your strategies. In the src/main/scala/com/constructiveproof/hackertracker folder, create a folder called auth, and inside it, create a folder called strategies.

Scalatra comes with one built-in strategy for you to extend: the BasicAuthStrategy. It requires that you pass a reference to your Scalatra application into the strategy's constructor, so that it can reference incoming HTTP params. It also requires that you specify an HTTP Basic authentication realm, so the user knows what they're authenticating to. This is a requirement of HTTP Basic authentication—it shows up at the top of the authentication box that opens when a user tries to log in.

Create the file OurBasicAuthStrategy.scala inside the strategies folder, and drop the following code into it.

Listing 11.1 `OurBasicAuthStrategy`

```
package com.constructiveproof.hackertracker.auth.strategies

import org.scalatra.auth.strategy.{BasicAuthStrategy}
import org.scalatra.{ScalatraBase}
import javax.servlet.http.{HttpServletResponse, HttpServletRequest}
import com.constructiveproof.hackertracker.models.User

class OurBasicAuthStrategy(
    protected override val app: ScalatraBase,
    realm: String)
    extends BasicAuthStrategy[User](app, realm) {

  protected def validate(userName: String, password: String)
    (implicit request: HttpServletRequest,
      response: HttpServletResponse): Option[User] = {
    if(userName == "scalatra" && password == "scalatra")
      Some(User("scalatra"))
    else None
  }

  protected def getUserId(user: User)
    (implicit request: HttpServletRequest,
    response: HttpServletResponse): String = user.id
}
```

Annotations:
- **Defines the strategy**
- **Defines an HTTP Basic authentication realm**
- **Passes the Scalatra app in the constructor**
- **Extends Scentry's built-in BasicAuthStrategy**
- **The validate() method is called by authenticate() in the superclass.**
- **If the username and password are both scalatra, authentication succeeds.**
- **Returns Option[User]—maybe a User, maybe None**
- **Returns Some[User] for a successful login**
- **Returns None for an unsuccessful login**
- **Provides a way to pull the user ID out of the session**

Scentry's built-in `BasicAuthStrategy` is an abstract class. It has its own `authenticate()` method—but that method calls `validate()`, which you've implemented here. In `OurBasicAuthStrategy`, validate returns an `Option[User]`, indicating that there's a possibility that it'll return either `Some(User)` or `None`. The body of the `validate` method checks whether the `userName` and `password` parameters that the app has received are both equal to `"scalatra"`.

You can put any authentication logic you want into your strategy. In a more complex system, you might, for instance, decide to do a database lookup on the username that came in on the app's HTTP params, and then check whether that `User`'s hashed and salted password was equal to the incoming password parameter.

11.3.3   *A basic authentication support trait*

Now that you have an authentication strategy defined, you need a way to *use* it in a controller. Let's make a trait that you can mix into your DatabaseSetupController, forcing it to use OurBasicAuthStrategy. Just as Scalatra has a built-in BasicAuthStrategy that you can extend, it also has a BasicAuthSupport trait to make your life a bit easier. All you need to do is extend that one, and it'll take care of the mundane details of HTTP Basic authentication redirects, HTTP headers, and status codes for you.

The trait should look like the following listing. Drop it into the auth folder you created earlier.

Listing 11.2   The OurBasicAuthenticationSupport trait

```
package com.constructiveproof.hackertracker.auth

import org.scalatra.auth.{ScentryConfig, ScentrySupport}
import org.scalatra.auth.strategy.BasicAuthSupport
import org.scalatra.ScalatraBase
import com.constructiveproof.hackertracker.auth.strategies.
   OurBasicAuthStrategy
import com.constructiveproof.hackertracker.models.User

trait OurBasicAuthenticationSupport extends ScentrySupport[User]
   with BasicAuthSupport[User] {
   self: ScalatraBase =>

   val realm = "Scalatra Basic Auth Example"

   protected def fromSession = { case id: String => User(id)  }
   protected def toSession   = { case usr: User => usr.id }

   protected val scentryConfig =
      (new ScentryConfig {}).asInstanceOf[ScentryConfiguration]

   override protected def configureScentry = {
      scentry.unauthenticated {
         scentry.strategies("Basic").unauthenticated()
      }
   }

   override protected def registerAuthStrategies = {
      scentry.register("Basic", app =>
         new OurBasicAuthStrategy(app, realm))
   }
}
```

Annotations:
- **Extends ScentrySupport and lets Scalatra know that your security subject is User**
- **Mixes in Scentry's built-in BasicAuthSupport trait**
- **Pulls user references out of the session**
- **Adds user references to the session**
- **Requires that any class this trait gets mixed into inherits from ScalatraBase**
- **Gets a reference to the Scentry configuration**
- **Uses Scentry's built-in handler for unauthenticated users**
- **Registers OurBasicAuthStrategy with Scentry**

The trait extends ScentrySupport with a user type of User for an authentication subject. It's worth pointing out the self: ScalatraBase => idiom used here, because you'll see it used in lots of Scala traits. In English, it would mean *any class that mixes in* the `BasicAuthenticationSupport` *trait must inherit from* `ScalatraBase`. In other words, this trait can only be mixed into Scalatra controllers.

You also hardcoded an HTTP Basic authentication realm into place. When a user attempts to view a protected URL, they'll see a login prompt pop up, and it'll have the title *Scalatra Basic Auth Example* set as the security realm.

The support trait must be able to pull a `User` object out of the session and serialize a user into the session, so that your users don't need to reauthenticate on every request. The `fromSession` and `toSession` methods do this in a simple way. Given a `User` object with an ID, `toSession` whacks the user's ID into the session and stores it between requests. When you want to pull a `User` out of session, `fromSession` instantiates a `User` with the proper ID. Once again, in a more complex application you'd likely be doing some sort of retrieval from your data store, but this is enough to get the job done here without getting bogged down in persistence details.

`scentryConfig` is a value in the constructor that gives you a reference to your application's Scentry configuration. It's used to define Scentry's behavior. In this case, you're using it to answer a fairly simple question: what should happen when an unauthenticated user hits a protected controller action?

The answer is here:

```
override protected def configureScentry = {
  scentry.unauthenticated {
    scentry.strategies("Basic").unauthenticated()
  }
}
```

You tell your support trait that if any unauthenticated user hits a protected controller action, it should look up Scentry's built-in `"Basic"` strategy and run its `unauthenticated()` method. If you nose around inside Scentry, you'll see that this causes a `halt(401, "Unauthenticated")`. Scalatra will stop the user from proceeding any further, and the user will see the word "Unauthenticated" as the response body.

The last thing you do in the support trait is register `OurBasicAuthStrategy` with Scentry's list of possible strategies. As you'll see in a little while, it's possible to define multiple Scentry strategies and fall back from one to another. For the moment, you're only registering the `"Basic"` strategy.

All the infrastructure you need is now set up, and you can protect your `Database-SetupController`. At present, the top of `DatabaseSetupController` looks like this:

```
class DatabaseSetupController extends HackerTrackerStack {

  before() {
    contentType = "text/html"
  }
```

Once again, you can take advantage of some built-in Scentry functionality: there's already a way to trigger a check for basic authentication. Just mix in `OurBasicAuthentication-Support` and add a call to `basicAuth` to the `before()` filter, so it looks like this:

```
class DatabaseSetupController extends HackerTrackerStack
  with OurBasicAuthenticationSupport {

  before() {
    contentType = "text/html"
    basicAuth
  }
```

That's it. All routes in the controller are now protected by the `basicAuth` call, which checks Scentry's list of registered strategies and triggers an authentication box if Scentry's built-in `BasicAuthStrategy` (or one of its subclasses) is registered.

11.3.4   *Protecting the DatabaseSetupController*

The result is wonderfully simple. Hit http://localhost:8080/database/drop. Instead of dropping the database as before, you're confronted with the browser's HTTP Basic authentication box asking you to log in, as shown in figure 11.3.

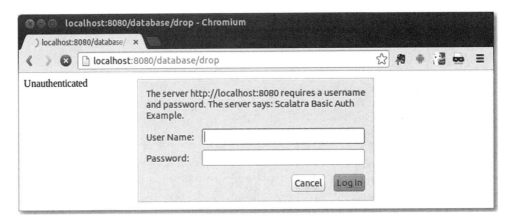

Figure 11.3   HTTP Basic authentication in action

If you enter *scalatra* as the username and *scalatra* as the password, the `validate()` method in `OurBasicAuthStrategy` will succeed, and Scentry will allow you to hit the route and drop the database. If you do anything else, you'll be shown the word *Unauthenticated* instead, as shown in figure 11.4.

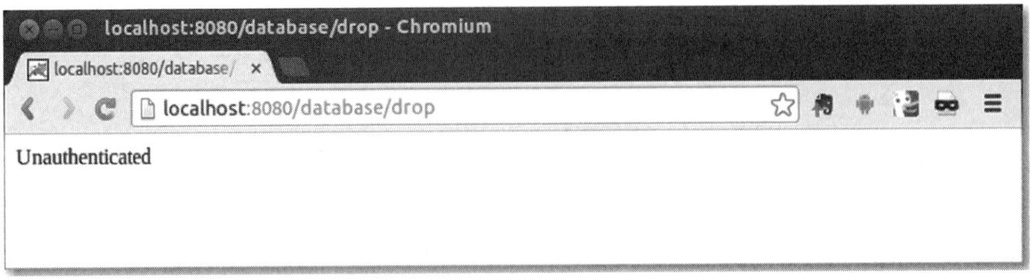

Figure 11.4   An unsuccessful login attempt

The Basic authentication strategy works, but that browser-specific login box is rather ugly. Most public-facing applications use a styled HTML login form instead. Let's see how to make a login form using a forms authentication strategy.

11.4 Using forms authentication

You don't want unauthenticated users to be able to add new hackers to the database, which they can currently do. The problem is, HackersController isn't protected. To fix this, let's turn our attention toward securing get("/new"), which displays the new hacker form, and post("/"), which creates a new hacker in the database.

Unauthenticated users who hit the new hacker route or try to create a new hacker should be redirected to a login page. After logging in, users should be able to see the new hacker form and create new hackers in the database. Scentry doesn't have a built-in strategy for doing this, so you'll write the code from scratch.

You want users to supply a username and password when users attempt to log in, so you'll call the strategy UserPasswordStrategy. You also want to have a Remember Me check box that allows the system to remember a user for a week, so the user can bypass authentication as long as a cookie is set. This requires a different strategy: RememberMeStrategy. You'll also make an AuthenticationSupport trait that you can mix into your controllers in order to protect them with your new strategies.

11.4.1 Creating a simple login form

You may as well start with the user interface. Add a new folder named sessions in your webapp/WEB-INF/templates/views folder, and create a file in it called new.ssp. That file is a simple login form, as follows.

Listing 11.3 A simple login form

```
<p>Please login:</p>
<form action="/sessions" method="post">
    <p>
        <label>Login:</label>
        <input type="text" name="username"/><br>
        <label>Password:</label>
        <input type="password" name="password"/><br/>
        <label>Remember Me:</label>
        <input type="checkbox" name="rememberMe" value="true" />
    </p>
    <p>
        <input type="submit">
    </p>
</form>
```

This form defines the user interface: a text input field for users to type their username into, a password field, and a check box that causes Hacker Tracker to remember the user for a week if it's selected when they log in successfully.

You'll now create a `SessionsController` so that you can display this form. Add the code from the following listing to it.

Listing 11.4   A basic sessions controller

```
package com.constructiveproof.hackertracker

class SessionsController extends HackerTrackerStack {
  get("/new") {
    contentType="text/html"
    ssp("/sessions/new", "allHackers" -> Hacker.all,
      "authenticated" -> isAuthenticated)
  }
}
```

Nothing too noteworthy here; it's a standard Scalatra action that renders the form. Remember to mount the controller in ScalatraBootstrap by adding `context.mount(new SessionsController, "/sessions")` to the `init()` method. Point your browser at http://localhost:8080/sessions/new, and you'll be able to see the form, as shown in figure 11.5.

11.4.2 *Building a UserPasswordStrategy*

At this point, you need to set up a Scentry strategy that can deal with form input and deal with login attempts by checking whether a user's username and password should

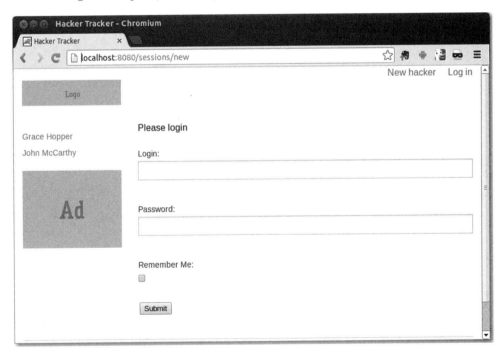

Figure 11.5   The login form

log them in. Create a new file called UserPasswordStrategy in auth/strategies/, and drop the following code into it.

Listing 11.5 The start of a `UserPasswordStrategy`

```
package com.constructiveproof.example.auth.strategies

import org.scalatra.ScalatraBase
import javax.servlet.http.{HttpServletResponse, HttpServletRequest}
import org.scalatra.auth.ScentryStrategy
import com.constructiveproof.hackertracker.models.User

class UserPasswordStrategy(protected val app: ScalatraBase)
  extends ScentryStrategy[User] {

    override def name: String = "UserPassword"

    def authenticate()
      (implicit request: HttpServletRequest,
        response: HttpServletResponse): Option[User] = ???
  }
```

Annotations:
- **Defines a strategy, and passes your Scalatra app into the constructor** → `class UserPasswordStrategy(protected val app: ScalatraBase)`
- **Inherits from ScentryStrategy [User]** → `extends ScentryStrategy[User] {`
- **Explicitly naming your strategy is a good idea.** → `override def name: String = "UserPassword"`
- **Stubs out the authenticate() method** → `response: HttpServletResponse): Option[User] = ???`

This looks very much like the minimal strategy from section 11.3.1, with one difference: it has an explicit name, which becomes important when multiple strategies with fallbacks are in play. The code will compile, but you only have a nonfunctional stub of the `authenticate()` method's functionality. Before you finish that, let's add a few convenience methods so your strategy can read incoming HTTP parameters.

You'll add one for reading the incoming `username` parameter and another for the incoming `password` parameter. Drop these into the body of the strategy class:

```
private def username = app.params.getOrElse("username", "")
private def password = app.params.getOrElse("password", "")
```

Both methods use the `app` val that this strategy was initialized with to read incoming form parameters. During authentication attempts, instances of this strategy will be created, and you can use these methods to either grab the parameters you want or return an empty string.

Now you're ready to finish the `authenticate()` method. Add code to that method so it attempts to authenticate the user:

```
def authenticate()
  (implicit request: HttpServletRequest,
    response: HttpServletResponse): Option[User] = {

  if(username == "foo" && password == "foo") {
    Some(User("foo"))
```

```
  } else {
    None
  }
}
```

This is a simple method that uses the convenience methods for `username` and `password` to check a user's credentials. If the user enters "foo" for both the username and password, `authenticate()` returns a `User` and authentication succeeds. Otherwise, the method returns `None`, and authentication fails.

Part of a Scentry strategy's job is to package up all authentication-related logic into one neat little bundle. Let's use Scentry to define what should happen when an unauthenticated user requests a protected resource. Add the function in the following listing to `UserPasswordStrategy`.

Listing 11.6 Defining what happens when someone accesses a protected resource

```
override def unauthenticated()            ◁─────    Overrides the unauthenticated()
    (implicit request: HttpServletRequest,          method from ScentryStrategy
  response: HttpServletResponse) {
  app.redirect("/sessions/new")   ◁─────   Redirects to
  }                                         the login form
```

When an unauthenticated user attempts to hit a route that's protected by this particular Scentry strategy, you issue a redirect to `"/sessions/new"` and the user sees the login form, requesting their username and password. Now let's create an `Authentication-Support` trait that you can use to protect the hacker-creation form, and see this in action.

11.4.3 Creating an AuthenticationSupport trait

As with the `UserPasswordStrategy`, you'll need to write the `AuthenticationSupport` trait from the ground up. Create a new trait beside `OurBasicAuthenticationSupport` in the `auth` namespace, and call it `AuthenticationSupport`. Its contents are shown in the following listing.

Listing 11.7 `AuthenticationSupport` trait for use across the app

```
package com.constructiveproof.hackertracker.auth

import org.scalatra.ScalatraBase
import org.scalatra.auth.ScentrySupport
import com.constructiveproof.hackertracker.models.User
import com.constructiveproof.example.auth.strategies.
  {UserPasswordStrategy}

trait AuthenticationSupport extends ScalatraBase
  with ScentrySupport[User] {
  self: ScalatraBase =>

  protected val scentryConfig = (new ScentryConfig {})
```

```
    .asInstanceOf[ScentryConfiguration]


protected def fromSession = { case id: String => User(id)  }
protected def toSession   = { case usr: User => usr.id }

protected def requireLogin() = {
  if (!isAuthenticated) {
    redirect("/sessions/new")
  }
}
```

A method you can use in the controller to define a protected route

Triggers an authentication check

Redirects to the login form if the user fails authentication

```
override protected def configureScentry = {
  scentry.unauthenticated {
    scentry.strategies("UserPassword").unauthenticated()
  }
}


override protected def registerAuthStrategies = {
  scentry.register("UserPassword", app =>
    new UserPasswordStrategy(app))
}

}
```

The trait defined in listing 11.7 is almost exactly the same as the OurBasicAuthenticationSupport trait you defined in section 11.3.3, but there's one crucial difference. When you used Scentry's built-in BasicAuthStrategy, you were able to protect a route by using the basicAuth method in the before filter of your DatabaseSetupController. That's what told Scentry to protect all the routes in that controller.

In the case of your new AuthenticationSupport trait, you need to build your own equivalent functionality, and that's what the requireLogin() method does. You can put requireLogin() either in a before() filter (to protect an entire controller) or in an action (to protect only a single action). It triggers a Scentry authentication check, and if the user is authenticated, it does nothing. But if a user isn't authenticated, they're redirected to the login form.

11.4.4 *Protecting your controllers with AuthenticationSupport*

Let's try it. You only need to make two small changes. Right now, the class definition for HackersController looks like this:

```
class HackersController extends HackerTrackerStack {
```

First, change the definition of HackersController so that it inherits from AuthenticationSupport in addition to HackerTrackerStack:

```
class HackersController extends HackerTrackerStack
  with AuthenticationSupport {
```

Second, add the `requireLogin` method call to the `get("/new")` route in Hackers-Controller. Right now, it looks like this:

```
get("/new") {
  val allHackers =  from(Db.hackers)(select(_))
  ssp("/hackers/new", "allHackers" -> allHackers)
}
```

All you need to do is drop the method call into place:

```
get("/new") {
  requireLogin                                          ◄─────────    The action with
  val allHackers =  from(Db.hackers)(select(_))                       requireLogin added
  ssp("/hackers/new", "allHackers" -> allHackers)
}
```

Now try hitting the URL http://localhost:8080/hackers/new. You're instantly redirected to the form asking you to log in. A small victory! The trouble is, currently there isn't any way for you to log in. Let's change that.

Open `SessionsController` again. At present, the controller definition looks like this:

```
class SessionsController extends HackerTrackerStack {
```

Change it by mixing in `AuthenticationSupport`:

```
class SessionsController extends HackerTrackerStack
  with AuthenticationSupport {
```

That gives the controller access to Scentry. You'll need that in a moment.

Next, paste a session creation action into it, as in the next listing.

Listing 11.8   Scentry login action

```
post("/") {
  scentry.authenticate()           ◄─────    Attempts to authenticate the user
                                             using the incoming "username"
  if (isAuthenticated) {           ◄─────    and "password" parameters
    redirect("/hackers")
  }else{                            Checks whether
    redirect("/sessions/new")       authentication succeeded
  }
}
```

This session-creation action is deceptively simple. The login form at webapp/WEB-INF/templates/views/sessions/new.ssp posts the parameters username and password to this action. When `scentry.authenticate()` is called, Scentry checks which strategies are currently registered for this controller. There's only one at the moment: `UserPasswordStrategy`.

Scentry instantiates an instance of `UserPasswordStrategy`, passing in the current controller as the strategy's app. Then it runs the `authenticate()` method on the strategy. You might want to reread that code right now to see what it does: it returns a `User` to Scentry if both the `username` and `password` parameters from the form submission are equal to the string `"foo"`.

The `authenticate()` method has another effect, though. If authentication succeeds, it stores a reference to the user in the session, using whatever the strategy has defined in the `toSession` method. At any time after that, you can call `isAuthenticated` and find out whether the current user has a login session.

The login code is complete, so let's stop talking about it and try it. Try a failure first: enter a username of *foo* and a password of *bar* into the form, and submit it. Authentication will fail, and you'll be redirected back to the login form to try again.

Now try logging in with a username of *foo* and a password of *foo*. Authentication will succeed this time. The user will have a login session, and Scentry will remember that the user is logged in, even over multiple requests (try hitting Refresh a few times).

Because you're logged in, you can also click the New Hacker link or visit http://localhost:8080/hackers/new. You'll see a form like the one shown in figure 11.6.

You've achieved your objective of protecting the new hacker action. You should add `requireLogin` to the `post("/")` action in `HackersController`, so you don't forget to protect that route. Now, let's optimize a little.

11.4.5 Deciding whether to run a strategy

The way the code is set up right now, `UserPasswordStrategy` will run in full every time the `scentry.authenticate()` method is called. But sometimes you won't want

Figure 11.6 You can visit the hacker-creation form again.

this to happen, depending on your application state. Let's see how you can tell Scentry to not bother running a strategy under certain conditions. The key to this is Scentry's isValid() method.

The isValid() method determines whether a strategy should run or not. It returns a Boolean, and you can use override in your strategies to determine the conditions under which they will run (or not).

Let's try it. You want the UserPasswordStrategy to run if and only if the strategy has received username and password params. Add the following code to UserPasswordStrategy.

Listing 11.9 Conditionally running authentication strategies

```
override def isValid(implicit request: HttpServletRequest) = {
  username != "" && password != ""
}
```

Your strategies will only run if their isValid methods return true; and by default, isValid set to true. The code in listing 11.9 tells Scentry to run UserPassword-Strategy's authenticate() method only if the user has entered both a username and password.

This isn't much of a gain from an efficiency point of view, but it illustrates that you can choose to run strategies conditionally. You might decide, for instance, that you shouldn't allow anyone to log in to your application between the hours of 10:00 p.m. and 8:00 a.m. on Tuesday nights.

The strategy is starting to become more full-featured. There's still a problem with the code as it stands, though: users can't log out.

11.4.6 Logging out

You need to add a Log Out link to the main navigation if the user is currently logged in, and a Log In link to the main navigation if the user is currently logged out. But first you need to make some additions to SessionsController and Hackers-Controller. You need to ensure that your Scalate templates know whether the user is currently logged in.

Open HackersController, and take a look at the get("/") action:

```
get("/") {
  ssp("/hackers/index", "allHackers" -> Hacker.all)
}
```

Add a new value, authenticated, to the outgoing template parameters:

```
get("/") {
  ssp("/hackers/index", "allHackers" -> Hacker.all,
    "authenticated" -> isAuthenticated)
}
```

You'll need to add the `authenticated` value to every one of your controller actions, in both `HackersController` and `SessionsController`. You're going to use it in the application's default layout, and everything will explode if it's not available.

Let's add a Log Out link to the top navigation. Open the Hacker Tracker's layout file at webapp/WEB-INF/templates/layouts/default.ssp. At the moment, the nav section looks like the following listing.

Listing 11.10   Navigation menu without Log In and Log Out links

```
<!-- Header and Nav -->
    <div class="row">
      <div class="large-3 columns">
        <h1><a href="/hackers">
        <img src="http://placehold.it/400x100&text=Logo" /></a></h1>
      </div>
      <div class="large-9 columns">
        <ul class="inline-list right">
          <li><a href="/hackers/new">New hacker</a></li>
        </ul>
      </div>
    </div>
<!-- End Header and Nav -->
```

Declare the `authenticated` value at the top of webapp/WEB-INF/templates/layouts/default.ssp:

```
<%@ val authenticated: Boolean %>
```

Now add conditional Log In and Log Out links to the default.ssp template.

Listing 11.11   Navigation menu with Log In and Log Out links

```
<!-- Header and Nav --> <div class="row">
  <div class="large-3 columns">
    <h1><a href="/hackers">
    <img src="http://placehold.it/400x100&text=Logo" /></a></h1>
  </div>
  <div class="large-9 columns">
    <ul class="inline-list right">
      <li><a href="/hackers/new">New hacker</a></li>
      #if(authenticated)
        <li><a href="/sessions/destroy">Log out</a></li>
      #else
        <li><a href="/sessions/new">Log in</a></li>
      #end
    </ul>
  </div> </div>
<!-- End Header and Nav -->
```

Your view code can now tell whether the user is authenticated: the `#if(authenticated)` conditional code will check to see whether the user is logged in.

If you're logged out, you'll see a link inviting you to Log In. It's in the upper-right corner of the page shown in figure 11.7. If you've logged in, you'll see a Log Out link instead, as shown in figure 11.8.

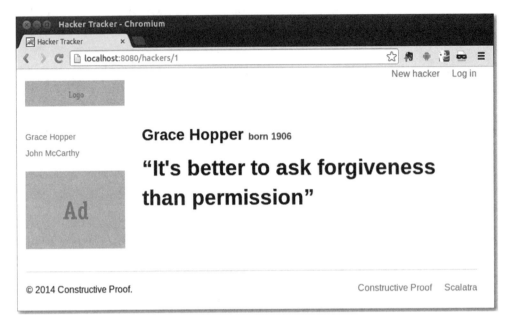

Figure 11.7   A conditional Log In link

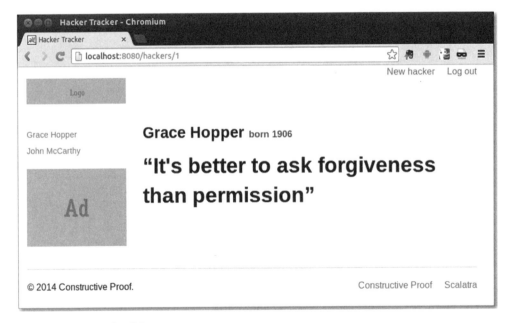

Figure 11.8   A Log Out link

Now it's time to wrap things up and fix the last problem. At present, clicking the Log Out link won't do anything. Open `SessionsController`, and add a route for destroying the session, as follows.

Listing 11.12   A session-destruction action

```
get("/destroy") {
  scentry.logout()
  redirect("/hackers")
}
```

Calling `scentry.logout()` tells Scentry to destroy the session for the current user and log them out. The servlet container that Scalatra is running inside destroys its reference to this user's session, and the user can no longer access any Scentry-protected routes without logging in again.

The `UserPasswordStrategy` is complete. You've defined your own strategy, built an `AuthenticationSupport` trait that you can mix into your controllers, and protected a couple of routes in the `HackersController` so that anonymous users can't access them. Now let's add a second strategy, so you can see how you can fall back when using multiple Scentry strategies.

11.5   *A fallback Remember Me cookie strategy*

Take another look at your login form, shown in figure 11.9. There's a Remember Me check box on the login form, but you haven't done anything with it yet. A check box like this typically sets a cookie and remembers the user for a week, so they don't need to log in again. Let's implement this functionality. To do so, you'll build another strategy, `RememberMeStrategy`, and register it with the `AuthenticationSupport` trait.

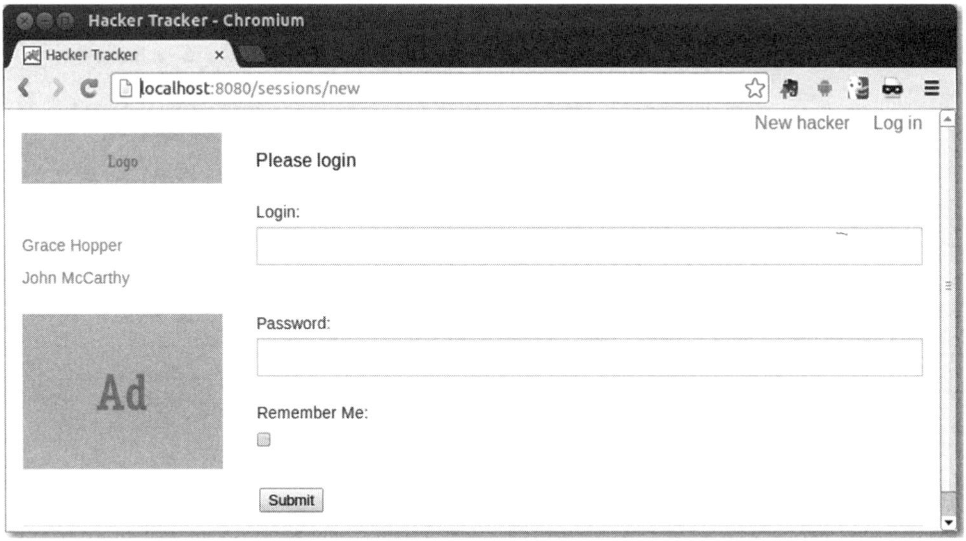

Figure 11.9   Note the Remember Me check box

You want to implement *fallback* behavior. When a user attempts to access a protected route, Scentry will first check to see if the user has a cookie set, and, if so, the user will be logged in without being asked for a username and password. This will happen using `RememberMeStrategy`.

If no cookie is set, Scentry will *fall back* to using `UserPasswordStrategy`, redirect the user to the login form, and ask for a username and password. If the user checks the Remember Me box in the form, you'll set a cookie so the user is remembered next time. Finally, you'll ensure that the Remember Me cookie is destroyed when the user logs out, so you don't inadvertently create a huge security hole.

11.5.1 Building the RememberMeStrategy class

The process of building authentication strategies should be familiar by now. Let's start by defining the `RememberMeStrategy` class. Create a RememberMeStrategy.scala file inside auth/strategies, and add the following code to it.

Listing 11.13   RememberMeStrategy

```scala
package com.constructiveproof.hackertracker.auth.strategies

import org.scalatra.{CookieOptions, ScalatraBase}
import javax.servlet.http.{HttpServletResponse, HttpServletRequest}
import org.scalatra.auth.ScentryStrategy
import com.constructiveproof.hackertracker.models.User
import org.slf4j.LoggerFactory


class RememberMeStrategy(protected val app: ScalatraBase)
  extends ScentryStrategy[User] {

  override def name: String = "RememberMe"

  val CookieKey = "rememberMe"
  private val oneWeek = 7 * 24 * 3600

  private def tokenVal = {
    app.cookies.get(CookieKey) match {
      case Some(token) => token
      case None => ""
    }
  }

  def authenticate()
    (implicit request: HttpServletRequest,
    response: HttpServletResponse) = {
      if(tokenVal == "foobar") Some(User("foo"))
      else None
  }

  override def unauthenticated()
    (implicit request: HttpServletRequest,
```

Grabs the value of the rememberMe cookie token from the app's cookies hash

Authenticates by checking the tokenVal

```
            response: HttpServletResponse) {
                app.redirect("/sessions/new")
        }
    }
```
⟵ **Redirects to the login form if the user isn't authenticated**

This strategy compiles, but it's not yet complete. So far, it looks almost exactly like Our-BasicAuthStrategy and UserPasswordStrategy. It inherits from ScentryStrategy, and it defines User as the authentication subject. It has an explicit name, RememberMe. Let's take a closer look at what it's doing.

The authenticate() method checks if there's an incoming cookie, using the tokenVal method. For simplicity's sake, you're only checking to see whether the incoming rememberMe cookie contains the string "foobar"; if it does, you return a User, which causes Scentry to log the user in.[1]

The main problem with the code as it stands is that nothing ever sets the rememberMe cookie, so the strategy will never log a user in. You can set and unset the rememberMe cookie at appropriate times using Scentry's callbacks.

11.5.2 Scentry callbacks

You'll often want to perform actions before, during, and after authentication or logout. In the case of Hacker Tracker, you want to set a rememberMe cookie if the user has checked the Remember Me check box during login, and destroy the rememberMe cookie when the user logs out. Other applications may need to do different things, such as notify all users that somebody has logged out, or log messages to a security audit log when a user logs in.

Scentry defines quite a few callbacks. Table 11.1 lists them.

Table 11.1 Scentry callbacks

Callback	What it does
beforeAuthenticate	Runs code before authenticating; is only run when the module is valid
afterAuthenticate	Runs code after authenticating; is only run when the module is valid
beforeSetUser	Runs code before setting the user in the session
afterSetUser	Runs code after setting the user in the session
beforeFetch	Runs code before fetching and deserializing the user from the session
afterFetch	Runs code after fetching and serializing the user from the session
beforeLogout	Runs code before logging the user out and invalidating the session
afterLogout	Runs code after logging the user out and invalidating the session

---

[1] A real-world application would save a randomized token value into the User object's backing data store when the user decided to be remembered, and would check the incoming cookie to see if it had the same value as the user has in the database.

Let's try a few of them. You want to set a cookie after authentication takes place if the user selected the Remember Me check box. Add the following code to your `RememberMeStrategy`.

Listing 11.14 `afterAuthenticate` callback to set the `rememberMe` cookie

```
override def afterAuthenticate(winningStrategy: String, user: User)
    (implicit request: HttpServletRequest,
    response: HttpServletResponse) = {
      if (winningStrategy == "RememberMe" ||
        (winningStrategy == "UserPassword" &&
          checkbox2boolean(app.params.get("rememberMe").
          getOrElse("").toString))) {

        val token = "foobar"
        app.cookies.
          set(CookieKey, token)(CookieOptions(
            maxAge = oneWeek, path = "/"))
      }
    }

/**
 * Used to easily match a checkbox value
 */
private def checkbox2boolean(s: String): Boolean = {
  s match {
    case "yes" => true
    case "y" => true
    case "1" => true
    case "true" => true
    case _ => false
  }
}
```

If the RememberMeStrategy authentication succeeded ...

... and the user selected the Remember Me check box in the form ...

... or the UserPasswordStrategy succeeded ...

... then set the rememberMe cookie

Converter function to grab the check box value from the params

In this code, you use Scentry's `afterAuthenticate` callback to set the `rememberMe` cookie. The cookie is set if the `winningStrategy` is `"RememberMe"`, and it's also set if the `winningStrategy` is `"UserPassword"` *and* the Remember Me check box form element was checked during login. Under any other conditions, the cookie doesn't get set.

The cookie is now being set, but there's nothing to trigger an authentication attempt. You need to add this code to the top of `SessionsController`:

```
before("/new") {
  if(!isAuthenticated) {
    scentry.authenticate("RememberMe")
  }
}
```

With this code in place, Scentry will attempt to authenticate users against the rememberMe cookie before they're shown the login form.

One last thing: you need to register `RememberMeStrategy` with Scentry. Open the `AuthenticationSupport` trait, and add the following code to it:

```
override protected def registerAuthStrategies = {
  scentry.register("UserPassword",
    app => new UserPasswordStrategy(app))
  scentry.register("RememberMe",
    app => new RememberMeStrategy(app))
}
```

You should now be able to select the check box when you log in. If you then restart your browser and attempt to hit a protected action, you'll automatically be logged in via the `RememberMeStrategy`. You may want to add a bit of code to the `get("/new")` route in the `SessionsController`, because it can be confusing to see a login form when you're already logged in:

```
get("/new") {
  if (isAuthenticated) redirect("/hackers")    ⟵┐  Redirects to /hackers if the
                                                │  user is already logged in
  contentType="text/html"
  ssp("/sessions/new",
    "allHackers" -> Hacker.all,
    "authenticated" -> isAuthenticated)
}
```

With this code in place, if you try to view the login form when you're already logged in, you'll be redirected to the `/hackers` route.

The last thing you need to do is destroy the `rememberMe` cookie when the user logs out. If you don't do this, users will have their sessions invalidated on the server when they click the Log Out link, but they'll be reauthenticated as soon as they attempt to view a protected part of the application, which probably isn't what anybody expects. You can use Scentry's `beforeLogout` callback to fix this, as follows.

> **Listing 11.15 `beforeLogout` callback to destroy the `rememberMe` cookie**

```
override def beforeLogout(user: User)
  (implicit request: HttpServletRequest,
  response: HttpServletResponse) = {
  if (user != null){
    user.forgetMe
  }
  app.cookies.delete(CookieKey)(CookieOptions(path = "/"))
}
```

In the callback examples in listings 11.14 and 11.15, you can see the use of Scentry's `winningStrategy`. There can be multiple strategies in play during any authentication attempt where more than one strategy is registered. The `winningStrategy` is the one that succeeded.

Scentry strategies for which `isValid` evaluates to `true` run successively until one of the following happens:

- A strategy succeeds
- All strategies have failed
- There are no more valid strategies

You've seen how to log in a user with a Remember Me cookie, and you've had a broad overview of using multiple Scentry strategies, falling back one after another. Like most things in Scalatra, the way in which your authentication strategies fall back on each other gives you maximum flexibility to structure your application in the way you want.

11.6 *Summary*

- Scentry is the authentication module shipped with Scalatra. To keep Scalatra as light as possible, Scentry isn't enabled by default. You need to add a dependency on `scalatra-auth` in order to use it.
- Scentry triggers a cookie-based HTTP session when it's used, so remember that you're setting a cookie on every request as soon as you extend Scalatra's `SessionSupport`.
- Scentry is ideally suited to stateful authentication scenarios, where credentials are submitted at the beginning of a session as opposed to per request.
- The pluggable design of Scentry makes it simple to support several authentication mechanisms, such as HTTP Basic or HTML login forms, or "remember-me" cookies.

Asynchronous programming

12

This chapter covers

- Scala, servlets, and mutable state
- Using Futures for asynchronous programming
- Using Akka Actors with Scalatra
- Big data in Scalatra with Spark

Scala makes multicore, distributed, and asynchronous programming easier. Its focus on immutability, as well as associated libraries such as Akka, lower the conceptual burdens of concurrency management by making it easier to reason about your code. Why is this important?

Most other languages still rely on old-style concurrency management tools like locks and threads, which can be extremely difficult to use because they are non-deterministic. That is, you can't necessarily reproduce your threading bugs when you want, because they can be the result of multiple threads interacting in strange and horrifying ways.

Older concurrency models were designed in an age of non-networked, single-core microcomputers, when building distributed systems was the exception rather than the norm. We now live in a very different world. New servers today typically have 32 or 64 cores, and high-performance applications are almost always built to

197

run across a network. Scala stands out from the language crowd as a great choice for this new hardware and networking environment. This is one of the reasons that it's being used by big organizations that need to build highly scalable distributed systems.

How does Scalatra fit into all this?

Scalatra runs on good old-fashioned servlets. This means that in order to understand asynchronous operations in Scalatra, you need to take the servlet threading model into account.

12.1 *Exploring concurrency in Scalatra*

To illustrate your options, let's build a simple web application. First, generate the project using g8:

```
g8 scalatra/scalatra-sbt
organization [com.example]: com.constructiveproof
name [My Scalatra Web App]: Crawler
version [0.1.0-SNAPSHOT]:
servlet_name [MyScalatraServlet]: CrawlController
package [com.example.app]: com.constructiveproof.crawler
scala_version [2.11.6]:
sbt_version [0.13.8]:
scalatra_version [2.4.0]:
```

With that done, let's build out a simple single-threaded web client. Hitting the route "/" on the controller in the following listing will trigger a call to Grabber.evaluate. Whatever URL you drop into the url parameter will be retrieved and evaluated. If it's a Scala site, you'll be congratulated. If it's not, you'll be admonished to choose more carefully next time.

Listing 12.1 Synchronous network retrieval

```
package com.constructiveproof.crawler

import java.net.URL
import java.nio.charset.StandardCharsets

import scala.io.Source

class CrawlController extends CrawlerStack {

  get("/") {                                              Calls the Grabber object
    contentType = "text/html"                             and gives it whatever's
    Grabber.evaluate(new URL(params("url")))    ◁──────   in params("url")
  }
}

object Grabber {
  def evaluate(url: URL): String = {          Makes a network call ...
    val content = Source.fromURL(     ◁──────
      url, StandardCharsets.UTF_8.name()   ◁────── ... to the URL specified
```

```
                 ).mkString
                 content.contains("Scala") match {
                   case true => "It's a Scala site, very cool."
                   case false => "Whoops, you've made some sort " +
                     "of mistake in your reading choices."
                 }
               }

             }
```

Returns the retrieved page as a string (annotation pointing to `.mkString`)

Judges the user on their reading choices and returns a string to the controller (annotation pointing to the match block)

You can easily try this code by hitting the URL http://localhost:8080/?url=http://scala-lang.org/. You should see a response like the one shown in figure 12.1.

In a world awash with HTTP APIs and networked machines, making network calls like this, and doing one thing or another based on the response received, is the sort of thing we need to do constantly. Whether you're dealing with upstream APIs, machine learning problems, or some other area of development, chances are you'll need to write code like this pretty often. The problem is that the preceding code isn't going to scale very well.

Servlet containers maintain a thread pool for dealing with incoming requests. By default, Apache Tomcat has a pool of 200 threads. When a request comes in, Tomcat uses a thread from the pool, and the thread stays tied up for the duration of the request.

In the case of the previous code, you're making a call to the network, which is potentially slow. You're tying up a thread for however long it takes the upstream server to respond. This call is *synchronous*. The `CrawlController` calls `Grabber.evaluate` and sits there waiting for the response.

The upstream server will probably come back within 1 second or so, but you're using 0.5% of the available thread resources to service this one request. It's wasteful, and it isn't going to scale well, especially if you need to make multiple requests to upstream APIs in order to build the response. You'd be able to handle a lot more traffic if you handed execution of `Grabber.evaluate` off to another thread pool, returned the controller's thread back to the servlet container while you waited for the long-running network operation to complete, and resumed execution once the upstream server had responded.

Figure 12.1   A response from the Grabber

This kind of *asynchronous* processing is what Scala excels at. Scala has a few different constructs for dealing with asynchronous tasks, and we'll look at two of them: *Futures* and *Actors*. Let's start with Futures.

12.2 *Using Futures in Scalatra*

A Future is part of the Scala standard library. It represents a possibly still-running computation. Futures let you program with results you don't have yet, and when the results become available, any transformations you've defined will run. You can attach callbacks to them—onSuccess, onFailure, onComplete—to take action whenever they're done.

If you return a Future from your Scalatra action, Scalatra suspends the request when it hands off to the Future, freeing up a thread. When the Future is completed, Scalatra will wake up the servlet thread and send the response back to the client. This can dramatically increase your throughput compared with hanging on to a thread for the duration of the process.

Futures are easy to use in Scalatra. All you need to do is add FutureSupport to your controller class definition and define a thread pool for the Future to do its work in. Futures run in their own thread pool, separate from the servlet container's thread pool. With these changes made, CrawlController looks as shown next.

Listing 12.2 CrawlController with FutureSupport

```
package com.constructiveproof.crawler

import java.net.URL
import java.nio.charset.StandardCharsets          Adds a few imports
                                                   to get access to
import org.scalatra.FutureSupport                  concurrency classes

import scala.concurrent.{ExecutionContext, Future}  ◁       Adds
import scala.io.Source                                      FutureSupport
                                                            to the class
class CrawlController extends CrawlerStack with FutureSupport {  ◁  definition

  protected implicit def executor = ExecutionContext.global  ◁  Defines a thread
                                                                pool for the
  get("/") {                                                    Futures to run in
    contentType = "text/html"
    Future {                                     ◁
      Grabber.evaluate(new URL(params("url")))       Uses a Future from inside
    }                                                the Scalatra action
  }
}

object Grabber {
  def evaluate(url: URL): String = {
    val content = Source.fromURL(
      url, StandardCharsets.UTF_8.name()
    ).mkString
```

```
  content.contains("Scala") match {
    case true => "It's a Scala site, very cool."
    case false => "Whoops, you've made some sort " +
    "of mistake in your reading choices."
  }
}

}
```

The code has hardly changed, but suddenly `Grabber.evaluate` is running inside its own thread pool, and the servlet container's thread will suspend execution until the `Grabber` does its work. The servlet thread will resume afterwards. It's asynchronous.

> **NOTE** We could easily use an asynchronous HTTP client, such as Apache's `HttpAsyncClient`, or Scala's Dispatch HTTP library, to decouple the outgoing HTTP calls from the servlet container's thread pool. These would solve the problem very well, in fact. But by using Scala's synchronous `Source.fromURL` function, we demonstrate the ways in which you can take *any* synchronous code and make it asynchronous, without needing any extra libraries. This is a much more flexible and general solution.

There are a few things to consider here. Adding `FutureSupport` means that you need to define an `ExecutionContext` for your Futures to run in. Adding `implicit def executor = ExecutionContext.global` is what accomplishes this. There are quite a few different kinds of `ExecutionContext`s that you can choose from, each with different qualities. If in doubt, use `ExecutionContext.global`. It uses a `ForkJoinPool`, which helps to minimize context switches and starts up the thread pool with a size equal to the number of processors. If you need more control over the behavior of your thread pool, you can instantiate a different one yourself. Examples include `CachedThreadPool`, `FixedThreadPool`, and `WorkStealingThreadPool`, each with their own trade-offs.

One thing to watch out for: never close a Future over mutable state. For instance, the servlet container makes the variable `request` available to you inside your Scalatra actions. The `request` is a reference to something that, by definition, lives *inside the servlet container's thread pool*. This raises a conundrum: the `request` is in the servlet container, but everything inside the `Future` executes in a totally different thread pool. What happens if you attempt to access the `request` from inside the Future? The answer is simple and potentially unexpected: it will be `null`, because `ExecutionContext.global` doesn't know anything about it.

This goes for Scala vars just as much as the servlet's `request` object, and it's a common pitfall when working with Scala async libraries. If you want to eliminate the problem in Scalatra, you can do so by wrapping your `Future` in some syntactic sludge: `AsyncResult`. At the cost of some extra boilerplate, this provides a stable identifier to the `request` object that's in scope for the Future. You can then use the `request` inside your Futures in complete safety. The `AsyncResult` version looks like the next listing.

Listing 12.3   Using `AsyncResult`

```scala
package com.constructiveproof.crawler

import java.net.URL
import java.nio.charset.StandardCharsets

import org.scalatra.{AsyncResult, FutureSupport}

import scala.concurrent.{ExecutionContext, Future}
import scala.io.Source


class CrawlController extends CrawlerStack with FutureSupport {

  protected implicit def executor = ExecutionContext.global

  get("/") {
    contentType = "text/html"
    new AsyncResult { val is =
      // this would have nulled out without AsyncResult
      println(request.getProtocol)
      Grabber.evaluate(new URL(params("url")))
    }
  }
}

object Grabber {
  def evaluate(url: URL)
    (implicit ctx: ExecutionContext): Future[String] = {
    Future {
      val content = Source.fromURL(
        url, StandardCharsets.UTF_8.name()
      ).mkString
      content.contains("Scala") match {
        case true => "It's a Scala site, very cool."
        case false => "Whoops, you've made some sort " +
          "of mistake in your reading choices."
      }
    }
  }
}
```

Wraps the Grabber in a new AsyncResult rather than a Future

This would have caused a NullPointerException if you weren't inside an AsyncResult

Wraps the Grabber's response in a Future

Passes the ExecutionContext implicitly to the Grabber

`AsyncResult` expects that whatever method it calls will return a `Future`, so the method signature of `Grabber.evaluate` has changed a little. Instead of giving back a `String`, it now returns a `Future[String]`.

Futures can be strange to work with. Instead of working with actual values, you work with a wrapper, which may or may not contain the value you expect at any given point in time. This is because you asynchronously wait for operations to complete, and you don't necessarily control when they will complete. The key thing to remember is that you don't need to have the value in order to define what should happen when it arrives.

Now that you've seen how to integrate Futures into Scalatra, the Akka documentation on Futures is a good thing to read next: http://doc.akka.io/docs/akka/2.3.4/scala/futures.html. Let's turn our attention to another way of dealing with concurrency in Scalatra: Akka Actors.

12.3 Using Akka Actors from Scalatra

Akka is a Scala library that gives you access to a software construct called *Actors*. An Actor is a container for application logic that's designed to send and receive messages. An Actor is lightweight—about 400 bytes before you start adding your domain logic—so you can have millions of them running at any given time. Like Futures, Akka Actors run in their own thread pool, which is detached from your Scalatra application's servlet thread pool. Unlike Futures, they can run on either a single machine or across a cluster of machines. The Akka library does all the thread management and scheduling and takes care of inter-Actor communication. On the other hand, setting up a distributed Akka `ActorSystem` is a lot more complex than just firing off a Future—each approach has its place.

To add Akka to your application, you'll need to add the following dependency to project/build.scala:

```
"com.typesafe.akka" %% "akka-actor" % "2.3.4",
```

Let's add an Actor that serves the same function as your `Grabber` object already does. Drop the code from the following listing into your application, in the `actors` namespace.

Listing 12.4   Akka Actor for retrieving URLs

```
package com.constructiveproof.crawler.actors

import java.net.URL
import java.nio.charset.StandardCharsets

import akka.actor.Actor

import scala.io.Source

class GrabActor extends Actor {          ⟵  GrabActor inherits
                                             from Actor.

  def receive = {                        ⟵  An Actor must
    case url: URL => evaluate(url)           implement a
    case _ => sender ! "That wasn't a URL."  receive method.
  }

  def evaluate(url: URL) = {
    val content = Source.fromURL(
      url, StandardCharsets.UTF_8.name()
    ).mkString
```

> An Actor can send messages to other Actors using the ! method.

```
content.contains("Akka") match {
  case true => sender ! "It's an Akka-related site, very cool."
  case false => sender ! "Whoops, you've made some sort of " +
    "mistake in your reading choices."
  }
}

}
```

As you can see, this is really just the `Grabber` object expressed as an Actor. Let's take a look at the component parts. There are two main differences between the `GrabActor` and the `Grabber` object.

First, the `GrabActor` has a `receive` method. All Actors must implement one of these: it's the key to their concurrency properties. Actors are completely opaque to other software components in your system. They communicate with each other *only* by sending immutable messages to the `receive` method. This keeps them isolated from each other, and it means that they can run across more than one machine: the immutable messages can easily be serialized and sent to an Actor that exists remotely. The requirement that messages must be immutable (that you can use `vals` but not `vars`) means that all of the problems stemming from using locks to access shared memory go away. An Actor instance never shares any state with any other code, so it can safely be executed on any available thread. Getting rid of locks, in turn, means higher performance and eliminates the chance of deadlocks, race conditions, thread starvation, and many of the other problems that have plagued programmers for the last several decades.

Second, the `receive` method returns `Unit`, which is Scala's way of saying it doesn't return anything to the caller. Instead of returning a value directly from its `receive` method, `GrabActor` does things the Actor way. It knows what sent it the message, and it stores this as a special reference in the value `sender`. When it's done evaluating the web page, it sends a message back to the sender using the syntax `sender ! "It's a Scala site, very cool."` The bang operator, `!`, is the `tell` operator. It means "Send a fire-and-forget message to whatever Actor reference is on the left side of me. The message to send is on the right side of me."

Let's integrate `GrabActor` with the rest of your Scalatra application. First, add a new controller, called `AkkaCrawler`.

Listing 12.5   Controller class integrated with an Akka Actor

```
package com.constructiveproof.crawler

import java.net.URL

import akka.actor.{ActorRef, ActorSystem}
import akka.pattern.ask
```

```
import akka.util.Timeout
import org.scalatra.{AsyncResult, FutureSupport}

import scala.concurrent.ExecutionContext
import scala.concurrent.duration._

class AkkaCrawler(system: ActorSystem, grabActor: ActorRef)
  extends CrawlerStack with FutureSupport {

  protected implicit def executor = system.dispatcher

  implicit val defaultTimeout = new Timeout(2 seconds)

  get("/") {
    contentType = "text/html"
    new AsyncResult {
      val is = grabActor ? new URL(params("url"))
    }
  }
}
```

Annotations:
- Passes in an ActorSystem and whatever Actors you want to use → `class AkkaCrawler(system: ActorSystem, grabActor: ActorRef)`
- Provides a Timeout, after which the Actor will return an exception → `implicit val defaultTimeout = new Timeout(2 seconds)`
- Instead of directly calling a method on the Actor, sends a message to it, this time using the ask pattern → `val is = grabActor ? new URL(params("url"))`

Again, it looks almost exactly the same as the original `CrawlController`, which used bare Futures. There are a few differences, though. First, you pass an `ActorSystem` and a reference to `GrabActor` in to the controller's constructor. You need to have the reference to the `GrabActor` in order to use it, which makes sense; but what's the `ActorSystem`? It's a set of Actors and a thread pool, which share a common configuration.

Second, you can see that although `AsyncResult` is still in use (just like with the Future example, earlier), you no longer invoke a method on an object in order to return a response. Instead, you send a message to the `grabActor` using the ? operator. The question mark operator, ?, is known as the *ask* pattern operator. It means "Ask whatever Actor reference is on the left side of me for a response to the message on the right side of me." The Actor being asked sends back a response as a Future, using ! (the tell operator). If you take a look back at `GrabActor`, you'll see that's exactly what it's doing.

The last main difference between the original `CrawlController` and this `AkkaCrawler` is the timeout. Akka requires that you explicitly set a timeout duration (in this case, 2 seconds) whenever you use the ask pattern. This forces you to think about how reactive you want your application to be. It also stops you from uselessly tying up resources with asks that will never complete. Any ask that exceeds its timeout will throw an exception. You should read the Akka documentation, which is extensive, or the book *Akka in Action* by Raymond Roestenburg, Rob Bakker, and Rob Williams (also from Manning) to get a feel for timeouts and exception handling with Akka.

Now that the controller is in place, you need to mount it in `ScalatraBootstrap`. Change the default `ScalatraBootstrap` so that it looks like the following listing.

Listing 12.6   Setting up for Akka in `ScalatraBootstrap`

```
import javax.servlet.ServletContext

import akka.actor.{ActorSystem, Props}          ◁──  A few new Akka-
import com.constructiveproof.crawler._               related imports
import com.constructiveproof.crawler.actors.GrabActor   ◁──  Imports GrabActor
import org.scalatra._                                       so it's available

class ScalatraBootstrap extends LifeCycle {

  override def init(context: ServletContext) {      Instantiates an
    val system = ActorSystem()              ◁──     ActorSystem
    val grabActor = system.actorOf(Props[GrabActor])    ◁──  Instantiates a
                                                             GrabActor
    context.mount(new CrawlController, "/*")
    context.mount(new AkkaCrawler(system, grabActor), "/akka/*")
  }
}
```

`ActorSystem` creation is a relatively heavyweight operation, and you typically only want one of them in your web app. You'll usually instantiate one when your application starts and then use it for all Akka-related purposes, as you're doing here.

This code also mounts the `AkkaCrawler` so it's available for web requests and passing references to the `ActorSystem` and `GrabActor` into the constructor.

Once you recompile your application and reload it, you can hit the URL http://localhost:8080/akka?url=http://akka.io/ and see that the `GrabActor` has asynchronously gone off to grab the Akka home page and evaluate it. Because it obviously has the word *Akka* in it, you'll see the message from figure 12.2 displayed in your browser.

Akka programming is something that entire books are written about. We've only scratched the surface here, but you've seen how easy it is to integrate Akka with a Scalatra web app.

When should you use a Future? When should you use an Actor? Futures execute on the same machine, whereas Actors can be on the same machine or they can run across a network. Futures can be easier to use, but Actors can encapsulate state very cleanly.

Figure 12.2   A message from your Akka `GrabActor`

12.4 Using Scalatra for big data

Scalatra can easily be used to provide an HTTP interface to your big data jobs. Using Spark, a successor to Hadoop, you can easily query datasets even if they're too big for comfortable processing using conventional tools. Spark is a big data framework that allows you to run batch jobs, query data interactively, and process incoming information as it streams into your system.

Spark runs on top of normal Hadoop data analysis infrastructure—if you already have a Hadoop Distributed File System (HDFS) cluster set up, you can run Spark on top of that, and run jobs on it without modifying or disturbing anything you're already doing. Like Hadoop, Spark can do batch processing, although it's typically quite a bit faster than Hadoop due to aggressive caching of data in RAM.

Hadoop workloads are usually batch jobs on large amounts of data, and Hadoop isn't usually used for interactive querying. In contrast, Spark has the ability to do interactive queries with quick response times. It has the potential to fundamentally transform the way people are doing big data.

To see this in action, find yourself any downloadable large dataset. We went to gov.uk's statistical datasets and grabbed the Price Paid data as a CSV file (http://mng.bz/bn9Y). It contains information about every house or apartment sold in the United Kingdom in the past 20 years. But the example analysis job will be non-specific enough that any big dataset should work fine.

We unzipped the downloaded zip file, moved it to a desktop, and renamed it data.csv. You should put yours in an easily accessible place; we'll reference the filename directly in a few moments.[1]

Next, you need to get Spark imported into your Scalatra application. Add the following dependency into `ScalatraBootstrap`:

```
"org.apache.spark" %% "spark-core" % "1.3.1",
```

Next, make a controller so that you can access Spark. It should look like the following listing.

Listing 12.7 Example Spark controller

```
package com.constructiveproof.crawler

import org.apache.spark.SparkContext
import org.scalatra.FutureSupport
import scala.concurrent.{Future, ExecutionContext}

class SparkExampleController(sc: SparkContext)      ◁——  Passes a SparkContext
  extends CrawlerStack with FutureSupport {                to the controller's
                                                           constructor
  protected implicit def executor = ExecutionContext.global
```

---

[1] Making the file location configurable rather than hardcoded would be the right thing to do, but it'd take us a little farther afield than we want right now.

```
get("/count/:word") {
  val word = params("word")
  Future {
    val occurrenceCount = WordCounter.count(word, sc)
    s"Found $occurrenceCount occurrences of $word"
  }
}

}

object WordCounter {

  def count(word: String, sc: SparkContext) = {
    val data = "/path/to/data.csv"
    val lines = sc.textFile(data)
    lines.filter(line => line.contains(word)).count()
  }

}
```

Annotations:
- Passes the SparkContext to the WordCounter
- Defines the data source
- Imports the data into Spark
- Uses Spark to count occurrences of the desired word

Intriguingly, there's not much code here. In the constructor for SparkExample-Controller, you pass in a SparkContext object. Spark is based on Akka, and like an Akka ActorSystem, a SparkContext is essentially a thread pool providing access to a configuration of Akka Actors. These actors may be local to the machine you're running on or may be a cluster of machines running remotely.

You define the route GET /count/:word, and because you expect this Spark job to be long-running, you run the WordCounter.count invocation inside a Future. The SparkContext gets passed into the WordCounter so that you can keep a reference to the thread pool where Spark is running. You then define a path to the data source (change this to suit where you put your data), and define it as a textFile for the SparkContext, sc. That takes care of the setup.

All the work is done in one line. Spark contains a set of distributed collection classes, which are very similar to the regular Scala collections but which can be run distributed inside a Spark cluster. The code lines.filter(line => line.contains(word)).count() counts all occurrences of whatever word you're interested in. If the Spark-Context is running locally, this will happen on the local machine. If the SparkContext points at a cluster, the job will be run there (although you'll need to do some additional configuration work to distribute your Spark job across the cluster).

Before you can see your job in action, you need to define a SparkContext and mount the new controller in ScalatraBootstrap. Change yours as follows.

Listing 12.8   ScalatraBootstrap with Spark

```
import javax.servlet.ServletContext

import akka.actor.{ActorSystem, Props}
import com.constructiveproof.crawler._
```

```
import com.constructiveproof.crawler.actors.GrabActor
import org.apache.spark.SparkContext
import org.scalatra._

class ScalatraBootstrap extends LifeCycle {

  val sc = new SparkContext("local", "Spark Demo")          ⟵  Creates a
                                                                SparkContext

  override def init(context: ServletContext) {
    val system = ActorSystem()                              Mounts the
    val grabActor = system.actorOf(Props[GrabActor])    SparkExampleController,
                                                         passing in the SparkContext
    context.mount(new CrawlController, "/*")
    context.mount(new AkkaCrawler(system, grabActor), "/akka/*")
    context.mount(new SparkExampleController(sc), "/spark/*")    ⟵
  }

  override def destroy(context: ServletContext) {    ⟵  Shuts down the SparkContext
    sc.stop()                                            when Scalatra stops, by
  }                                                      calling sc.stop()
}
```

Creating a `SparkContext` is relatively easy. In its simplest form, it takes only two parameters: the address of a Spark cluster (or the word *local*), and a human-readable name. You then mount the `SparkExampleController`, passing the `SparkContext` to the controller's constructor. Finally, you tell the `SparkContext` to shut down, using `sc.stop()` when Scalatra shuts down, by adding a `destroy()` method to `ScalatraBootstrap`.

You're now ready to run the code. Exit sbt by typing `exit`, and rerun `sbt`—that way, the servlet container will create a `SparkContext` when it starts up. The results look like figure 12.3.

Figure 12.3   Running the Spark job and viewing its output

Impressively, Spark was able to rip through our 3.4 GB file in about 8 seconds. This would be considered too slow for your average web application, but for doing data analytics work, it's quite acceptable in our view.

Running in local mode like this is great for demonstrating how easy Spark is to use, but it isn't very useful if you've got multiple users accessing your application at the same time. When you're running in local mode like this, there's no concurrency available to you. Your Spark jobs are all submitted to the same SparkContext, and they'll run in order rather than simultaneously. If you want to have concurrent access to multiple Spark jobs running at the same time, you'll need to set up a Spark cluster, and let the cluster handle concurrency and resource-sharing.

If you're running on a multicore system, it's possible to use a trick to speed things up a bit. When you defined your SparkContext in ScalatraBootstrap, it looked like this:

```
val sc = new SparkContext("local", "Spark Demo")
```

When you define your SparkContext as "local", you're telling Spark to use only one processor. But you likely have more than one available. If you set your SparkContext as "local[X]" where X is equal to the number of processors in your machine, your job will speed up. We've set ours like this:

```
val sc = new SparkContext("local[8]", "Spark Demo")
```

Doing this allows processing to speed up quite a bit: from 8 seconds on average to about 2.4 seconds. Pretty good!

Spark is itself written in Scala, so it takes advantage of the same kinds of technologies (Akka Actors and Futures) that we've discussed in this chapter. If you really want to see the performance benefits of Spark, try running it on a cluster—it's designed to efficiently share the resources of dozens or hundreds of machines, and you'll see massive performance increases from running it this way.

12.5   Summary

- You can use Scala's Futures to decouple work that Scalatra's HTTP thread pool does from the main work in your application. Use Futures when you want a simple, lightweight concurrency construct.
- Akka is more complex, but potentially much more powerful, than the Futures approach. Using Akka Actors gives you a very large number of independent concurrency units that can interoperate with each other. Because Akka can handle execution over a network, this gets your code running on more than one machine at the same time.
- Using the Spark library, which is built on top of Akka, you can do parallel processing of very large datasets.

Creating a RESTful JSON API with Swagger

Scalatra is commonly used as a way to build HTTP application programming interfaces (APIs). An API is a way for one computer system to talk to another. It usually exposes business processes and data from one computer system, making it available for another computer system to talk to.

If you've done any web development over the past several years, you'll be aware that large web companies—Google, Facebook, Twitter, Amazon—all have APIs that you can integrate with. This functionality often mirrors what you get from their websites. In the case of Google, for instance, you can send machine-readable requests to and from the Google Maps API, just as you can request human-readable information from the Google Maps web interface. With the web interface, you get back HTML that your browser allows you to read yourself. With the API, you get back JSON or XML responses that your programs can use.

Now that you know what an API is, let's make one.

13.1 An API for the Hacker Tracker

At present, the Hacker Tracker application is set up solely for use by a person, using a web browser. You're going to build a simple REST API that will allow you (or other people) to access and update the information inside the Hacker Tracker's data store programmatically.

> **What's a REST API?**
>
> The example API will be a RESTful one. The term *REST* (short for *Representational State Transfer*) is one of the most meaningless acronyms ever, but RESTful APIs aren't difficult to understand. A RESTful API uses the standard HTTP verbs combined with route matchers to define functionality.
>
> In your API, you'll have method names like GET /hackers (which brings back a list of hackers), POST /hackers (which creates a single hacker), and GET /hackers/1 (which gets the first hacker). REST APIs tend to be self-describing, and they usually operate on a single well-defined resource (such as a hacker).

13.2 Adding an API controller

You'll start with the Hacker Tracker as it last appeared, at the end of chapter 11. Before you start coding, let's consider what you can reuse and what you'll need to add to the application.

At the moment, you've got a functional data storage system that uses Squeryl for persistence. It allows you to create new hackers and to list all hackers in the database. You don't need to modify any of this.

You need to add a new controller to deal with incoming API requests. Just like the existing `HackersController`, the new controller will have operations for creating and retrieving hackers. The big difference is that it'll return JSON instead of HTML responses.

Let's add the API controller. Create a new file called ApiController.scala at the same level as HackersController.scala. Because you won't have a user interface, there's no need to inherit from `HackerTrackerStack`, which has references to `ScalateSupport` and `FlashMapSupport`. Instead, you can inherit directly from `ScalatraServlet` (which gives you the HTTP DSL) and `MethodOverride` (which allows you to support HTTP's PUT and DELETE operations in addition to GET and POST). Your controller should look like the following listing.

Listing 13.1   The API controller

```
package com.constructiveproof.hackertracker

import com.constructiveproof.hackertracker.init.DatabaseSessionSupport
import org.scalatra.{MethodOverride, ScalatraServlet}

class ApiController extends ScalatraServlet with MethodOverride
  with DatabaseSessionSupport {

  /**
   * List all hackers.
   */
  get("/") {
    // retrieve all hackers from the database
    // return a JSON representation
  }

  /**
   * Retrieve a specific hacker.
   */
  get("/:id") {
    // retrieve a single hacker from the database
    // return a JSON representation
  }
```

⟵——— **Notice that there's no "new" action.**

```
  /**
   * Create a new hacker in the database.
   */
  post("/") {
    // create a new hacker in the database
    // return a JSON representation of the new hacker
  }

}
```

This is just a skeletal controller, and it should look familiar. It's structurally similar to the `HackersController`, with one difference. There's no need for a `get("/new")` action, because the API has no reason to show an HTML form.

You need to mount the `ApiController` in `ScalatraBootstrap`, so that it becomes available to the outside world, as shown in the next listing.

Listing 13.2   Mounting the `ApiController`

```
import com.constructiveproof.hackertracker._
import com.constructiveproof.hackertracker.init.DatabaseInit
import org.scalatra._
import javax.servlet.ServletContext

class ScalatraBootstrap extends LifeCycle with DatabaseInit {
```

```scala
override def init(context: ServletContext) {
  configureDb()
  context.mount(new ApiController, "/hackers-api", "hackers-api")
  context.mount(new DatabaseSetupController, "/database")
  context.mount(new HackersController, "/hackers")
  context.mount(new SessionsController, "/sessions")
}

override def destroy(context:ServletContext) {
  closeDbConnection()
}
}
```

Mounts the
ApiController
at /hackers-api
and names it
"hackers-api"

All the functionality you define in the `ApiController` will now be available at http://localhost:8080/hackers-api. In REST terms, you've defined some of the operations of a `Hacker` resource and made it addressable via standard HTTP routes. See chapter 3 for a refresher on the standard REST routes, if you need one.

13.2.1 Returning Hacker JSON from the ApiController

We covered JSON handling in chapter 5. Now we'll look at interacting with the database and returning JSON from your routes.

As in chapter 5, you'll need to add the line `"org.json4s" %% "json4s-jackson" % "3.2.11"`, to your `libraryDependencies` in project/build.scala and restart to pick up the dependencies.

Now let's add the necessary JSON-handling traits and return JSON from the controller. You can see what you need to add in the following listing.

Listing 13.3   Adding JSON support

```scala
package com.constructiveproof.hackertracker

import com.constructiveproof.hackertracker.init.DatabaseSessionSupport
import org.json4s.{DefaultFormats, Formats}
import org.scalatra.{MethodOverride, ScalatraServlet}
import org.scalatra.json.JacksonJsonSupport

class ApiController extends ScalatraServlet with MethodOverride
  with DatabaseSessionSupport with JacksonJsonSupport {

  protected implicit lazy val jsonFormats: Formats = DefaultFormats

  before() {
    contentType = formats("json")
  }

  /**
   * List all hackers.
   */
  get("/") {
```

Adds
Jackson
support

Adds JSON formats

All responses
should return JSON.

```
    // retrieve all hackers from the database
    // return a JSON representation
}
```

You add the `JacksonJsonSupport` trait so that you can parse JSON and import the `DefaultFormats` implicit so that you can transform case classes and JSON. You also ensure that you always respond with JSON by setting the `contentType` in the `before` filter. If any of that is unfamiliar to you, please refer back to chapter 5 for a detailed explanation.

You'll work directly with the `Hacker` model, so make sure you've got a reference to it in your controller:

```
import org.scalatra.json.JacksonJsonSupport
import com.constructiveproof.hackertracker.models.Hacker       ◁——
```
Reference the Hacker model class.

```
class ApiController extends ScalatraServlet with MethodOverride
  with JacksonJsonSupport {
```

Now it's time to implement the actions inside your routes. All the actions in `Api-Controller` will be functionally similar to the corresponding actions in `Hackers-Controller`, but they'll respond with JSON. First up: the `get("/")` action.

Currently the action body is blank. Change it so it looks like the following listing.

Listing 13.4 Implementing `get("/")`

```
/**
 * List all hackers.
 */
get("/") {
  Hacker.all.toList
}
```

Pretty simple. Because you've added all the JSON support code, you should be able to run your application now. Hit http://localhost:8080/hackers-api, and you'll get a JSON representation of the hackers in your database. Ours looks like figure 13.1.

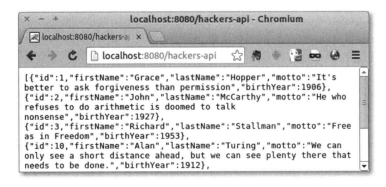

Figure 13.1 Hacker API output

As you can see, Scalatra has serialized the Hackers into a list structure and given it back as JSON output. Yours may be different if you've already input different hackers, or it may be empty if you haven't entered any yet (you can log in and enter some hackers if so).

Next, let's add the show action, which returns a single hacker. Change the get ("/:id") method so that it looks like the next listing.

Listing 13.5 Hacker retrieval action

```
/**
 * Retrieve a specific hacker.
 */
get("/:id") {
  val id = params.getAs[Int]("id").getOrElse(0)
  Hacker.get(id)
}
```

Once again, JSON serialization is handled automatically by Json4s and Scalatra. Assuming that you've got at least one hacker in your database, you should be able to hit http://localhost:8080/hackers-api/1 and retrieve data for a single hacker, as shown in figure 13.2.

Figure 13.2 Hacker API output for a single retrieval

The JSON output this time is for a single Hacker. You can retrieve different hackers by changing the :id parameter in the URL.

Now on to the final action, post("/"), which creates a new Hacker in the database. Add the following code to the action body.

Listing 13.6 Hacker creation action

```
/**
 * Create a new hacker in the database.
 */
post("/") {
```

```
  val firstName = params("firstname")
  val lastName = params("lastname")
  val motto = params("motto")
  val birthYear = params.getAs[Int]("birthyear").getOrElse(
    halt(BadRequest("Please provide a year of birth.")))

  val hacker = new Hacker(0, firstName, lastName, motto, birthYear)
  if(Hacker.create(hacker)) {
    hacker
  }
}
```

You can try it with the following `curl` invocation:

```
curl -X POST \
--data "firstname=Richard&lastname=Stallman" \
--data "motto=Free+as+in+Freedom&birthyear=1953" \
http://localhost:8080/hackers-api
```

This will post a new `Hacker` to the API and save it to the database. If you refresh the list view, you'll see that the hacker has been inserted, as shown in figure 13.3.

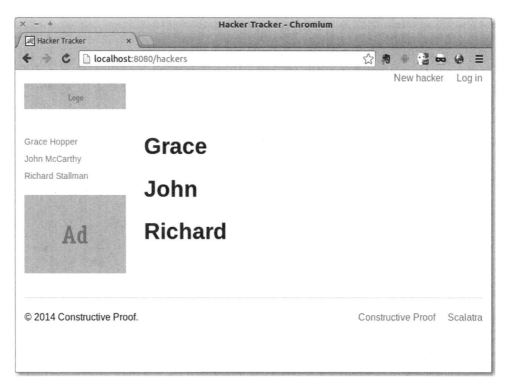

Figure 13.3   A new `Hacker` added to the tracker

13.2.2 *Refactoring to remove duplication*

Let's pause and take stock. The functionality of the application has grown, and with the addition of the API controller, things are starting to get a bit messy. Time for some refactoring.

There are several problems you can easily clean up. First, the traits being mixed into the `ApiController` and `HackersController` have some duplication (and as you know, duplication is maintainability's greatest enemy). Here's what you currently have mixed into the `ApiController`:

```
class ApiController extends ScalatraServlet with MethodOverride
   with DatabaseSessionSupport with JacksonJsonSupport {
```

This is strikingly similar to your `HackerTrackerStack`, which is mixed into the `Hackers-Controller`:

```
trait HackerTrackerStack extends ScalatraServlet with ScalateSupport
   with DatabaseSessionSupport with FlashMapSupport with MethodOverride {
```

Several traits are duplicated between the two: `MethodOverride`, `DatabaseSession-Support`, and `ScalatraServlet`. These three traits are core to your application, and almost every controller will probably use them. But only controllers that serve HTML will need `FlashMapSupport` or `ScalateSupport`.

The solution is simple: you need to refactor these traits so that you have a `CoreAppStack` trait that can be used by all controllers, a `BrowserStack` that can be used by controllers that serve HTML, and an `ApiStack` that you can mix into your API controllers. Because you're now multiplying your stacks, you might as well give them a home. Create a package directory for the new stacks to live in, as shown in figure 13.4.

Next, create the `HackerCoreStack` trait in the new `stacks` package, and mix in the traits you'll want to use in every controller:

Figure 13.4 Creating a package for your stacks

```
package com.constructiveproof.hackertracker.stacks

import org.scalatra.{MethodOverride, ScalatraServlet}
import com.constructiveproof.hackertracker.init.DatabaseSessionSupport
```

```
trait HackerCoreStack extends ScalatraServlet
  with DatabaseSessionSupport with MethodOverride {

}
```

Rename the current `HackerTrackerStack` so it's called `BrowserStack`, move it into the `stacks` package, and replace the core traits by mixing in `HackerCoreStack`. You'll end up with a trait declaration that looks like this:

```
trait BrowserStack extends HackerCoreStack with ScalateSupport
  with FlashMapSupport {
```

Finally, create an `ApiStack` that extends the `HackerCoreStack` with JSON support:

```
package com.constructiveproof.hackertracker.stacks

import org.scalatra.json.JacksonJsonSupport

trait ApiStack extends HackerCoreStack with JacksonJsonSupport{

}
```

You can now proceed to clean up your controllers. `HackersController`, for instance, can be simplified quite nicely:

```
class HackersController extends BrowserStack
  with AuthenticationSupport {
```

The `SessionsController` cleans up in a similar way:

```
class SessionsController extends BrowserStack
  with AuthenticationSupport {
```

The `DatabaseSetupController` mixes in a different authentication trait, but it's otherwise the same:

```
class DatabaseSetupController extends BrowserStack
  with OurBasicAuthenticationSupport {
```

The `ApiController` also sheds a lot of declarative weight:

```
class ApiController extends ApiStack {
```

With the refactoring complete, you have a much more rational structure of traits mixed into your controllers. The final directory structure looks like figure 13.5.

There are several other refactorings you could apply. Usually, we prefer to have controllers in their own package.

We'd probably rename Api-Controller to something like HackersApiController so that future API controllers could be added more easily. You can also drop in a business logic layer to abstract communication between controllers (which should only handle user input and response generation) and the persistence layer (which should handle persistence but not much application logic). But the application is clean enough for now, so let's move on.

Let's turn our attention back to the ApiController and add another hacker:

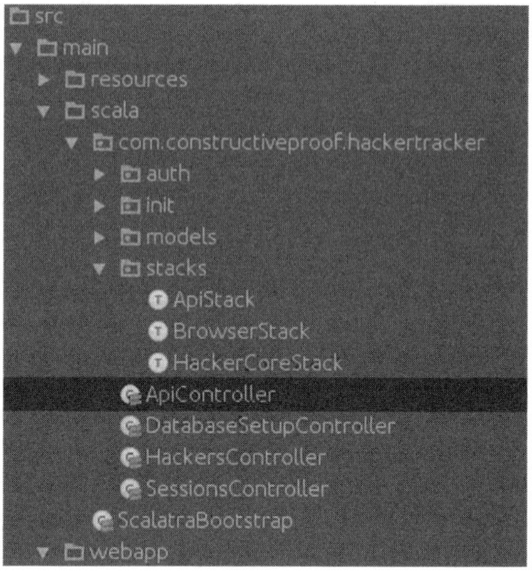

```
curl  -X POST \
--data firstname=Alan \
--data lastname=Turing \
--data motto="We can only see a short distance ahead, \
  but we can see plenty there that needs to be done." \
--data birthyear=1912 http://localhost:8080/hackers-api
```

Figure 13.5   The stacks package after refactoring

It works, but it's pretty cryptic. Anyone wanting to use the API would need to read your code to figure out what routes are available, what parameters are required, and what the return values of each action are. This is impractical, especially if you don't want to publish your source code.

13.3   *Self-documenting APIs using Swagger*

There are two common solutions to the problem of API documentation. Typically, people write up a spec document and email it to prospective implementers as a PDF. A more advanced, but still very manual, approach is to make a web page detailing available routes, parameters, and return types, and update it by hand.

These options are terrible. Even with the best of intentions, the code and documentation will probably drift apart eventually—and it's potentially a lot of work to document all this information for even a small API. Because (as Larry Wall argues) laziness is one of the cardinal virtues of a programmer, it seems like this isn't the right way to do things. How can you fix this? The Scalatra community solves it by integrating with a library called Swagger.

13.3.1   *Swagger—what is it?*

Swagger is a specification and complete framework implementation for describing, producing, consuming, and visualizing RESTful web services. Scalatra integrates Swagger so that your API always has autogenerated documentation that you can easily keep in step with your application code. Swagger also lets people try out API methods using auto-generated forms in a web browser.

Swagger is an open source project from Wordnik, the word-meanings people. It's a specification that allows you to create simple JSON-based documents that describe your API. These JSON specs can then be used for several things.

First, there's a project called swagger-ui. This is a simple idea—it's a set of HTML/CSS/JavaScript that reads Swagger JSON specs and kicks out a web page allowing you to explore a REST API. Let's take a look at the Swagger Petstore, which is their sample app.

Go to http://petstore.swagger.io/ and wait a moment. The HTML interface will load up, and you'll be presented with a page that allows you to explore a sample Petstore API, which will look something like the one in figure 13.6. It may have slightly different names and methods as the Swagger people update their demo. The important thing is to get a feel for how easy Swagger makes it to browse REST APIs.

Figure 13.6   The Swagger Petstore as viewed in Swagger-ui

You can see all the APIs that this application exposes: pet, store, and user. Click the pet link to see what operations you can perform on pets, as shown in figure 13.7.

Figure 13.7   Exploring the pet resource

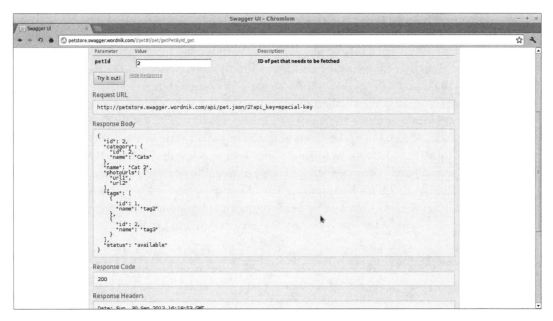

Figure 13.8   Exploring the GET /pet/{petId} method

This API has some methods similar to what you've got, plus a few more—this API allows you to retrieve a single pet, add a new pet, update a pet, and find pets by tags or status.

Let's see what parameters you'd need to use to add a new pet. Click the GET /pet.json link. You'll be presented with a form input such as figure 13.8, allowing you to retrieve a pet by its petId. Enter the number 2 in the petId input field, and click the Try It Out button.

This gives you information related to this pet, including its name (Cat 2), what categories it's in, and the API's response status (200 OK). All of this information came from the Swagger spec file for the Petstore API, which you can see by clicking the Raw link on the right side of the /pet definition. It looks like figure 13.9.

Figure 13.9   A raw machine-readable JSON spec

This machine-readable JSON is what the swagger-ui HTML client is reading in order to autogenerate documentation for the pet store or, potentially, for your Hacker Tracker API.

In addition to the documentation, the Swagger spec for this application can be used to automatically generate client code (in multiple languages) in order to speed the process of creating integrations with an API. This is part of the swagger-codegen project (https://github.com/wordnik/swagger-codegen). There's also support for generating server-side code in Scala and Java.

You might be thinking that all of these benefits sound wonderful, but if you need to build a JSON file by hand for each of your APIs, and keep it up to date manually whenever you make any changes, you're not very far ahead. Luckily, this isn't the case.

Scalatra has Swagger support baked right into it. This means you can annotate your controller and your actions with a few extra bits of information, and Scalatra will automatically generate a full Swagger spec for the APIs and models in your application.

13.3.2 *Swaggerize the application*

Let's set your application up to use Swagger. First, add the Swagger dependencies to your build.sbt file:

```
"org.scalatra" %% "scalatra-swagger" % ScalatraVersion,
```

Exit your sbt console, and again type `sbt` in the top-level directory of your application in order to pull in the dependencies. Then run `~jetty:start` to start the server and get code reloading going again.

Any Scalatra application that uses Swagger support must implement a Swagger controller. Those JSON specification files, which you'd otherwise need to write by hand, need to be served by something, after all. Let's add a standard Swagger controller to your application. Drop the code in the following listing into a new file next to ApiController.scala. You can call it HackersSwagger.scala.

Listing 13.7 Standard Swagger controller to serve JSON spec files

```
package com.constructiveproof.hackertracker

import org.scalatra.swagger.{Swagger, JacksonSwaggerBase}
import org.scalatra.ScalatraServlet
import org.json4s.DefaultFormats

class HackersSwagger(implicit val swagger: Swagger)
  extends ScalatraServlet with JacksonSwaggerBase {
}
```

That code will automatically produce Swagger-compliant JSON specs for every Swagger-documented API method in your application. The rest of your application doesn't know about it yet, though. In order to get everything set up properly, you need to change your

`ScalatraBootstrap` class so that the container knows about this new controller, and provide some summary information about the API; see the next listing.

Listing 13.8   Mounting the Swagger docs controller

```
import com.constructiveproof.hackertracker._
import com.constructiveproof.hackertracker.init.DatabaseInit
import javax.servlet.ServletContext
import org.scalatra._
import org.scalatra.swagger.{ApiInfo, Swagger}
```
← Adds Swagger-related imports

Defines an apiInfo val

```
class ScalatraBootstrap extends LifeCycle with DatabaseInit {
```

Sets the API's title

```
  implicit val apiInfo = new ApiInfo(
    "The HackerTracker API",
    "Docs for the HackerTracker API",
    "http://www.constructiveproof.com/hacker-tracker/tos.html",
    "apiteam@constructiveproof.com",
    "MIT",
    "http://opensource.org/licenses/MIT")
```
Sets the API's description · Specifies a person to contact about the API

Specifies a terms-of-service URL for the API

← Specifies a URL providing a pointer to the API's license terms

Provides a brief description of the API's license terms

```
  implicit val swagger = new Swagger("1.2", "1.0.0", apiInfo)
```
←

```
  override def init(context: ServletContext) {
    configureDb()
    context.mount(new ApiController, "/hackers-api", "hackers-api")
    context.mount(new HackersSwagger, "/api-docs")
    context.mount(new DatabaseSetupController, "/database")
    context.mount(new HackersController, "/hackers")
    context.mount(new SessionsController, "/sessions")
  }
```

Mounts the Swagger controller

Defines a Swagger object you can pass to controllers

```
  override def destroy(context:ServletContext) {
    closeDbConnection()
  }
}
```

`val apiInfo` holds global information about the Hacker Tracker API—what it's called, a brief description, contact details so that implementers know who to talk to about the API, and licensing information. This information will presumably be constant for all methods in the API, so it's defined at the application level in `ScalatraBootstrap`.

Next, you instantiate a new `swagger` object, which will implicitly be passed to all Swaggerized controllers. Finally, you mount the `HackersSwagger` controller at the location `api-docs/*`. The `HackersSwagger` controller will now automatically spit out Swagger JSON spec files for any route in your application that you'd like to document. Let's document your `ApiController` to see how this works.

Currently, the `ApiController` declaration should look like this:

```
class ApiController extends ApiStack {
```

This needs to change a bit. You need to ensure that the `ApiController` has a reference to the `swagger` object you just defined in `ScalatraBootstrap`. Change the constructor parameters so that they look like the following listing.

Listing 13.9   Adding Swagger constructor parameters

```
class ApiController()(implicit val swagger: Swagger)
  extends ApiStack with SwaggerSupport {
```

Because Swagger already implements `jsonFormats`, you need to remove the following line from your `ApiController`:

```
protected implicit lazy val jsonFormats: Formats = DefaultFormats
```

The `ApiController` is now Swagger-enabled.

What have you accomplished so far? You've got a controller, which, given information from Swagger annotations in your controllers, can automatically generate machine-readable descriptions of your API's methods. These machine-readable descriptions can, in turn, be read by an HTML5/JavaScript user interface, allowing easy browsing of the API documentation in a web browser.

You can see Swagger starting to work already. Take a look at http://localhost :8080/api-docs/resources.json (figure 13.10). You should see a JSON description of your API's capabilities, built from the `apiInfo` you entered into `ScalatraBootstrap`.

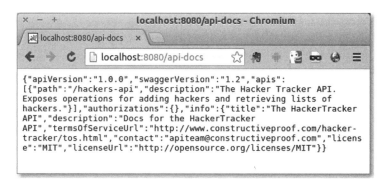

Figure 13.10   The resources.json API descriptor file

That's pretty much it for setup. Now you can begin documenting the API methods with Swagger.

13.3.3 Documenting the routes

You've already added an `apiInfo` to `ScalatraBootstrap` to add some information about the API. Now you should add some information about the `ApiController`. Drop a controller name and description into the body of the `ApiController` class, as in the following listing.

Listing 13.10   Adding controller information

```
class ApiController()(implicit val swagger: Swagger)
  extends ApiStack with SwaggerSupport {

  before() {
    contentType = formats("json")
  }

  protected val applicationDescription =
    """The Hacker Tracker API. Exposes operations for adding
    hackers and retrieving lists of hackers."""

  /**
   * List all hackers.
   */
  get("/") {
    Hacker.all.toList
  }
```

Provides a human-readable description of the controller's functionality

It's time to document a route. Swagger annotations are fairly simple in Scalatra. You describe each route as an ApiInfo object and decorate each of your routes with it, and Scalatra generates the JSON spec for your route.

Let's do the get("/") method first. Right now, it looks like this:

```
/**
 * List all hackers.
 */
get("/") {
  Hacker.all.toList
}
```

You'll need to add some information to the controller in order to tell Swagger what this method does, what parameters it can take, and what it responds with. Drop a new apiOperation val into the body of the controller class, and start describing the get("/") method. Then add the apiOperation into the method call.

Listing 13.11   Documenting the get("/") route

Sets up an apiOperation and notes the method's return type and name

```
val listHackers = (apiOperation[List[Hacker]]("listHackers")
    summary("Show all hackers")
    notes("Shows all available hackers."))

  /**
   * List all hackers.
   */
  get("/", operation(listHackers)) {
    Hacker.all.toList
  }
```

Provides a simple human-readable description

Notes any special behavior

Adds the apiOperation to the route

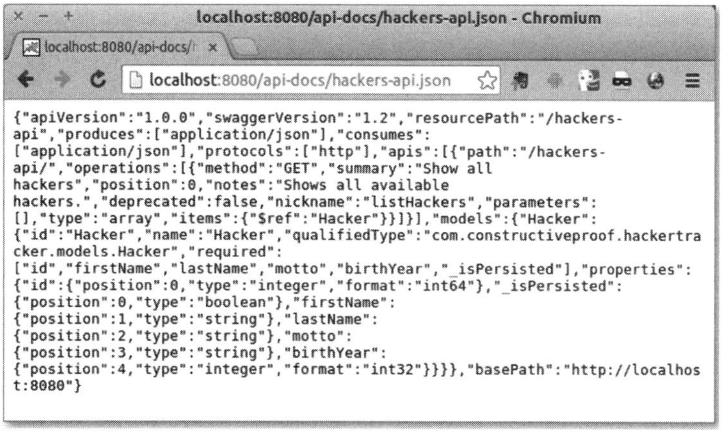

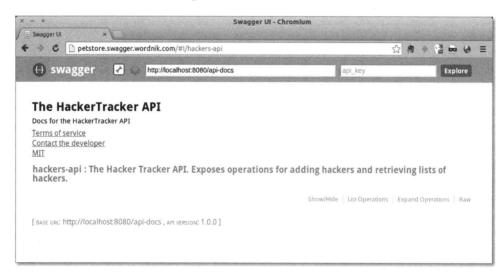

**Figure 13.11
Swagger spec file for
the `ApiController`**

These annotations are used by Scalatra's Swagger integration to automatically generate Swagger spec files for your API's methods. You can see the spec file in raw JSON form at http://localhost:8080/api-docs/hackers-api.json (see figure 13.11).

Swagger-ui can read this JSON spec and show you a set of dynamic forms. These allow you to interact directly with your API, seeing the methods available and each method's required and optional parameters.

To try out your API using swagger-ui, go to http://petstore.swagger.io/ in a browser. By default, this shows you the Swagger Petstore API, but you can use it to browse your own local APIs as well.

Paste the path to your application's resources.json file, http://localhost:8080/api-docs, into Swagger UI's location field, and then click Explore. You'll be presented with a view like that shown in figure 13.12.

Figure 13.12   Browsing local API docs using Swagger UI

> **NOTE** Swagger UI can be used to browse any Swagger-compliant API. You can run your own local copy by grabbing the wordnik/swagger-ui project code from GitHub. There are no dependencies.

Clicking the Hackers-api link will present you with a list of all the Swagger-annotated RESTful API methods in your `ApiController`. Clicking the `GET /hackers-api/` route will give you an interactive user interface, as shown in figure 13.13, which you can use to explore that route.

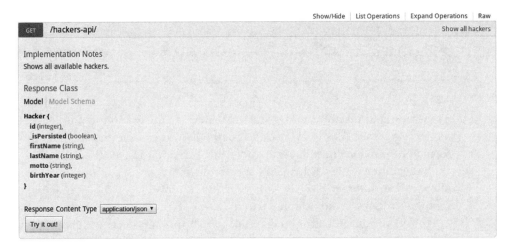

Figure 13.13 Getting a list of hackers

You can now document the `post("/")` route, which allows you to add a new hacker to your list. Right now the route definition looks like this:

```
/**
 * Create a new hacker in the database.
 */
post("/") {
```

You can add Swagger information to the route, so it looks like the next listing.

Listing 13.12 Documenting the hacker creation action

```
val createHacker = (apiOperation[Hacker]("createHacker")
  summary("Create a new hacker")
  notes("firstname, lastname, motto, and year of birth are required")
  parameters(
    Parameter(
      "firstname",
      DataType.String,
      Some("The hacker's first name"),
      None,
```

Declares that this apiOperation has a list of parameters

Creates a new Parameter object

Documents the type of the parameter

Documents the parameter name

Provides a human-readable description of the parameter

Provides optional notes about the parameter

Specifies the type of the parameter (possible types are Body, File, Path, Query, and Header)

Specifies whether the parameter is required

```
        ParamType.Body,
        required = true),
      Parameter(
      "lastname",
      DataType.String,
      Some("The hacker's last name"),
      None,
      ParamType.Body,
      required = true),
      Parameter(
      "motto",
      DataType.String,
      Some("A phrase associated with this hacker"),
      None,
      ParamType.Body,
      required = true),
      Parameter(
      "birthyear",
      DataType.Int,
      Some("The year that the user was born in"),
      Some("A four-digit number"),
      ParamType.Body,
      required = true))
    )

  /**
   * Create a new hacker in the database.
   */
  post("/", operation(createHacker)) {
```

Adds the createHacker operation to the route

Each parameter to the API method is documented as a `Parameter` object within a `List` of parameters. Each parameter is thoroughly documented and includes information about the parameter name; what data type is acceptable; a human-readable description; any notes about the parameter that implementers need to know about; and whether the parameter should be sent in a `POST` body, as a file, within the URL path, on the query string, or as a header. Finally, you can specify whether the parameter is required or optional. Adding these annotations increases the JSON specs at http://localhost:8080/api-docs/hackers-api.json by a considerable amount, as shown in figure 13.14.

Clicking Explore again in the Swagger UI browser and expanding the `POST /` route will show you the documentation for the route, as you can see in figure 13.15. Note that this form is fully interactive, and it generates real API requests that you can use to explore your application. Click the Try It Out button to see your API method in action.

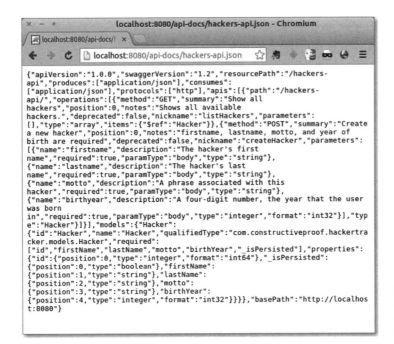

```
{"apiVersion":"1.0.0","swaggerVersion":"1.2","resourcePath":"/hackers-
api","produces":["application/json"],"consumes":
["application/json"],"protocols":["http"],"apis":[{"path":"/hackers-
api/","operations":[{"method":"GET","summary":"Show all
hackers","position":0,"notes":"Shows all available
hackers.","deprecated":false,"nickname":"listHackers","parameters":
[],"type":"array","items":{"$ref":"Hacker"}},{"method":"POST","summary":"Create
a new hacker","position":0,"notes":"firstname, lastname, motto, and year of
birth are required","deprecated":false,"nickname":"createHacker","parameters":
[{"name":"firstname","description":"The hacker's first
name","required":true,"paramType":"body","type":"string"},
{"name":"lastname","description":"The hacker's last
name","required":true,"paramType":"body","type":"string"},
{"name":"motto","description":"A phrase associated with this
hacker","required":true,"paramType":"body","type":"string"},
{"name":"birthyear","description":"A four-digit number, the year that the user
was born
in","required":true,"paramType":"body","type":"integer","format":"int32"}],"typ
e":"Hacker"}]}],"models":{"Hacker":
{"id":"Hacker","name":"Hacker","qualifiedType":"com.constructiveproof.hackertra
cker.models.Hacker","required":
["id","firstName","lastName","motto","birthYear","_isPersisted"],"properties":
{"id":{"position":0,"type":"integer","format":"int64"},"_isPersisted":
{"position":0,"type":"boolean"},"firstName":
{"position":1,"type":"string"},"lastName":
{"position":2,"type":"string"},"motto":
{"position":3,"type":"string"},"birthYear":
{"position":4,"type":"integer","format":"int32"}}}},"basePath":"http://localhos
t:8080"}
```

**Figure 13.14
Hackers-api.json with
a second annotated
method**

Implementation Notes
firstname, lastname, motto, and year of birth are required

Response Class

Model Model Schema

Hacker {
  id (integer),
  _isPersisted (boolean),
  firstName (string),
  lastName (string),
  motto (string),
  birthYear (integer)
}

Response Content Type [application/json ▾]

Parameters

Parameter	Value	Description	Parameter Type	Data Type
firstname	(required) Parameter content type: application/json ▾	The hacker's first name	body	string
lastname	(required) Parameter content type: application/json ▾	The hacker's last name	body	string
motto	(required) Parameter content type: application/json ▾	A phrase associated with this hacker	body	string
birthyear	(required)	A four-digit number, the year that the user was born in	body	integer

Figure 13.15   Swagger UI for POST /

Let's document the last API method, `get("/:id")`. Add the code from Listing 13.13 to the `ApiController`. The process is fairly similar to the previous two examples. First define an `apiOperation`, and then add the operation to the route so that it gets documented.

> **Listing 13.13 Documenting `get("/:id")`**

```
val getHacker = (apiOperation[Hacker]("getHacker")
  summary("Retrieve a single hacker by id")
  parameters(
    Parameter(
      "id",
      DataType.Int,
      Some("The hacker's database id"),
      None,
      ParamType.Path,
       required = true)
  ))

/**
 * Retrieve a specific hacker.
 */
get("/:id", operation(getHacker)) {
```

The id in this case is expected to be on the URL path.

Adds the operation to the route

That's it—the API methods are now documented with Swagger. But there are a few security-related mysteries. Why does the documentation browser work at all (the docs are on a remote server and your API is local)? Also, what's that empty `api_key` text field doing there in the Swagger documentation browser? We'll deal with these questions in the next few sections.

13.3.4 Cross-origin API security and Swagger UI

How is it possible that you can use a form on the internet, at http://petstore.swagger .io/, to browse an application running on http://localhost:8080? Why does Swagger UI work at all? Shouldn't the JavaScript security sandbox, which normally blocks these kinds of cross-domain shenanigans, swing into action and deny the request?

Normally, this would be true. But Scalatra has built-in support for cross-origin resource sharing (CORS), and it's enabled by default whenever you mix `SwaggerSupport` into a servlet.

You can restrict access to the documentation browser (or to your API itself) by setting the init parameter `org.scalatra.cors.allowedOrigins` to a comma-separated list of values, in your ScalatraBootstrap file:

```
context.initParameters("org.scalatra.cors.allowedOrigins") =
 "http://example.com:8080 http://foo.example.com"
```

13.4 Securing your API

API security is a complex subject—there are a lot of ways to do it. Because you've built a RESTful API here, it's normal to want to keep things stateless. This means API clients don't log in first to pick up a session and then use the session as their authentication mechanism. Every request needs to authenticate itself separately from every other request.

There are many ways to accomplish this. Probably the simplest way is to use the same HTTP Basic authentication mechanism you used back in chapter 11, and send the username and password to the API with every request. It's not particularly pretty, but if secured with an SSL connection, it'll do the job with minimum fuss for low-ceremony applications.

Other ways to do it are more complex. Popular ways to secure APIs include HMAC request signing using shared secrets, multiple authentication flows using OAuth2, and heavyweight solutions such as SAML.

Which authentication method you choose will depend on many different factors. What kinds of clients do you plan to support? What degree of technical sophistication do you expect your API client implementers to have? What's your strategy for protecting shared secrets? Do you need to support JavaScript clients?

These subjects warrant a book of their own, and they're way beyond the scope of what we can cover in detail here. But we can look at simple API security using HMAC signing.

13.4.1 HMAC—what is it?

Hash-based message authentication codes (HMACs) are a way to guarantee two things: that an incoming request was sent by a client your application knows about *(authentication)* and that the request data hasn't been tampered with in transit *(data integrity)*. The API server and the API client both have access to a *shared secret*. The client cryptographically signs requests to the API, using the shared secret. It then makes the request, and submits the signature alongside the request.

When the server receives a request, it uses the same shared secret to sign the incoming request data, and compares the resulting hash with the submitted signature. If the two values match, the server knows that the request originated from someone with access to the shared secret. To illustrate this in a practical way, let's try it out using Amazon's signing strategy as a guide.

If you've ever used the popular Amazon S3 API, you've used HMAC signing to authenticate, although you might not have realized it. S3 uses HMAC signatures to guarantee a lot of things about the data integrity of each request: the HTTP verb, the path being requested, the date, the Content-Type, submitted HTTP headers, and incoming parameters. It's worth reading Amazon's HMAC article.[1]

---

[1] Amazon Web Services, "Signing and Authenticating REST Requests," http://mng.bz/DlDH.

For the purposes of this chapter, you'll use a simplified version of the S3 signatures. It will look like this pseudocode:

```
Signature = Base64( HMAC-SHA1( secretKey, stringToSign ) );
```

In this case, `stringToSign` will contain two things: the HTTP verb for the request, and the path you're going to hit on the server, concatenated together in order as a comma-separated list. You'll use the string `thisisthesecretkey` as a shared secret. So for a request such as `GET /hackers-api`, you calculate the signature as follows:

```
Base64 ( HMAC-SHA1 ( "thisisthesecretkey", "GET,/hackers-api" ) )
```

If the client signs its request this way and sends the signature along with the request, the API will know whether the client had access to the shared secret. It will also be able to tell that neither the requested path nor the HTTP verb were tampered with in transit.

13.4.2 An HMAC calculator in Scala

Let's build an HMAC calculator in Scala, borrowing from the Java security libraries included in the standard library. Create a new package inside the existing `auth` package and call it `utils`. Then create the file HmacUtils.scala inside that package. It should look like the following listing.

Listing 13.14   HmacUtils.scala

```
package com.constructiveproof.hackertracker.auth.utils

import javax.crypto.Mac
import javax.crypto.spec.SecretKeySpec
import sun.misc.BASE64Encoder

object HmacUtils {

  def sign(secretKey: String,
    signMe: String): String = {
    val secret = new SecretKeySpec(secretKey.getBytes(),
      "HmacSHA1")
    val mac = Mac.getInstance("HmacSHA1")
    mac.init(secret)
    val hmac = mac.doFinal(signMe.getBytes)
    new BASE64Encoder().encode(hmac)
  }

}
```

With the secret key ...
... and the string you want to sign ...
... transform the secret key into its bytes ...
... and specify the HMAC-SHAl algorithm
Next, initialize a new message authentication code (MAC) ...
... and initialize it with the secret bytes
Sign the string's bytes ...
... and return a Base64-encoded string

It's a pretty straightforward translation of the pseudocode into Scala. The secret key is used to cryptographically sign a string called `stringToSign` and hash it with the bytes of the `secretKey` using the `HmacSHA1` hash function.

What does this get you? You can now sign a string with a shared secret to produce a cryptographic signature. If you drop the code in listing 13.15 into HmacUtils.scala, you'll see the verification part. It adds the ability to verify that a submitted `hmac` matches a signed string.

Listing 13.15   Verifying the signature

```
def verify(secretKey: String, stringToVerify: String,
  hmac: String): Boolean = {
  sign(secretKey, stringToVerify) == hmac          Returns true if a submitted
  }                                                 HMAC matches the signature
                                                    you calculate for a given string
```

Now you're getting somewhere. Let's use the new `HmacUtils.verify` function to protect the Hacker Tracker's API.

13.4.3   *Protecting the API with a trait*

In chapter 11 you saw various uses of Scentry to secure the Hacker Tracker: HTTP Basic authentication, a username/password strategy, and using a Remember Me cookie to let users back in without re-authenticating. This time, let's try something a bit more lightweight: you'll secure the API using a simple trait with a `before` filter. Drop the code from the following listing into a file called ApiAuthenticationSupport in the auth directory.

Listing 13.16   `ApiAuthenticationSupport` trait

```
package com.constructiveproof.hackertracker.auth

import java.net.URLEncoder

import com.constructiveproof.hackertracker.auth.utils.HmacUtils
import org.scalatra.{ScalatraBase, Unauthorized}
```

This trait can only be mixed into subclasses of ScalatraBase.

```
trait ApiAuthenticationSupport extends {
  self: ScalatraBase =>
```

Defines the shared secret

```
  protected val secretKey = "thisisthesecretkey"
```

This will be called by a before() filter in protected API controllers.

```
  protected def validateRequest() = {
    if (!HmacUtils.verify(secretKey, signMe, hmac)) {
      unauthorized
```

If the incoming HMAC parameter doesn't match the one you compute from the current request ...

... halt execution

```
    }
  }
```

Gets the hmac parameter or stops execution

```
  protected def hmac = params.getOrElse("sig", unauthorized)

  protected def unauthorized = {
    halt(Unauthorized("Please provide a valid sig parameter. "
      + notifySig()))
  }

  protected def signMe = {
```

Concatenates the HTTP verb and
request path for the current
request, separated by a comma

Outputs the proper
HMAC if request
signing has failed

```
        request.requestMethod + "," + request.scriptName + requestPath  <┘
    }

  protected def notifySig() = {
      val base64hmac = HmacUtils.sign(secretKey, signMe)
      val urlEncodedHmac = URLEncoder.encode(base64hmac, "UTF-8")
      val notification =
        """Append the following to this request
            in order to sign it: ?sig=""" + urlEncodedHmac
      println(notification)
      notification
    }

  }
```

Let's take this one step at a time. You've built a trait that you can mix into either the
ApiController or the ApiStack. It has a validateRequest method, which you can
execute in a before() filter to check that requests have been properly signed.

The secretKey defines a shared secret. When making requests, API clients need to
concatenate a string consisting of the HTTP verb and the request path, separated by a
comma, and sign it with the shared secret. The signed hash is then submitted as a
query string parameter sig, as ?sig=thisiswherethesignaturegoes.

The ApiAuthenticationSupport trait's validateRequest function reads the signature sig from the query string, and then concatenates the HTTP verb (GET, PUT, POST, or
DELETE) and the request path, separated by a comma, in the signMe function. It then
sends both these values, and the secret key, to HmacUtils.verify to see whether the
incoming request is properly signed (that is, whether the request being received has a
hashed value equal to the incoming signature). Requests with incorrect or nonexistent
signatures will be stopped in their tracks when the unauthorized function is called. Additionally, both the sbt console and the response have the correct signature added to them,
for your learning convenience. Obviously, it'd be a bad idea to do this in production.

Let's see it in action. First, add the ApiAuthenticationSupport trait to the
ApiStack:

Adding ApiAuthenticationSupport
to ApiStack

```
trait ApiStack extends HackerCoreStack with ApiAuthenticationSupport  <┘
  with JacksonJsonSupport {

  override protected implicit lazy val jsonFormats = DefaultFormats

}
```

Now you have the ability to use the validateRequest function in your controllers.
Let's try it. Add the validateRequest function call to the before() filter in the Api-
Controller, as in the next listing.

Listing 13.17   Adding API request validation

```
before() {
  contentType = formats("json")
  validateRequest()          ◁──── | Adds the validateRequest()
}                                    | function call to the before
                                     | filter in the ApiController
```

Your API is now protected from access by unauthenticated clients. Try it by hitting the URL http://localhost:8080/hackers-api, and you'll see a message like that in figure 13.16.

Figure 13.16   API authentication is now required.

As you can see, the API no longer allows access without a valid HMAC signature. The error message in the response tells you the proper `sig` parameter to append. You can see it in action in figure 13.17.

It works! Now you can sleep easy, knowing your API has been secured from use by world + dog.

There are several other things you'll want to do in production. First, you should include a timestamp in the request and include it in the request signature, so that anyone who gets hold of a signed request can only replay the request within a fairly small

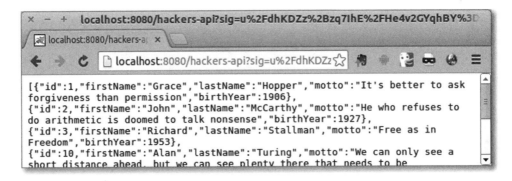

Figure 13.17   A request with a good HMAC signature

time period (Amazon uses 15 minutes). This prevents what are called *replay attacks*, where an unauthorized person gets hold of signed requests after they're made and executes the same actions as the original client.

Unless your API has only one user, you'll probably also want to include some kind of `keyid` parameter so you can have one shared secret per user, or per client application. When a request comes in, you'll read the `keyid` parameter, retrieve the shared secret for that account from your data store, and use the shared secret to verify the incoming request.

If you have an account-based setup that allows external parties to register apps, like Twitter and Facebook do, you might generate a shared secret when a user decides to create a new client app, and show it to users in their account area.

This is just the start of your API construction journey; there's lots still to learn. But this should be enough to get you started.

13.5 Summary

- You've seen the basics of constructing and interacting with a RESTful HTTP API using Scalatra.
- The Hacker Tracker now sports an API, so it can be accessed not only by humans using a web browser but also via machine-to-machine interactions on the internet.
- The Swagger API documentation framework lets your API users browse methods and data. You can use Swagger docs as a way to communicate with both technical and non-technical people about the capabilities of your API. You can also send requests directly to your API and see them in Swagger's handy human-usable web interface.
- API security is just as important as securing HTML-based information and forms. You can use HMAC request signing to authenticate requests and guarantee data integrity for requests to your API.

And with that, the book comes to an end. We hope it proves useful to you. Stop by for a chat on https://gitter.im/scalatra/scalatra if you need to discuss any aspects of the framework in real time, have questions, or just want to hang out.

From the Scalatra crew, thanks for reading. We wish you good luck in your use of the framework!

appendix
Installation
and development setup

Installation

In order to run the code in this book, you need to set up your development machine with several components that will help you generate, build, and run Scalatra applications. This appendix will give you a quick start.

Installing JDK 7

Scalatra runs on the Java Virtual Machine (JVM), so you need a Java Development Kit (JDK). Many systems come with a JDK preinstalled; let's check first to see whether you've got one. Run this in a DOS or Unix console:

```
java -version
```

This should give back the following:

```
java version "1.7.0_65"
Java(TM) SE Runtime Environment (build 1.7.0_65-b17)
Java HotSpot(TM) 64-Bit Server VM (build 24.65-b04, mixed mode)
```

Also run this:

```
javac -version
```

You should see something like this:

```
javac 1.7.0_65
```

If both commands spew forth responses like those shown here, you're all set. The key thing is the number 1.7 in the responses. If you see 1.6, your version of Java is too old, and you'll need to upgrade.

Scalatra 2.4.0 requires Java 7 (a JVM version of 1.7). As of this writing, the Scala 2.11.x language has experimental support for Java 8 (JVM 1.8.x). This means Java 8 may work for you, but you probably shouldn't depend on it in a production situation until Scala 2.12 is available. If you don't already have a JDK, or if your version is too old, go here and follow the install instructions: http://docs.oracle.com/javase/7/docs/webnotes/install/index.html.

Now that you've got Java installed and working, you need to install some tools to generate code and build your application.

Installing conscript and giter8

Although it's theoretically possible that you could open your favorite code editor and start working on your first Scalatra application, it would take you a long time to get all the files into place and lay them out with the proper structure. To simplify this process, most people use a tool called giter8.

Giter8, which depends on another tool called conscript, generates customized Scalatra projects for you. When you run giter8, it uses conscript to retrieve template files from GitHub, and it asks you several questions about your project—its name and version number, for example. Once you've answered these questions, giter8 injects your answers into the retrieved template code, and the result is a customized, buildable, runnable project skeleton on your machine. This is the recommended way of getting started with Scalatra.

Install conscript first by following the instructions for your platform at https://github.com/foundweekends/conscript. Conscript will install itself into your home directory, in a folder called bin. You'll probably need to add this folder to your system's PATH variable so you can run the conscript utility, cs.

SETTING PATH ON WINDOWS
There are quite a few versions of Windows in use, and each version has a slightly different way of setting the PATH environment variable. Go to https://www.java.com/en/download/help/path.xml, and follow the instructions for the version of Windows you're using.

In the PATH editing box, type a ; (semicolon) character at the end of it, and then enter the path to your new bin folder. On our system, it's at C:\Users\IEUser\bin. Once this is set, close and open your terminal. If you've entered your PATH correctly, you should now be able to type cs at the DOS prompt and see the output shown in figure A.1.

SETTING PATH ON MAC OR LINUX
Setting PATH on a Mac OS X or a Linux system is a fairly simple matter. If you're on Linux, open the .bashrc file in your home directory. On Mac OS X, open the .bash_profile file in your home directory.

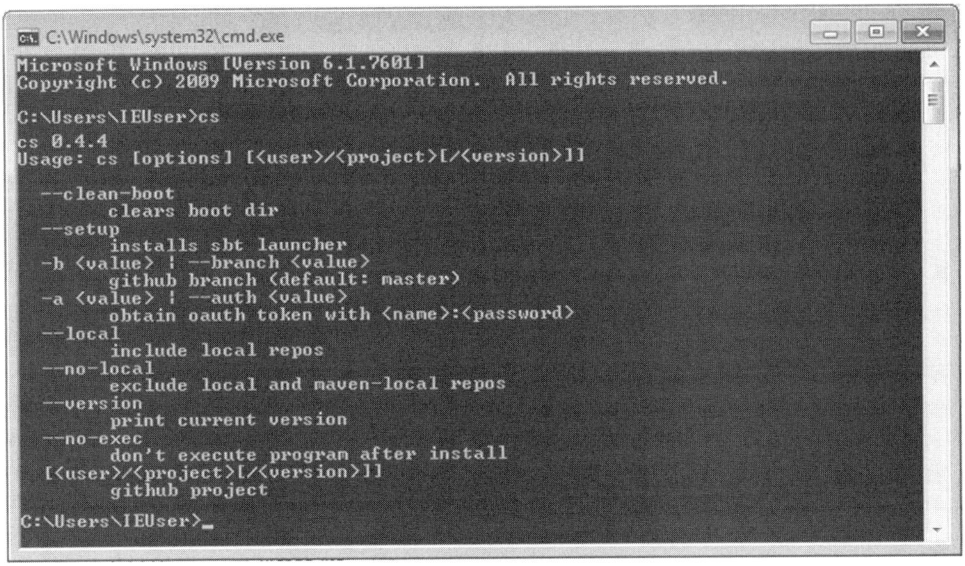

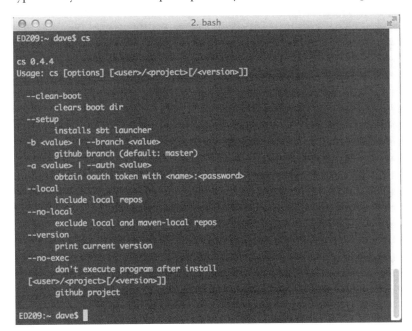

Figure A.1   Making sure conscript works on Windows

Add the following line at the end of the file: export PATH=$PATH:~/bin. Close and reopen any terminals you have open so that you pick up the new $PATH variable. Now, type cs at your command prompt, and you should see the output shown in figure A.2.

Figure A.2   Making sure conscript works on Mac or Linux

INSTALLING GITER8

Now that conscript is installed, you can proceed with installing giter8. This is much easier. Run the following command from a DOS or Unix terminal, and giter8 will be retrieved from GitHub:

```
cs foundweekends/giter8
```

Conscript will download the giter8 utility into the bin folder in your home directory and make it available as the command-line utility g8. To test that it works, run it. The output should be like that shown in figure A.3.

With conscript and giter8 installed, you have everything you need to generate a Scalatra project. You'll try it in the next section.

Generating your first Scalatra project

The Scalatra team maintains a giter8 template for a standard Scalatra project skeleton on GitHub. To generate your own project code from it, run the following code in your terminal:

```
g8 scalatra/scalatra-sbt
```

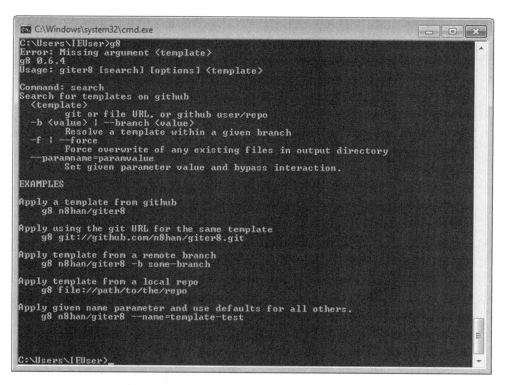

Figure A.3   Making sure giter8 works

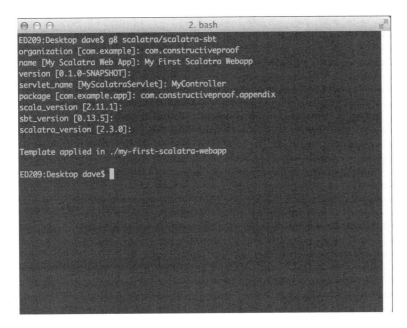

Figure A.4 Generating a Scalatra project

Giter8 will reach out to GitHub and download a full Scalatra application skeleton. It will then ask you a series of questions about your project. Answer as shown in figure A.4.

Each question customizes a specific aspect of your application:

- organization is used for publishing. Most people use either their organization's domain name (such as com.constructiveproof in our case) or the reverse of their GitHub username (for example, com.github.futurechimp).
- package is the namespace you want to use for this particular application. Use something unique for each of your web apps.
- name is the particular name for this application. Type it as a free-form sentence; giter8 will automatically turn it into a project name.
- servlet_name is the name of the first servlet, or controller, that you want to generate.
- version is the version number of your application. It starts at 0.1.0, and you can increment it in your build file as you do releases.
- scala_version is the version of the Scala language you'd like to use.

If you don't know the answers to some of the questions, press Enter to accept the default; you can always change the generated code later. When you're finished answering, giter8 injects your answers into the templates it downloaded from the internet. The template files for any giter8 project are typically stored on GitHub. The ones you downloaded are found in the project https://github.com/scalatra/scalatra-sbt.g8.

Using conscript and giter8, you can generate a new project. Next, you need the build tool that lets you run your generated project.

Building your code with the simple build tool (sbt)

The simple build tool (sbt) is the standard build system for Scala projects. Like any software with the word *simple* or *lightweight* in it, sbt is complex. It has quite a few functions:

- It automatically downloads and installs a full Scala installation, including a Scala compiler, on first use.
- It builds your application.
- It runs your automated tests.
- It manages dependencies, rather like Maven, Ruby Gems, and Python Eggs do in other languages.
- It can automate common tasks, as Ant and Rake do in other languages.

Scalatra conveniently bundles its own copy of sbt for use on Unix-style systems. This means that on Linux and Mac systems, you don't necessarily need to install sbt, if all you're using it for is Scalatra development. But if you want to do general non-Scalatra development in Scala, or if you're on Windows, follow the installation instructions for your platform at http://scala-sbt.org to install sbt.

Let's run your newly generated Scalatra project using sbt. To do so, `cd` into the top-level my-scalatra-web-app project by typing `cd my-scalatra-web-app`. Then type either `./sbt` (Linux or Mac) or `sbt` (Windows) at the command prompt to start sbt. The first time you do this, you may as well go get a cup of coffee; sbt will download an entire Scala development environment, including the language, a compiler, and the Scala standard libraries, and then grab all the dependencies needed to run a Scalatra application. This can take a while, depending on the speed of your internet connection. At the end, you'll see the `>` character, which is the sbt command prompt, as shown in figure A.5.

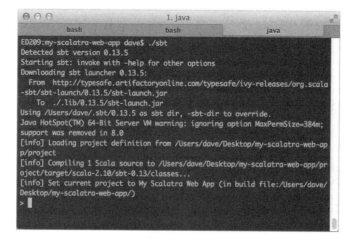

Figure A.5   Running Scalatra using sbt

```
> jetty:start
[info] Compiling Templates in Template Directory: /home/dave/Desktop/my-scal
atra-web-app/src/main/webapp/WEB-INF/templates
SLF4J: Failed to load class "org.slf4j.impl.StaticLoggerBinder".
SLF4J: Defaulting to no-operation (NOP) logger implementation
SLF4J: See http://www.slf4j.org/codes.html#StaticLoggerBinder for further de
tails.
[info] starting server ...
[success] Total time: 1 s, completed Mar 29, 2016 1:00:07 PM
> 2016-03-29 13:00:07.154:INFO::main: Logging initialized @28ms
2016-03-29 13:00:07.159:INFO:oejr.Runner:main: Runner
2016-03-29 13:00:07.224:INFO:oejs.Server:main: jetty-9.2.1.v20140609
2016-03-29 13:00:09.135:WARN:oeja.AnnotationConfiguration:main: ServletConta
inerInitializers: detected. Class hierarchy: empty
13:00:09.452 [main] INFO  o.scalatra.servlet.ScalatraListener - The cycle cl
ass name from the config: ScalatraBootstrap
13:00:09.506 [main] INFO  o.scalatra.servlet.ScalatraListener - Initializing
 life cycle class: ScalatraBootstrap
13:00:09.654 [main] INFO  o.f.s.servlet.ServletTemplateEngine - Scalate temp
late engine using working directory: /tmp/scalate-2048513183786683943-workdi
r
2016-03-29 13:00:09.656:INFO:oejsh.ContextHandler:main: Started o.e.j.w.WebA
ppContext@24aa663f{/,file:/home/dave/Desktop/my-scalatra-web-app/target/weba
pp/,AVAILABLE}{file:/home/dave/Desktop/my-scalatra-web-app/target/webapp/}
2016-03-29 13:00:09.657:WARN:oejsh.RequestLogHandler:main: !RequestLog
2016-03-29 13:00:09.669:INFO:oejs.ServerConnector:main: Started ServerConnec
tor@538f1db2{HTTP/1.1}{0.0.0.0:8080}
2016-03-29 13:00:09.670:INFO:oejs.Server:main: Started @2561ms
>
```

Figure A.6 Starting the Scalatra app in a web server

Scalatra's sbt setup packages a web server, so you can get to work right away. To run your new project, type the command `jetty:start` at the sbt prompt. You'll see output something like that shown in figure A.6.

sbt will start a web server and make your application available on port 8080. You can view your application by going to http://localhost:8080. To enable automatic code reloading, so the web server reloads itself to pick up changes whenever you save a file, use this command:

```
~jetty:start
```

You now have all the mandatory components installed, and you've seen how to generate and run a Scalatra application. If you were in the middle of chapter 1 and you're eager to get busy constructing your application, you can go back there now. The rest of this appendix will guide you through the Scalatra project structure and give you a few tips on working with sbt, adding and removing project dependencies, and setting up Scalatra with your favorite IDE.

The structure of a Scalatra project

The structure of your new project will look like that shown in figure A.7. Let's take a quick tour of the project.

The project directory contains project-related files. The build.properties file specifies which version of sbt should be used to build the project. build.scala is the project's build file, and it's where you can configure all aspects of the build. This is one of the most important files in the entire application, and you'll open it frequently when you want to add dependencies to or remove them from your project. The plugins .sbt file allows you to add sbt plugins to your project, extending the capabilities of sbt itself.

The src/main/scala directory is where you'll do most of your application development work. By default, the giter8 template generates package directories for you, composed of your organization name and the package name you entered when you generated the project. There's no reason to use packages like this if you don't want to; you can, for instance, put all your Scala code in src/main/scala, and everything will build and run without any trouble.

The src/main/resources directory can contain any project-specific resource files that you

Figure A.7   A Scalatra project's structure

need to build into your web application. Configuration files, I18N files, and any other files you want to bundle into your application go here.

The src/main/webapp directory is where your web resources live. Except for WEB-INF, all files and directories placed in webapp are served publicly. This is where you'll typically keep any static HTML, CSS, and JavaScript needed to serve your application. The contents of the WEB-INF directory aren't served; this is where Scalatra keeps the files for its web-templating system by default (see chapter 7 for details).

The src/main/test directory is where you keep your automated test code. The sbt file in the project root contains the sbt launcher, so you don't need to install sbt globally on your system if you're on Mac OS X or Linux.

With the overview out of the way, let's zoom in and focus specifically on two files: we'll look at dependency management in project/build.scala and also examine the ScalatraBootstrap init file.

Configuring your application with sbt

As mentioned, you can configure most aspects of your project's build settings, including what dependencies it pulls in, using the configuration file at project/build.scala. This is an sbt configuration file.

One thing you may find confusing when you're first using Scala is that sbt can have its configuration in two locations. Simple sbt projects typically have a build.sbt file in the project root; this file lets you configure your application with a limited subset of Scala. More-complex projects, including Scalatra, instead use the file at project/build.scala. This file is an actual Scala file, laid out in a specific structure, and it provides for more-complex configurations than build.sbt. It's worth noting that you can use project/build.scala and build.sbt in the same sbt project, and settings in both will work.

Let's turn our attention to dependency management in sbt. Scalatra depends on Java JAR files to make dependencies available. A JAR file is basically a zip file containing JVM bytecode, laid out in a specific structure.

When you want to make a new capability available to your Scalatra application, you add a new dependency listing to project/build.scala. sbt will then take care of downloading the JAR file for this dependency and making it available to your application. Let's see how this works. Open project/build.scala; halfway through the file, you'll see a series of lines like the following.

Listing A.1 Dependencies in sbt

```
"org.scalatra" %% "scalatra" % ScalatraVersion,
```

In the Java (and thus Scala) world, every library JAR has at least three pieces of information associated with it:

- An organization, typically defined by its domain name
- A name
- A version number

Those are the pieces of information you see here. The organization name of this file is `"org.scalatra"`, the library's name is `"scalatra"`, and the version number is `ScalatraVersion` (look further up the file, and you'll see that it's `"2.4.0"`).

Any time you want to add a new dependency to your Scalatra application, you determine these three pieces of information and put them in the file. Any Scala library will list an sbt dependency line in this format.

You also have the entire world of Java libraries available to you. If you want to use a Java library, it may not have an sbt dependency line listed in its documentation. Your best bet is to go to http://search.maven.org and search for the library name. Clicking a library name and then clicking the Scala sbt link in the Dependency Information box on the left side of the window will display the sbt dependency line, as shown in figure A.8.

To add a dependency, add the dependency line to project/build.scala, adding a comma at the end of the line if it's not the last line in the Seq. Then you can type the reload

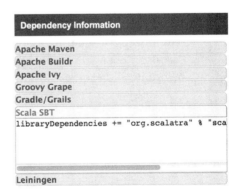

Figure A.8 sbt dependencies on search.maven.org

command at the sbt prompt, which will cause sbt to look for any new dependencies. Alternately, you can type the `exit` command to leave sbt; the dependency will become available the next time you run sbt. For more-detailed information on sbt project definitions, see chapter 9.

sbt tasks

When you run `jetty:start` to start your web server, you're running an sbt command. It's not the only one available; to see a list of available sbt tasks, run `tasks`. Other useful tasks include the following:

- `compile`—Compiles without running the web server
- `jetty:stop`—Stops the web server
- `reload`—Reloads the sbt environment to pick up new dependencies
- `test`—Runs your application's tests
- `testQuick`—Runs all tests that failed during the previous test run

Mounting servlets in ScalatraBootstrap

The default generated template contains only a single servlet, or controller (the terms are used interchangeably by many Scalatra developers). If you've generated a fresh project and specified `ArticlesController` as the default servlet when answering g8's questions, the file src/main/scala/ScalatraBootstrap.scala will contain the following lines.

Listing A.2 `ScalatraBootstrap` with a single mounted controller

```
import com.example.app._
import org.scalatra._
import javax.servlet.ServletContext

class ScalatraBootstrap extends LifeCycle {
  override def init(context: ServletContext) {
    context.mount(new ArticlesController, "/*")     ◁──┐  A single controller is
  }                                                     │  available via HTTP.
}
```

In a real application, it's unlikely that you'll have only a single controller—you may have dozens of them in a large application. If you add another controller, such as a `CommentsController`, you need to mount it in `ScalatraBootstrap`'s init method before it will become available to your application. The next listing shows a stubbed `CommentsController`.

Listing A.3 The `CommentsController`

```
package com.example.app

import org.scalatra._
import scalate.ScalateSupport
```

```
class CommentsController extends MyScalatraWebAppStack {

  get("/") {
    //We would list comments here
  }

  get("/new") {
    //We would show a new comment form here
  }
}
```

The controller is now defined, but it's not available for HTTP requests. You need to mount it so that it becomes requestable. To do so, you add it to the list of instantiated classes using `context.mount`.

Listing A.4   Mounting a second controller

```
override def init(context: ServletContext) {
  context.mount(new ArticlesController, "/*")
  context.mount(new CommentsController, "/comments/*")    ◁─┐  Mounts the
}                                                             CommentsController
```

The `CommentsController`'s routes are now available at GET `http://localhost:8080/comments/` and GET `http://localhost:8080/comments/new`. To keep things clean, it's a good idea to also mount `ArticlesController` at the path `"/articles/*"`.

Note that you could just as easily have mounted `CommentsController` at `"/*"` and then set up the controller class's routes as in the following listing. As with most things in Scalatra, how you structure your routes is up to you.

Listing A.5   Namespaced routes in the controller

```
package com.example.app

import org.scalatra._
import scalate.ScalateSupport

class CommentsController extends MyScalatraWebAppStack {

  get("/comments") {              ◁──────────┐  Namespaces the index
    //We would list comments here              action to /comments
  }

  get("/comments/new") {          ◁──────────┐  Namespaces the new action
    //We would show a new comment form here     to /comments/new
  }
}
```

You can also run any other initialization code you want in the `init` method of `ScalatraBootstrap`. Add a `destroy` method if you want to do some cleanup when your application exits, as shown next.

Listing A.6 Cleaning up at application shutdown

```
override def destroy(context: ServletContext) {
  // clean up database connections, close resources, etc.
}
```

For a more detailed discussion of `ScalatraBootstrap`, see chapter 9.

Do you need an IDE?

The short answer is no: nothing about Scala requires an IDE. If you're thinking about trying Scala but the thought of losing your regular text editor gives you the shudders, take heart: nothing in this book assumes or requires that you have an IDE. If you're a happy vi, Emacs, Sublime, gedit, or jEdit user, you should probably stick with a familiar setup for the moment. There's a lot to learn, and learning an entirely new IDE while you're learning all about sbt, Scala, Scalatra, Scalate, servlet configuration, and the million other details of an unfamiliar environment may be too much.

But speaking from experience as former Rubyists, we were pleasantly surprised by the speed boost we got when we started using IntelliJ Idea and its Scala plugin, which is now our environment of choice for Scalatra development. The refactoring, code completion, and integrated docs support make it much easier to learn Scalatra, Scala, and dozens or hundreds of libraries. The syntax highlighting is nearly perfect, making it easy to see when you've made a mistake before you compile. Having said that, you're spoiled for choice. If you don't care about compiler-aware syntax highlighting, automated typesafe refactoring, and integrated docs, you can skip this section. If you're interested in these things, there are three ways to get them: Emacs, IntelliJ, or Eclipse.

Emacs

If you're an Emacs user, you can use the Enhanced Scala Interaction Mode for text Editors (ENSIME). It has quite a few features, including the following:

- Showing the type of the symbol under the cursor
- Contextual completion for `vars`, `vals`, and `defs`
- Adding imports for the symbol under the cursor
- Classpath search for types and members
- Browsing packages and type hierarchies
- Finding all references to a symbol
- Refactorings such as (rename, organize imports, extract method)
- A REPL with stack-trace highlighting
- Red squiggles for errors and warnings in your code
- Debugger support

You begin by installing the scala-mode2 Emacs mode from https://github.com/hvesalai/scala-mode2. Once that's running, follow the installation instructions at https://github.com/ensime/ensime-server to install ENSIME. Next, install the

ENSIME sbt plugin and generate an .ensime configuration file by following the instructions at https://github.com/ensime/ensime-sbt.

Eclipse

If you're already an Eclipse user, you can add the Scala plugin to your current installation. Alternately, you can download a version of Eclipse with the Scala plugin already installed. In either case, go to http://scala-ide.org, which is where the downloads live.

Eclipse requires an Eclipse project file to be present so it can figure out dependencies for syntax highlighting and other IDE features. Follow the instructions at https://github.com/typesafehub/sbteclipse to install the `sbteclipse` plugin.

If you want to use Eclipse's integrated debugging, start sbt like this:

```
./sbt -jvm-debug 8000
```

You can then set up your Eclipse debugger. Go to Run > Debug configurations, select Remote Java Application, and click New Configuration. Select Remote to make a new remote debugging configuration, and give it a name. The default debugging port should already be 8000 (matching the port you started sbt with earlier), so clicking Debug and setting some breakpoints should result in a working debugger.

IntelliJ IDEA

You can use the Community Edition of IntelliJ IDEA and add the Scala plugin. There's no need to add any extra sbt plugins to your projects, because IDEA's Scala plugin recognizes sbt projects without any further configuration.

To debug in IntelliJ IDEA, start sbt like this:

```
./sbt -jvm-debug 5005
```

Next, go to Run > Edit Configurations. Click the + button, and select Remote to make a new remote debugging configuration. Give it whatever name you like, such as Scalatra Debug. The default run configuration, `-agentlib:jdwp=transport=dt_socket`, `server=y,suspend=n,address=5005`, should work (note that the port 5005 you started sbt with should match the run configuration).

Set some breakpoints and refresh your browser. The debugger should start up when you select Run Debug 'Scalatra Debug'.

index